The Good Guide to
Employment

Wendy Blake Ranken

workforce hub

Change**Up**

FUNDEI

**Northern College
Library**

NC06896

Published by NCVO
Regent's Wharf
8 All Saints Street
London N1 9RL

Published April 2008

Design by Steers McGillan Ltd
Printed by Short Run Press

British Library Cataloguing in
Public Data
A catalogue record for this book is
available from the British Library

ISBN 978-0-7199-1749-3

Acknowledgements

Lai-Har Cheung of the UK Workforce Hub and Wendy Blake Ranken would like to thank the following people and organisations for their support and assistance:

This edition of the Good Guide to Employment would not have been possible if Capacitybuilders had not supported NCVO's programme of work promoting good employment practice in the voluntary and community sector. We would like to thank several readers of the previous edition of the Good Guide to Employment , particularly members of NCVO's Personnel Network, for giving detailed and constructive feedback. We have tried to take your comments into account and make this edition the best ever! Unfortunately, we do not have everyone's names so have decided to thank you all as a 'group'.

We would also like to thank: Rachael McIlroy of the TUC for reviewing a draft of Chapter 12;

Mark Restall of Volunteering England for reviewing a draft of Chapter 18;

Peter Harwood, Margaret McMahon and Sue Terry of the Acas Knowledge Directorate, for reading a draft of the entire publication, and for making detailed comments which were very helpful. We are also grateful to Acas for giving permission to extensively cite their material.

Katie Hall and Rob Stevens of NCVO for reading earlier drafts and giving their feedback.

The UK Workforce Hub paid Sherrards Employment Law Solicitors www.harrysherrard.com to review the final draft of the publication to ensure that the law was accurate as at January 2008.

The publication makes extensive reference to other sources of information such as RoSPA, HSE, and Business Link. We have tried to acknowledge all sources of information whenever possible.

If we have accidentally omitted any acknowledgements or thanks, we apologise. Please contact NCVO publications team so that we can make the corrections when the publication is reprinted.

A note about the law

Employment law changes very rapidly. Our understanding of and statement of employment law was correct, to the best of our knowledge, in January 2008.

If you wish to check the latest legal position, you can do this by following the references in each chapter of the guide.

If you are operating in Scotland or Northern Ireland, please note that legislation may be different in some circumstances.

Introduction

Lai-Har Cheung
Employment Practice Manager
UK Workforce Hub

The voluntary sector as an employer
The voluntary sector is a major force in the UK economy, with an annual income of £27.7 billion and employing over 611,000 people – that's one in 50, or 2.2%, of the UK workforce (source: UK Voluntary Sector Workforce Almanac 2007). This is a growth in the paid workforce of 26% in the last ten years.
Although voluntary and community organisations are aware that employment law must be complied with, many struggle to understand and implement it, and often lack the knowledge and skills that will help them to be good employers. We know that two-thirds of voluntary and community organisations do not have dedicated Human Resources (HR) staff.

We also know that 39% of the UK voluntary sector work part-time, which is higher than either the public or the private sector. We also know that one-third of workers (32%) are employed in workplaces with fewer than ten employees, and that 69% of the sector's employees are female; this all has implications on how organisations are able to deliver good employment practice.

Voluntary and community organisations are founded on passion and they need passionate people to keep them thriving. Go to a housing charity and you'll struggle to find anyone who isn't committed to solving housing problems. The sector is also more diverse than many people realise – numerous arts organisations, from galleries to music festivals, sports clubs and other societies, are also registered charities. The beauty of the voluntary and community sector is that whatever cause interests you, the chances are that a charity exists to support it.

However, the voluntary and community sector is no different from other sectors in experiencing recruitment and retention difficulties. We need to recruit the right skills and expertise, and when we do, we want to keep those staff. Being a poor employer can be expensive. The Chartered Institute of Personnel and Development has estimated the average cost of filling a vacancy per employee is £4,333. This increases to £7,750, when associated costs, such as costs of training the new recruit, are added (CIPD Recruitment, Retention and Turnover Survey 2007).

However, there are also indirect costs such as the impact on existing staff who may experience an increase in workload, time spent interviewing new candidates and if you don't appoint first time round, starting the process all over again. Perhaps more significantly, when someone leaves your organisation, they take with them vital knowledge of how your organisation works, and so even when you do appoint someone new, there will be a period of induction and probation before they are fully up to speed.

High staff turnover, poor staff performance and high levels of sickness absence, will all cost your organisation money. Can you afford this? What is the impact on your beneficiaries or service users – would they suffer because your staff perform poorly? Could your organisation survive being taken to an employment tribunal through poor employment practice?

We know that our staff are our most vital resource. It therefore makes sense that we take care in how we recruit, train and develop our employees. A good employer will be exploring ways to reward staff and to retain them for as long as possible. Being a good employer will mean you remain a strong competitor in attracting the right people in the first place.

On behalf of the UK Workforce Hub and NCVO, I am very pleased that Wendy Blake Ranken, the author, has done such an excellent job in revising the Good Guide to Employment.

I hope that you find this guide informative, straightforward to use and that it shows you how your organisation can be a good employer.

Who is this guide for?

Employment law is changing all the time. For those voluntary and community organisations recruiting their first paid worker, this guide offers a clear basis from which to start thinking about and recruiting that first member of staff.

Even those who currently employ staff, will benefit from updating their employment practices, keeping up with good practice and finding out about new resources.

What the guide covers

The guide 'walks you through' all the main stages of recruiting, developing and managing your staff and also helping you to understand the rights of employees and volunteers. Hopefully, the guide is here to answer some of the main 'how do I?' questions such as:

How do I...
- Attract the right person?
- Pay and reward staff?
- Draft their contract of employment?
- Appraise them?
- Comply with the law?
- Deal with performance, attendance or conduct problems?
- Handle disputes and differences of opinion?
- Deal with requests for maternity, paternity or adoption leave?
- Tackle redundancy?
- Respond to requests for flexible working?
- Follow the correct procedure for retirement?
- Pay expenses for volunteers?
- Ensure that all employment practices meet equal opportunities/ good diversity practice?

Having read this guide, you should be more confident about the basics of employing people and managing them well. You will also find a list of resources where you can find out more information.

Making the most of this guide

Chapter summaries
Each chapter starts by telling you what the chapter is about. Read this information first, as it will help you decide what you want to read in more detail.

Case studies and good practice examples
Throughout the guide, we have included case studies and examples of good practice. Several of these are based around a fictitious voluntary organisation, the Westwich Association. Others are from a variety of real voluntary organisations. We hope these will provide some context and 'bring to life' the different employment issues.

Checklists
At the end of each chapter, you will find a checklist of the main points covered in the chapter. You can use the checklists to review your current employment practices and to help you plan your future developments.

Index
This guide also has an index at the back, which we hope will make it easier for you to refer to the relevant information you need.

Further information
At the end of each chapter, there are references to where you can find out more. There are lots of references to online resources such as websites. The Internet is a quick and effective way of gaining information. If you do not have access to the Internet, telephone numbers are also provided where possible. You may also wish to note that many public libraries provide free Internet access.

In addition, there is a comprehensive list of resources at the back of the guide.

Other NCVO Good Guides
This publication is one of a suite of NCVO Good Guides. Others in the series include: the Good Campaigns Guide; the Good Financial Management Guide; the Good Guide to Working with Consultants; the Good Investment Guide; the Good Management Guide; the Good Membership Guide; and the Good Trustee Guide. You can go to www.ncvo-vol.org.uk/publications for more information or call NCVO on 0800 2 798 798 or textphone 0800 01 88 111, or to order any of the above call 0800 2 798 798.

NCVO Networks
NCVO's Personnel Network is free and open to anyone who has responsibility for human resources/personnel within a voluntary organisation.

NCVO's Charity Trainers' Network is free and open to anyone who has responsibility for training within a voluntary organisation and those who deliver training to the sector.

NCVO's Diversity Forum is free and open to anyone who is responsible for promoting and enabling diversity within a voluntary organisation.

The purpose of these networks is to enable members to share good practice, information and resources. Members receive regular emails which update on relevant issues, and each network runs up to four half day events a year.

If you would like further details about these networks or NCVO's other networks and forums, visit NCVO's website at www.ncvo-vol.org.uk/networks, contact NCVO's HelpDesk free on 0800 2 798 798 or textphone 0800 01 88 111.

Tell us what you think
We welcome your comments on this guide, to help us make sure that future editions are as relevant as possible. If you would like to comment, you can or e-mail publications@ncvo-vol.org.uk or write to: Information and Publishing, NCVO, Regent's Wharf, 8 All Saints Street, London N1 9RL

Contents

About the author

Wendy Blake Ranken is an independent NCVO-approved consultant. She has over 20 years' experience in Human Resources. Prior to becoming a consultant, she was Head of Personnel of a large UK voluntary sector organisation.

Wendy provides consultancy on a broad range of Human Resources matters, including diversity, performance management, recruitment and selection, reward and job evaluation, managing and communicating change, management training, employment disputes, mediation, employment policies and employment law. Her work is underpinned by a commitment to quality, fairness and good practice.

As well as her consultancy work, Wendy is an Employment Tribunal panel member.

Wendy has a degree in Mandarin Chinese, and a Masters degree in Human Resource Management. She is a Chartered Member of the Chartered Institute of Personnel and Development.

As well as writing this Good Guide, Wendy is the author of the following NCVO publications and documents:

A diversity and recruitment publication 'Are you looking at me?'

A publication on Staffing a Collaborative Project

Fact sheets on Transfers of Undertakings and sources of HR support.

Wendy Blake Ranken
wendy@blakeranken.clara.co.uk

One

Overview of rights, responsibilities and good employment practice

This chapter gives an overview of the essential things you need to know about employing people. It explains the legal obligations between employer and employee, and the legal rights of employees.

It also gives some ideas on how to be a good employer.

You might find this chapter of particular use if you are a first time employer. Alternatively, you might find that the chapter is a helpful route map to the rest of this Good Guide.

The chapter includes a practical case study of an employer appointing their first employee, including how they ensured they complied with their employment obligations.

General obligations in the employment relationship

Regardless of what is actually written down in an employment contract, employees and employers are expected to abide by certain unwritten obligations.

The employee must:
- render faithful service to the employer and not compete with the employer
- obey lawful and reasonable orders (consistent with their contract)
- exercise reasonable care and skill
- provide a personal service
- maintain confidentiality.

The employer must:
- pay agreed wages
- provide work
- provide a safe workplace
- pay out of pocket expenses
- provide reasonable notice
- maintain the relationship of trust and confidence by behaving reasonably towards the employee.

Legal rights of employees

Over the years, the law has provided a number of legal rights for employees.

The following information is adapted from the Acas Advisory Handbook, 'Employing people – a handbook for small firms' (downloadable from www.acas.org.uk). Acas is a government organisation that provides employment advice and support to employers and employees.

All employees have the right to certain benefits and conditions legally, they cover the areas of equality; leave; pay; contracts/conditions:

Equality
All employees have the right...

- not to be discriminated against or to suffer a detriment (including the right not to be dismissed) – on grounds of age, race, sex, marriage, disability, sexual orientation or religion or belief. See chapter 2 for further information.
- to equal pay – with members of the opposite sex if it can be shown that they are doing like work or work of equal value.
- to protection from being required to work on Sundays – shop workers have the right to opt out of the requirement to work on Sundays.

- for part-time workers to be treated no less favourably than comparable full-timers – the Part-time Workers (Prevention of Less Favourable Treatment) Regulations 2000 aim to ensure that part-time workers have the same terms and conditions as comparable full-timers. Less favourable treatment must be objectively justified. See chapter 4 for further information.
- for employees on fixed-term contracts to be treated no less favourably than comparable permanent employees – the Fixed-term Employees (Prevention of Less Favourable Treatment) Regulations 2002 aim to ensure that employees on contracts of fixed duration have the same terms and conditions of employment as comparable permanent employees. Less favourable treatment must be objectively justified. See chapter 4.

Leave

All employees have the right to...

- maternity leave – see chapter 8 for details
- paternity leave – see chapter 8
- adoption leave – see chapter 8
- parental leave (unpaid) – of up to 13 weeks in total (over 5 years) for each child. See chapter 8 for full details
- sick leave – see chapter 6
- time off for dependants – all employees have the right to take a reasonable period of unpaid time off work to deal with an emergency involving a dependant and not to be dismissed or victimised for doing so. See chapter 8.
- time off
  - for public duties (civic, magistrate, etc)
  - to look for work if declared redundant with at least two years' service
  - for trade union activities, duties and training (including acting as a Union Learning Representative) where a trade union is recognised for collective bargaining
  - for duties as an employee representative, or as a candidate for election, for purposes of statutory consultation over redundancies or business transfers or European Works Councils

- for carrying out functions as a safety representative (trade union or non trade union) or as a candidate for election as a representative of employees not in groups covered by trade union safety representatives
- for performing the functions of a pension fund trustee or undergoing relevant training
- to study, if employees aged 16 or 17 have not attained a certain standard of education
- for medical suspension if continued employment would endanger health (eg in the case of pregnancy).
- annual leave and working time limits – under the Working Time Regulations 1998, workers are entitled to 24 days paid leave (as of 1 April 2009 this will increase to 28 days) per year (pro-rata for part time staff), to rest periods and in-work rest breaks and health assessments in certain circumstances. The regulations also limit the average working week to 48 hours and limit night working to an average of eight hours in any 24-hour period. Special rules apply to young persons. See chapters 6 and 11 for further information.

Pay

All employees have the right to...

- maternity pay – see chapter 8
- adoption pay – see chapter 8
- paternity pay – see chapter 8
- redundancy pay – employees with at least two years' service are entitled to redundancy payments, the size of which depends on the individual's pay, age and service. See chapter 13 for further information.
- statutory sick pay (SSP) – paid by the employer (provided the employee meets the qualifying conditions) for up to 26 weeks. However, where an organisation has an exceptionally high level of sickness in any month, the employer may be able to claim reimbursement of a proportion of SSP paid out. For further information about SSP including the current rates, see the Business Link website www.businesslink.gov.uk.
- not have unlawful deductions from pay – employers must not deduct from an employee's pay unless the deduction is required or authorised by law or by a relevant provision of the employee's contract; or if the worker has previously given written agreement or consent for the deduction to be made.
- minimum pay – under the National Minimum Wage Act 1998, workers are entitled to be paid at least the level of the National Minimum Wage. See chapter 6 for further information.
- an itemised pay statement.

Contract/conditions

As part of their contract, or under terms and conditions employees have the right...

- to a written statement – of the main terms of the contract. See chapter 4 for further information.
- not to be unfairly dismissed – employees have the right to complain to an Employment Tribunal within three months of their dismissal, provided they have at least one year of continuous service. However, there are several circumstances where no continuous service is required; these are known as 'automatically unfair dismissals'. For example, if an employee is dismissed for: trade union activities; for seeking to assert a statutory right; for taking action on health and safety grounds; because of pregnancy and childbirth; or because of taking or seeking to take parental leave.
- to apply for flexible working – employees who are parents of children under the age of six or disabled children under the age of eighteen have the right to apply to their employer to work flexibly. Carers of adults also have the right to make this application. See chapter 8.
- to notice of termination of employment – most employees are entitled to receive from their employers at least one week's notice after one month's service, two weeks' after two years and an additional week's notice for each complete year of employment up to 12 weeks for 12 years' service.
- to a safe system of work – when an employer hires someone, the employer becomes legally responsible for their health and safety at work. See chapter 11 for further information.
- to trade union membership – employees have a number of rights, including the right:
  - to belong or not to belong to a trade union
  - to time off to take part in trade union activities/duties
  - not to be refused employment because of membership or non-membership of a trade union. See chapter 12 for further information on trade union matters.
- to protected employment rights – employees have the right to be transferred automatically, on the same terms without loss of service-related employment rights, from one employer to another when the business or part of the business in which the employee is then employed is transferred to a new employer or there is a service provision change eg outsourcing or in-sourcing ('TUPE' transfer). See chapter 14.
- to written reasons for dismissal on request – provided they have at least one year's service. If an individual feels they have been dismissed for reasons related to pregnancy or maternity, however, they have the right to written reasons for dismissal, even if they do not have one year's service and even if they do not request it.
- to be accompanied at disciplinary and grievance hearings – workers are entitled to be accompanied by a fellow worker or a trade union official of their choice at disciplinary and grievance hearings provided that they make a reasonable request to be so accompanied. See chapter 9 for further information.
- to protection when making disclosures of wrongdoing to the employer – the Public Interest Disclosure Act 1998 protects employees from being subjected to a detriment eg dismissal/disciplinary action who have a reasonable belief that they are disclosing information relating to criminal offences, miscarriages of justice, danger to health and safety or the environment or breaches of legal obligations to their employer. See chapter 12 for further information.

Legal obligations of employers

As well as the obligations to provide all the above rights to employees, employers must:

Register with HM Revenue and Customs if they are taking on an employee
HM Revenue and Customs will then send a new employer's starter pack with all the forms and tables required to run a payroll. You can call the New Employer's Helpline on 0845 60 70 143 to find out more.

Adhere to data protection principles
Some employee data is considered to be personal data and the Data Protection Act therefore applies to the processing of that data. The Data Protection Act 1998 covers both computer and manual records and works in two ways:

- it gives individuals certain rights, including the right to see information that is held about them and to have it corrected if it is not right. For a fee employees can ask to see the data you hold on them.
- it says anyone who records and uses personal information (data controllers) must be open about how the information is used and must follow eight principles of good information handling.

The eight principles of good information handling are that data must be:

- fairly and lawfully processed
- processed for limited purposes
- adequate, relevant and not excessive
- accurate
- not kept for longer than is necessary
- processed in line with the data subject's rights
- secure
- not transferred to countries outside the EU without adequate protection.

As an employer, you may need to register under the Data Protection Act. You can find out whether you need to register by calling the Information Commissioner on 01625 545740.

For a first time employer the information above can be a bit daunting. The followng case study will help you think about what you may actually need to do when you are thinking of employing a first member of staff.

'Anyone who records and uses personal information must be open about how the information is used'

Case study – first time employer

The Westwich Association began in 1995, in response to local concerns about a lack of facilities for young people.

The Association's first steering committee was elected from local residents, mainly comprising parents.

Money for the Association was raised via jumble sales and community events. A weekly youth club, run by volunteers, was established in a local hall.

By 2001, the Association had obtained charitable status. The Management Committee found that there was more work than could be done by the available volunteers. Several youth groups had been formed, but the youth work was somewhat disjointed and there was a feeling that resources could be used better. It was decided to employ a youth worker, whose job would be to co-ordinate all youth work. Funding was applied for and gained from a local charitable trust to employ a youth worker for two years.

In preparation for employing the youth worker, the Association did the following:

Looked on the Acas website www.acas.org.uk and downloaded a copy of 'Employing People: a handbook for small firms.' As they did not have internet access at the association premises, they made use of free internet access at the local library.

Acas advised them that they could attend a training session on employing people – which at the time was free as they employed less than five people.

They contacted HM Revenue and Customs (New Employer's Helpline 0845 60 70 143) to register as an employer and the Revenue sent them a new employer's starter pack, with all the tables, forms and information they would need to operate their payroll.

They also contacted the Information Commissioner to check if they needed to register as a data processor under the Data Protection Act (tel: 01625 545740). They downloaded information from the Business Link website www.businesslink.gov.uk on data protection, so that they knew their responsibilities.

Subsequent to the training, the Association drafted a written statement ('contract of employment') for the new employee – based on a model written statement downloaded from the Acas website.

The Association also used resources from the Acas website to draft brief disciplinary and grievance procedures.

The Association wanted to be a fair employer and so put together an equality statement of intent, to which all should comply. Having such a statement was also a condition of receiving funding for the youth worker post. They used the Acas handbook Tackling discrimination and promoting equality – good practice guide for employers to guide them.

The management committee checked whether they needed to provide a pension. They found that as they had less than 5 employees, they did not have a legal obligation to provide a pension scheme.

The Management Committee agreed who would manage the new employee.

Continued overleaf...

'Good managers genuinely listen to and consider their employees' views so everyone is actively involved in making important decisions'

They also agreed how the individual's salary would be administered, who would do returns to HM Revenue and Customs and who would arrange for the employee to be given an itemised pay statement each month.

The Association considered health and safety matters. Although there is a legal requirement to have a health and safety policy only when an organisation has five employees, they decided to draft a policy, using the free leaflet from the Health and Safety Executive called 'Starting your business: Guidance on preparing a health and safety policy document for small firms.' They downloaded the leaflet from www.hse.gov.uk. They already had first aiders amongst their volunteers, procedures for reporting accidents and fire procedures.

They found information on the Working Time Regulations from the website of the Department for Business, Enterprise and Regulatory Reform, www.berr.gov.uk/employment, and found out what rest breaks they needed to give. As a result, they made sure that if the youth worker worked late one evening, he or she would not be required to work the next day until 11 hours had passed.

They decided that as soon as the new employee was recruited, they would undertake a risk assessment on Display Screen Equipment use. They would also do a risk assessment on any danger to safety that may arise for the employee, due to working with some vulnerable and potentially volatile young people.

They were ready to recruit!

Become an employer of choice

Judith Leary-Joyce, in her book Becoming an employer of choice, analyses the practices of the Times Top 100 organisations to work for. She finds that these organisations:

- build a sense of belonging
- offer the best benefits possible
- are flexible and responsive
- provide support and care
- demonstrate trust
- develop people
- practice 'servant leadership' (leaders who help staff to achieve their best)
- recognise good work
- deal with poor performance (don't ignore it)
- communicate.

Acas has also undertaken some work, called the Acas Model Workplace, on what makes a great employer.

Acas divides the model workplace into three areas outlined below:

1. Put systems and procedures in place

- formal procedures for dealing with disciplinary matters, grievances and disputes that managers and employees know about and use fairly
- ambitions, goals and plans that employees know about and understand
- managers who genuinely listen to and consider their employees' views so everyone is actively involved in making important decisions

- a pay and reward system that is clear, fair and consistent
- a safe and healthy place to work

2. Develop relationships

- people to feel valued so they can talk confidently about their work and learn from both successes and mistakes
- everyone to be treated fairly and valued for their differences as part of everyday life
- work organised so that it promotes initiative and innovation and encourages people to work together
- an understanding that people have responsibilities outside work so they can openly discuss ways of working that suit personal needs and the needs of the business
- a culture where everyone is encouraged to learn new skills so they can look forward to further employment either in the business or elsewhere

3. Work together

- A good working relationship between management and employee representatives that in turn helps build trust throughout the business.

You can download a booklet about the Acas Model Workplace from www.acas.org.uk.

Case study – developing a positive place to work

Children's Links is a small voluntary sector organisation that has undertaken work to improve staff retention.

A first step was to assess information, including: absence statistics; feedback from exit interviews; and staff surveys. Children's Links also assessed reports from its IiP (Investors in People) review and ALI (Adult Learning Inspectorate) inspections. From this assessment, an action plan was developed.

Actions included:

- training for managers on appraisal skills
- an organisational training plan, which considered both organisational training needs and individual training needs.
- encouraging more informal communication within the office environment, including recognising achievements.
- introducing return to work meetings, if there were more than 3 separate absences within a year.
- reviewing the exit interview procedure, so that the HR Officer conducted the interview rather than the line manager.

If you would like more information about this case study, or would like to see other case studies, please refer to the UK Workforce Hub website at www.ukworkforcehub.org.uk.

Checklist

	Make sure you know the basic rights of employees, and the obligations of employers, outlined in this chapter
	Draft a health and safety policy, if you do not have one. Undertake any risk assessments that are required
	Produce a written statement of terms and conditions of employment. This document forms the basis of the contract of employment. It has to be given to employees within the first two months of employment, but ideally, you should give it when confirming a job offer, to avoid misunderstandings
	Set yourself up as an employer with HM Revenue and Customs. Make sure you deduct your new employee's tax and National Insurance contributions from their salary and pay this money to HM Revenue and Customs under PAYE
	Draft disciplinary and grievance procedures, which comply with statutory minimum requirements, as soon as you are able
	Draft an equality and diversity statement of intent or policy, as soon as you are able
	Audit yourself against the good practice standards outlined in 'Becoming an Employer of Choice' or in the Acas model workplace. What is your organisation already good at? What could it do next?

Further information

The following organisations offer advice and resources about the subjects covered in this chapter to new and existing employers, often free of charge:

Acas
www.acas.org.uk

Business Link
www.businesslink.gov.uk

Department for Business, Enterprise and Regulatory Reform (DBERR)
www.berr.gov.uk

HM Revenue and Customs
www.hmrc.gov.uk

NCVO
www.ncvo-vol.org.uk

UK Workforce Hub
www.ukworkforcehub.org.uk

A listing of all the useful organisations referred to in this Good Guide can be found at the back of this book with full contact details.

Two

Non-discrimination and good diversity practice

Exceptions to discrimination legislation

There are a small number of exceptions to discrimination legislation. These are outlined below.

Genuine occupational qualification/ genuine occupational requirement (GOQs and GORs)
Discrimination may be lawful in limited circumstances, if being of a particular group is a necessary (and not just desirable) genuine occupational qualification or requirement for a job.

Here are some examples to illustrate this:

1 An adviser on sickle cell anaemia to African-Caribbean people might be sought from the African-Caribbean community, on the grounds that someone from the same racial group is most able to provide the necessary services.

2 A women's refuge may state that its care assistants must be female, for reasons of decency or privacy.

3 A faith based care home may be able to show that being of a particular faith is a genuine requirement of its carers because they are required to carry out their duties in a manner that fulfils both the physical and spiritual needs of its patients. However, they may not be able to justify a similar requirement for their maintenance or reception staff whose jobs do not require them to provide spiritual leadership or support to service users.

If a GOQ or a GOR is to be applied to a job, this must be stated in the recruitment advertisement.

If you are in doubt about whether it is appropriate to apply a genuine occupational qualification/ requirement in a particular circumstance, you are advised to seek advice.

Positive action
It is possible to take certain steps to redress the effects of previous inequality of opportunity. This is called positive action and it is taken to encourage people from particular groups to take advantage of opportunities for work and training. This can be done when under representation of particular groups has been identified in the previous year.

Examples of positive action are:

1 Stating in recruitment advertisements that you particularly encourage disabled people or people from a certain gender, ethnic origin, sexual orientation or religion/belief to apply.

2 Providing additional training for these groups.

You should note that there is a difference between 'positive action' and 'positive discrimination'. Positive discrimination could be, for example, selecting someone for employment specifically because they are Black, in order to address under-representation in your organisation. Positive discrimination is unlawful in the UK. Whilst positive action enables you to encourage people from certain groups to apply, you should make clear that selection will be on merit without reference to background.

Disability charities
Disability charities are allowed to favour, in recruitment, those individuals who have a disability applicable to that charity. So, for example, a learning disability charity may specifically decide to recruit people with a learning disability.

'It is likely that your funders will require you to be able to demonstrate how you promote diversity and equality in your organisation'

The UK population is changing. For example:

- by 2025, half the adult population will be aged 50 and over
- women make up nearly half the workforce in the UK, double the number 25 years ago
- it is estimated that over 14% of the adult population of the UK are disabled
- people from Black and minority ethnic communities will account for more than half of the increase to the working age population in the next 10 years
- by 2010, it is predicted that only 20% of the UK working population will be white, male, able-bodied and under 45.

These changes will mean some radical rethinking by employers about how they encourage and retain a variety of workers and are flexible to different needs.

To be able to recruit the most appropriate people for your jobs, you will need to ensure that your organisation is one that celebrates diversity and is attractive to people from lots of different backgrounds.

There are also other reasons to promote equality and diversity:

- legislation requires that you do not discriminate against certain groups. If you are actively working towards equality and diversity, you are less likely to discriminate
- defending a discrimination claim can be expensive. It is important that you are clear about your responsibilities in respect of discrimination legislation, including the new age discrimination legislation, so that you make sure you do not discriminate without realising it

- as a voluntary organisation, you may be working to champion the rights of people who may suffer discrimination or be marginalised. If you are to reach the whole community in your work, it makes sense that your workforce and volunteers reflect the make-up of that wider community
- it is likely that your funders will require you to be able to demonstrate how you promote diversity and equality in your organisation.

Equality legislation

The law says that you must not discriminate against others on the grounds of:

- race, ethnic origin or national origins (Race Relations Act 1976 and Race Relations (Amendment) 2000)
- gender, marital status, transgender status or pregnancy (Sex Discrimination Act 1975, Equal Pay Act 1970 and Gender Reassignment Regulations 1999)
- disability (Disability Discrimination Act 1995 and Disability Discrimination Act 2005). The Disability Discrimination Act now applies to all employers, regardless of their size
- part-time status (Part-time Workers (Prevention of Less Favourable Treatment) Regulations 2000)
- fixed-term status (Fixed-term Employees (Prevention of Less Favourable Treatment) Regulations 2002)
- sexual orientation (Employment Equality (Sexual Orientation) Regulations 2003)
- religion, belief (including philosophical belief) or non-belief (Employment Equality (Religion or Belief) Regulations 2003)
- taking maternity, paternity, adoption or parental leave (Employment Rights Act 1996)
- age (Employment Equality (Age) Regulations 2006).

Forthcoming change
Please note that at the time of writing, government consultation had just closed on the proposal to implement a Single Equality Act, which would bring together all the above equality strands within the one Act. The intention is to make the law more effective, as well as simpler to understand and enforce.

Direct and indirect discrimination
The law says that both direct and indirect discrimination are unlawful.

Direct discrimination
This is when you specifically treat someone less favourably on one of the grounds covered by legislation. The following are examples of direct discrimination:

- not appointing a woman to a job because she is deemed to be 'of childbearing age'. This would be direct discrimination on the grounds of her gender and her age
- not appointing someone to a job because of their actual or perceived sexual orientation
- giving less favourable benefits to a part time member of staff, simply because they are part time
- failing to offer employment to a wheel chair user who was the best person for the job, on the grounds that the wheel chair might 'get in the way' in the office

- promoting someone because they would be younger than the people they would be managing.

Indirect discrimination
This is more subtle and may not be intentional. Whether it is intentional or not, it is unlawful. It involves applying a 'provision, criterion or practice' which considerably fewer people of the relevant group can comply with and which cannot be objectively justified. The following are examples which may constitute indirect discrimination:

- the imposition of a height requirement of 6 foot or over – because fewer women and individuals from certain minority ethnic groups would be able to comply
- refusing a request from an employee who wishes to reduce their working hours in order to be able to leave early on Friday afternoons in winter – so as to be home before nightfall – a requirement of their religion. This would be indirect discrimination unless you could justify the refusal (eg being certain that the employee's work had to be done at that time and no one else could do it)
- requiring a person whose second language is English to complete an employment application form, when written skills are not a requirement of the job.

'The proposed Single Equality Act will bring together all equality strands, making the law more effective'

A key issue with indirect discrimination is whether or not it is justified. In the examples above, if you can show that: you really need employees to be at least 6 foot; or if no one else can do the work on Friday afternoon; or if you need someone to be able to write English to do the job, then the requirements are justified, even though they may have a disproportionate effect on certain groups.

Reasonable adjustments in the Disability Discrimination Act (DDA) 1995

Disabled people are defined under the DDA as having a "physical or mental impairment which has a substantial and long term adverse effect on their ability to carry out normal day to day activities". The definition of disabled is quite wide and includes: people with HIV, cancer, or multiple sclerosis (MS) from the point of diagnosis; as well as severe disfigurements and mental illness, where that mental illness has a substantial and long term adverse effect.

The term indirect discrimination as such is not found in the DDA, but instead there is a requirement for employers to make reasonable adjustments to remove unreasonable physical, organisational or communication barriers, which a disabled person may encounter and which put them at a substantial disadvantage compared to others.

The Act does not specify what is reasonable and what is not, but the following examples highlight what adjustments could be considered:

- reallocating duties
- altering hours of work
- providing a reader or interpreter
- giving time off for therapy or rehabilitation
- modifying instructions and reference manuals
- assigning a disabled worker to a different place of work, eg the ground floor
- making adaptations to the written test used in an interview
- allowing job applications to be submitted on tape
- providing a blind or partially sighted person with a reader or adapted computer with large character, Braille display or speech output
- reallocating some minor duties to another colleague.

The Act says that an employer should pay regard to:

- the extent to which making the adjustment would assist the disabled person
- the practicability of taking the step
- the financial and other cost in making the adjustment and the extent to which taking it would disrupt any of the organisation's activities
- the extent of the employer's resources
- the availability of financial or other assistance for making the adjustment
- the nature of the employer's activities and the size of the undertaking.

This means that in some circumstances, an adjustment may not be 'reasonable' for you to make and you may be justified in refusing the adjustment. Also if the adjustment would not rectify or limit the substantial disadvantage in which the disabled person has been placed, it cannot be reasonable under the DDA to make it. However, do make sure you have explored all possible options before you refuse.

You should note that there is a government funded scheme called Access to Work. The service provides practical advice and financial help, of up to 100% of the cost of an adjustment for a new employee. You can contact your local Disability Employment Adviser (DEA) through your nearest JobcentrePlus office. The DEA will put you in touch with an Access to Work adviser.

'If you have a male and female employee doing the same job, or a job of equal value, and if one is earning more than the other, you must be able to justify the pay difference'

Victimisation and harassment
Victimisation or harassment of another employee are unlawful, on any of the grounds covered by legislation, such as sex, race, disability, sexual orientation, religion or belief and age.

Victimisation
would occur if you treated someone less favourably (for example, by denying them promotion) because they made a complaint of discrimination under one of the discrimination laws.

Harassment
is where one individual engages in unwanted conduct that has the effect of violating the dignity of another person, or creates an intimidating, hostile, degrading, humiliating or offensive environment for that person, for a reason related to one of the grounds covered by legislation eg disability, age, sex etc.
Here are some examples of what might constitute harassment:

- an employee making remarks about 'July 7th', and relating this to all Muslims. This is likely to be offensive to Muslim employees (harassment on the grounds of religion)
- the display of calendars and posters displaying nude or semi-nude women could be deemed to be harassment of female staff (sexual harassment)
- making derogatory remarks to colleagues about an employee with a learning disability (disability harassment)
- constantly calling an older worker 'grandad' or describing a younger worker as 'wet behind the ears', especially when the workers concerned have made it clear that they do not like such remarks (harassment on the grounds of age).

Equal Pay
Men and women have the right to an equal wage when the work they do is: the same or like work; or of equal value; or rated as equivalent.
For example, if you have a male and a female employee doing the same job, or a job of equal value, and if one is earning more than the other, you must be able to justify the pay difference if challenged. A justification might be, for example, that the pay difference is based on a difference in performance. However, if you cannot justify the difference objectively, it could be deemed to be discriminatory on the grounds of gender.

It is normally (but not exclusively) women who make equal pay claims against men.

For more information about equal pay, see chapter 6.

Positive duty to promote equality

There are three items of equality legislation that place duties on employers in the public sector to do more than simply not discriminate, but to positively promote equality. These items of legislation are: the Race Relations (Amendment) Act (RR(A)A) 2000; the Disability Discrimination Act 2005; and the Equality Act 2006.

Each of the Acts imposes a General Duty on public authorities, plus Specific Duties which explain how they must meet the General Duty, via race, disability and gender equality schemes.

The General Duty under the RR(A)A is to:

- eliminate unlawful race discrimination
- promote equality of opportunity
- promote good race relations.

The General Duty under the Disability Discrimination Act is to:

- promote equality of opportunity between disabled people and other people
- eliminate discrimination that is unlawful under the Disability Discrimination Act
- eliminate harassment of disabled people that is related to their disability

- promote positive attitudes towards disabled people
- encourage participation by disabled people in public life
- take steps to meet disabled people's needs, even if this requires more favourable treatment.

The General Duty under the Equality Act is to:

- promote equality of opportunity between women and men
- not to unlawfully discriminate between women and men.

Impact of the positive duties on the voluntary sector

These pieces of legislation primarily apply to the public sector, but the General Disability and Gender Equality duties (not currently the Race Equality Duty) also apply to those parts of voluntary organisations that are performing functions of a public nature. This includes the service delivery aspects of voluntary organisations, which have been outsourced from public authorities – such as the provision of care homes. The Specific Duties under the Acts, requiring public authorities to produce equality schemes, do not apply to the voluntary sector.

What voluntary sector organisations should do

If your organisation performs functions which are of a public nature, then you need to demonstrate how you are meeting the General Disability Equality and Gender Equality Duties. You could do this via an action plan – see the example shown later in this chapter. Alternatively, you could include specific equality actions within your strategic plan.

Even if your organisation does not perform functions of a public nature, there are other reasons for having objectives and actions related to equality:

- it is good practice to do so
- it is increasingly a condition of funding, from whatever source, that you can demonstrate how you are promoting equality. One reason for this is that public bodies need to be able to demonstrate that the organisations they fund are also meeting the General Duties in respect of race, disability and gender.

Exceptions to discrimination legislation

There are a small number of exceptions to discrimination legislation. These are outlined below.

Genuine occupational qualification/genuine occupational requirement (GOQs and GORs)

Discrimination may be lawful in limited circumstances, if being of a particular group is a necessary (and not just desirable) genuine occupational qualification or requirement for a job.

Here are some examples to illustrate this:

1 An adviser on sickle cell anaemia to African-Caribbean people might be sought from the African-Caribbean community, on the grounds that someone from the same racial group is most able to provide the necessary services.

2 A women's refuge may state that its care assistants must be female, for reasons of decency or privacy.

3 A faith based care home may be able to show that being of a particular faith is a genuine requirement of its carers because they are required to carry out their duties in a manner that fulfils both the physical and spiritual needs of its patients. However, they may not be able to justify a similar requirement for their maintenance or reception staff whose jobs do not require them to provide spiritual leadership or support to service users.

If a GOQ or a GOR is to be applied to a job, this must be stated in the recruitment advertisement.

If you are in doubt about whether it is appropriate to apply a genuine occupational qualification/ requirement in a particular circumstance, you are advised to seek advice.

Positive action

It is possible to take certain steps to redress the effects of previous inequality of opportunity. This is called positive action and it is taken to encourage people from particular groups to take advantage of opportunities for work and training. This can be done when under representation of particular groups has been identified in the previous year.

Examples of positive action are:

1 Stating in recruitment advertisements that you particularly encourage disabled people or people from a certain gender, ethnic origin, sexual orientation or religion/belief to apply.

2 Providing additional training for these groups.

You should note that there is a difference between 'positive action' and 'positive discrimination'. Positive discrimination could be, for example, selecting someone for employment specifically because they are Black, in order to address under-representation in your organisation. Positive discrimination is unlawful in the UK. Whilst positive action enables you to encourage people from certain groups to apply, you should make clear that selection will be on merit without reference to background.

Disability charities

Disability charities are allowed to favour, in recruitment, those individuals who have a disability applicable to that charity. So, for example, a learning disability charity may specifically decide to recruit people with a learning disability.

The Equality and Human Rights Commission

With effect from October 2007, a new body, the Equality and Human Rights Commission, has been established. It brings together the work of the following three Commissions, which now no longer exist:

• Commission for Racial Equality
• Disability Rights Commission
• Equal Opportunities Commission

The websites of these commissions have been incorporated into the new Equality and Human Rights Commission website, which is www.equalityhumanrights.com.

The role of the Commission is to enforce equality legislation on age, disability and health, gender, race, religion or belief, sexual orientation or transgender status, and encourage compliance with the Human Rights Act 1998. The Commission brings together equality experts and acts as a single source of information and advice. The aim is that the Commission will be able to tackle discrimination on multiple levels, because people may face more than one type of discrimination.

Codes of practice

Codes of practice exist on race, sex and disability discrimination. Whilst they are not part of the legislation, they may be taken into account by an employment tribunal as evidence that an employer was or was not following good procedure. The Codes have lots of useful information on how to promote equality and diversity and how to avoid discrimination.

The Codes can be downloaded from the website of the Equality and Human Rights Commission, at www.equalityhumanrights.com.

In addition, Acas has published the following guides:

• Guidance on Age and the workplace: a guide for employers
• Guidance on Religion or belief and the workplace
• Guidance on Sexual orientation and the workplace

The guides can be downloaded from the Acas website at www.acas.org.uk.

Institutional discrimination

Sometimes, discrimination can take place in an organisation, not because individuals discriminate, but because different needs are not taken into account. Policies and practices that have hitherto gone unchallenged may lead to unthinking ways of doing things that put some groups at a disadvantage. One way that institutional discrimination can happen is if, in our policies and practices, we make majority assumptions about other people, based on how we see the world.

Here are some examples of practices that may lead to institutional discrimination:

• recruitment practices which favour younger people, when there is no objective justification for this
• long salary scales, which may discriminate against women because they tend to have shorter service due to career breaks
• buildings and work arrangements that take into account the needs of able-bodied people, but not disabled people.

By developing an equality and diversity policy and action plan (outlined later in this chapter), you can avoid or work to eliminate institutional discrimination.

Diversity and equal opportunities

Equal opportunities is concerned with keeping within the law and ensuring that all personnel decisions concerning pay, recruitment and promotion are based only on an individual's ability to do their job well. Equal opportunities is about recognising that certain groups in society (such as people from Black and minority ethnic groups, disabled people and gay people) have experienced and do experience more discrimination than others.

Managing diversity complements, and expands on, equal opportunities. Diversity recognises that each individual is different in lots of different ways, not just the ways covered by law. This might not just be about who we are but also about our likes and dislikes, and how we lead our lives, our socio-economic differences and our educational background.

Valuing diversity can help develop your organisation, because people who are different can bring different ideas. This can help broaden your view on every aspect of the work of your organisation.

Developing a diversity and equality policy

The importance of a policy

Your starting point in promoting diversity and equality in your organisation is to develop a policy, with an action plan to back it up.

It is important to have a policy and action plan because:

- it will help to clarify the main issues and priorities for your organisation
- it is a basis for making required changes
- it sends a clear statement to staff about what is and is not acceptable, and on how they can be expected to be treated
- it may be required by your funders
- it helps you comply with the law.

Make sure you consult with your staff when developing your policy and action plan – your staff may have useful insights and they are also more likely to help with implementing change if they have been involved.

Your policy

You could follow the format below for your policy:

Introduction
Make a statement of your organisation's commitment to eliminate discrimination and promote diversity and equality and its desire to reflect the make-up of the community it serves.

Scope
You could list the main areas where you will ensure that discrimination does not occur. Include at least the areas that are covered by legislation, namely sex (including marital status and gender reassignment), race (including ethnic origin, colour, nationality and national origin) disability, age, part time status, sexual orientation and religion. Consider also including other factors which may lead to unfair discrimination, such as family background and educational background.

Expectations
You could list here the expectations of behaviour that you have of all staff. You could explain, for example, that you expect all staff members to treat each other with respect, regardless of personal differences.

You should also explain what staff can expect from your organisation. This might include:

'Valuing diversity can help develop your organisation, because people who are different can bring different ideas.'

- a work environment where individuals are judged on the work they do, not on who they are
- a work environment where harassment and bullying are not tolerated
- that if staff feel they are being treated unfairly or being harassed, they may use the grievance procedure and that their complaint will be dealt with swiftly and with due regard to confidentiality.

Note that some organisations have a specific policy on harassment, but for smaller organisations, it is normally sufficient for employees to be able to raise their concerns via the grievance procedure.

Commitments
You could list your commitments, which might include:

- developing an annual action plan
- communicating the policy and action plan to all employees and volunteers
- providing training on equality awareness
- regular review of employment policies and procedures, to eliminate any discrimination or unnecessary barriers
- monitoring (eg the workforce, applicants for employment, volunteers and service users) and taking action as a result of monitoring
- procedures for reviewing your equality and diversity policy.

Example
Equality policy, from the Acas handbook: Tackling discrimination and promoting equality – good practice guide for employers

(Organisation name) is committed to eliminating discrimination and encouraging diversity amongst our workforce. Our aim is that our workforce will be truly representative of all sections of society and each employee feels respected and able to give of their best.

To that end the purpose of this policy is to provide equality and fairness for all in our employment and not to discriminate on grounds of gender, marital status, race, ethnic origin, colour, nationality, national origin, disability, sexuality, religion or age. We oppose all forms of unlawful and unfair discrimination.

All employees, whether part-time, full-time or temporary, will be treated fairly and with respect. Selection for employment, promotion, training or any other benefit will be on the basis of aptitude and ability. All employees will be helped and encouraged to develop their full potential and the talents and resources of the workforce will be fully utilised to maximise the efficiency of the organisation.

Our commitment:

- to create an environment in which individual differences and the contributions of all our staff are recognised and valued
- every employee is entitled to a working environment that promotes dignity and respect to all. No form of intimidation, bullying or harassment will be tolerated
- training, development and progression opportunities are available to all staff
- equality in the workplace is good management practice and makes sound business sense
- we will review all our employment practices and procedures to ensure fairness
- breaches of our equality policy will be regarded as misconduct and could lead to disciplinary proceedings
- this policy is fully supported by senior management and has been agreed with trade unions and/or employee representatives. (Insert details if appropriate)
- the policy will be monitored and reviewed annually
- we will implement the intentions in this policy via an annual action plan.

'Tell staff about your parental leave policies
and flexible working polices, so that they know
what is available to them.'

Your action plan
Your action plan should state each
objective, how it will be achieved, by
whom and by when.

Example equality action plan

Target	Actions	Who?	By when?
To encourage people from the whole community to work and volunteer for us	Hold open day	Director to organise	June 2008
	Introduce an equality statement in all our advertisements.	Agree with Trustees; administrator to ensure the statement is used.	By November 2008
	Advertise in places accessed by the whole community eg doctor's surgeries	Staff team to agree best places to advertise; administrator to follow up	From now, with ongoing review of effectiveness
Update our recruitment documentation	Revise letters to applicants – offer to make adjustments	Joe to take on as a project	Review with Director end November 07 and end Jan 08
	Review our person specifications to ensure that there are no unjustifiable criteria		Complete by end Feb 08
	Remove date of birth from application form and enlarge font size		

Whilst the above actions are focused on employment matters, you could also build into your plan anything you want to achieve with regard to delivering your services or with regard to attracting and retaining volunteers. For example, you might want to take specific actions to reach a certain part of the local community which does not currently access your services.

Become an organisation that promotes diversity

Below are some practical steps that you could consider taking, to become an employer that promotes diversity. In addition to the steps below, you will find that throughout this guide, there are hints and tips on good diversity practice.

Be flexible
For job applicants:

- offer to produce documentation in alternative formats eg large print, online, Braille
- offer different ways of contacting you for an application pack eg email and fax as well as phone
- offer to receive application forms in different media, such as on tape (provided you have the capacity to listen)
- state in your documentation that you are committed to employing disabled people and ask all candidates if there are any adjustments they may require to the selection process
- offer flexible times to attend interviews, so that, for example, candidates can avoid times of religious observance or can accommodate child care responsibilities

- state that if a candidate is offered the job, you will be happy to discuss at that stage adjustments required and that this will not form a part of the selection process
- make adjustments that are requested.

For existing employees and new recruits:

- offer flexible working (eg flexible start/finish times, compressed week, working from home, job share or term time only working), as appropriate to the job
- tell staff about your parental leave policies and flexible working policies, so that they know what is available to them
- allow flexibility where possible in the way employees approach tasks: concentrate on results being achieved, on time and to standard; be less concerned about where, how and when the work was undertaken. You may need to train and support managers in this
- if possible, provide to all staff the right to take annual leave on the days of their major religious festivals.

Check your image

- undertake a review of the images you use in your publications and website. Make changes if needed
- consult with your existing staff, volunteers and service users about the image they consider that your organisation portrays
- make sure that the images you portray and the wording you use convey your positive stance to people from a variety of backgrounds, eg from Black and minority ethnic groups, carers, those with different religions, different ages etc
- consider becoming a 'two ticks' positive about disabled people symbol user. For further information, contact your local JobCentre Plus, or see www.jobcentreplus.gov.uk

Be welcoming

- train those (such as receptionists) who 'meet and greet' applicants for employment to treat everyone appropriately and with respect
- provide a work environment that is welcoming and accommodates individual lifestyles and needs (eg providing a room which is available during part of the day for quiet or prayer, providing a special chair for a back pain sufferer).

Show commitment

- adopt and implement fair employment practices – use this Good Guide as a start
- use an equal opportunities or diversity statement in your advertisements. If you have one already, check if it needs to be updated
- include in application packs your organisation's equal opportunities or diversity policy. Give brief details of what you have done to implement the policy as it will give the message that it is not just a piece of paper.

Improve your skills in assessing and appraising others

- make sure you and other managers are trained in interviewing skills – an unskilled interviewer may not be able to draw out the information needed to make a selection decision – and may therefore fall back on their assumptions
- focus your selection criteria more on the skills that are required and less on where or how the skills have been acquired: it is not only university graduates who are able to think analytically, for example
- consider and question stereotypes and 'baggage'. Such 'baggage' might include unconscious perceptions of the right sort of person in a job – a female secretary, for example

- in appraisals, ensure you focus on the job requirements, not on individual and irrelevant personal characteristics
- check that your training and development practices are sufficiently flexible. Are there alternatives to residential courses, for example?

Be willing to experiment and learn

- advertise your jobs in a variety of media – experiment to see what works
- have a look at the job advertisements placed by other organisations – obtain ideas for good practice
- listen to the views of others (volunteers, staff, trustees, service users) and learn from these views – don't always stick to 'this is how we do things around here'.

'Consider and question stereotypes and 'baggage'.
Is there an unconscious perception that secretaries
are female?'

Influence others
- even in the smallest charity, you'll need to influence others about what you want to do – you can't recruit and retain a diverse workforce on your own
- think about who you need to influence and why, such as managers, staff, volunteers, the Board
- consider what other people's viewpoints might be – and how you will deal with objections or concerns
- use statistics and data to persuade people (use the statistics as the beginning of this chapter, together with monitoring information from your organisation – see later in this chapter)
- have diversity as a standing item at meetings
- establish a network eg an equality and diversity working group with other similar voluntary organisations.

Case study – diversity in practice

We probably all want to have a workplace which is positive about diversity, but where do we start? Below is some information about what two organisations have done.

Glasgow Association for Mental Health is an independent organisation and is established as one of the principal providers of mental health services in Greater Glasgow.

GAMH took the following actions to promote diversity:

Senior managers wrote down all the functions in the organisation, eg recruitment, service delivery etc. This helped them to analyse each area of work in relation to equality.

An Equalities Action Group was established, followed by smaller groups relevant to each equality task.

The senior management team attended equality training. The aim was then for all staff to attend the training.

GAMH appointed a Senior Project Worker to support project staff on inclusive practice development.

GAMH is now considering equality in relation to the full journey of staff through the organisation. They have started with recruitment, for example considering where they place their adverts and updating their application form so that it is anonymised.

GAMH intend to continue reviewing the staff 'journey', by looking at issues in relation to staff training and development, secondment, acting up opportunities etc, up to and including leaving the organisation.

'If you want to improve the diversity of your workforce, you'll need to monitor both job applicants and existing employees.'

Case study– diversity training

The Diversity Hub is an organisation that runs a programme of open community workshops on a range of diversity topics. The Hub also delivers training contracts to institutions, organisations, groups and in neighbourhoods.

The Diversity Hub trains all their new staff, trustees and volunteers in their 'welcoming diversity and prejudice reduction' workshop. They have found that this workshop provides a really useful vehicle for:

– welcoming people for who they are

– providing an opportunity for people to get to know a lot of others faster

– demonstrating that the Hub takes diversity and equality very seriously

– setting a culture that leaves little space for prejudice, discrimination and bullying to flourish

– providing a foundation to diversity and equalities work and practical skills to work for change

– alerting people to the expectation that the Hub views every individual as a champion for diversity.

The Hub found that this was a very lively, upbeat way to introduce someone to the organisation and the organisation to new people.

The Hub reports that people continually refer back to their first workshop with them as a turning point in their understanding of diversity issues, as well as how quickly they felt integrated within the organisation.

For more information about these case studies please refer to the UK Workforce Hub website at www.ukworkforcehub.org.uk.

The Investors in Diversity Standard

The Investors in Diversity (IiD) standard is a relatively new standard, from the National Centre for Diversity. The standard provides a route map to help organisations to adopt, develop and benchmark behaviours and practices, which promote inclusion, equality, diversity and achievement.

The standard allows organisations to measure their progress and receive recognition for their achievements.

If you are interested in becoming an Investor in Diversity, you can register online at www.nationalcentrefordiversity.com /iid/register.

Once you have registered, you will be contacted by the National Centre for Diversity, in order to arrange a visit by one of their approved IiD advisors. You then receive two days of support, prior to formal assessment.

During the first day of support, the IiD standard will be explained to you. Following the first day of support, you will be given a mutually agreed amount of time to make progress against the requirements of the IiD standard.

The second day of support is a shared review between you and the IiD advisor. At the end of the day, the advisor will give you an indication of how much progress you have made and when you may be ready to undertake an assessment.

When you are ready, you will have a formal assessment by an independent Centre for Diversity Approved IiD assessor. If you are successful you will assume the status of an Investors in Diversity accredited organisation for a period of two years, after which you will be able to be re-assessed.

Once it is possible to measure the impact of your work on in the longer term, not less than two years, you may be able to become accredited as a Leader in Diversity.

For further details and costs, go to www.nationalcentrefordiversity.com, or phone 0113 283 7100.

Equality monitoring

If you want to improve the diversity of your workforce, you'll need to monitor both job applicants and existing employees.

Monitoring can:
- highlight possible inequalities
- enable an investigation of possible causes
- allow you to remove unfairness or disadvantage.

Monitoring is not a legal requirement in the voluntary sector, but it is good practice and your funders may also expect you to do it.

Workforce monitoring

If yours is a very small organisation, formal monitoring of your workforce may not be necessary. You are likely to know the age, gender, ethnic group and any disability of your staff. However, if your organisation is larger, it can be useful to monitor the percentages of people from different groups. This can help you to assess, for example, whether disabled people or people from a particular minority ethnic group are under-represented in your organisation or not.

You could monitor your workforce as follows:
- numbers of staff from different ethnic groups
- numbers of disabled staff
- numbers of male and female staff
- age ranges of staff
- sexual orientation and religion or belief (but note that this information is particularly sensitive and staff may not wish to divulge it).

You could analyse this information by salary level and grade.

Recruitment monitoring

It is good practice to monitor applicants for employment, because this will tell you whether you are attracting applicants from all sections of your local community. It will also tell you how applicants from different groups fare during the selection process.

Further information on recruitment monitoring is given in chapter 3.

Starting to monitor

Start monitoring at a level you can cope with – and don't collect more information than you will use. You might decide, for example, to focus on ethnic origin in one year, and disability, gender, age, sexual orientation or religion in other years.

If your organisation is small, you may want to analyse the data less frequently, eg every few months as the data will be more meaningful. It may also be several years before clear patterns emerge.

You should note that monitoring sexual orientation may be particularly sensitive. Think carefully about why you need the information and how you are going to use it, so that you can explain it to your staff. Your main reason for collecting it will probably be to assess whether you are under-represented by people who are gay, lesbian or bisexual, so that you can consider why and take action accordingly.

However, if, in fact, your main focus in the coming year is on increasing the ethnicity or age range of your workforce, then don't collect data on sexual orientation if you are not going to use it to develop your organisation.

Qualitative monitoring

As well as the statistical monitoring outlined above, you could also consider:

- surveying staff to gain their views about equality in the organisation (see chapter 12 for an example staff survey)
- surveying successful and unsuccessful applicants to gain their impressions of how they were treated during the recruitment and selection process.

Benchmarking your monitoring data

In order to assess whether your workforce is representative of the local community, you will need to compare (benchmark) your data with external data. The main source of information is the 2001 census, which you can get from www.statistics.gov.uk/census. In addition, you can benchmark your data against internal data from previous years, or from department to department (if you are a larger organisation).

What to do with the results

Differences between groups are not, in themselves, evidence of discrimination. However, you will need to study the results further, find out why there are differences, and tackle any barriers you find.

The Equality and Human Rights Commission identifies three categories of actions:

1. Removing unfair barriers for example, considering whether the qualifications you are asking for are strictly necessary and whether they are barring certain groups in the community from applying for your jobs.

2. Examining decision making considering, for example, whether you and your managers are taking fair decisions, or whether there may be a tendency to 'recruit like me; or 'recruit like the previous post holder.'

3. Outreach and positive action considering what you could do to encourage people to work for you. Experiment with advertising in different areas or with putting positive statements on your recruitment advertising. See chapter 3 for further information.

'Start monitoring at a level you can cope with – and don't collect more information than you will use'

Keep monitoring

Think carefully about implementing a monitoring system that is easy to maintain and make sure you keep the momentum up with monitoring. The Equality and Human Rights Commission (in its publication 'Ethnic Monitoring – a guide for public authorities') comments that: 'Monitoring is part of an ongoing process of analysis, asking questions, investigation and change.'

Case study– monitoring

Below is an example of how one organisation has monitored lesbian, gay, bisexual and transsexual people in its organisation.

Nacro, the crime reduction charity describes its vision as enabling "a safer society where everyone belongs, human rights are respected and preventing crime means tackling social exclusion and re-integrating those who offend". Nacro has been established since 1966 and has about 1400 staff. It is very proud of being listed number 24 out of 100 employers in Stonewall's Corporate Equality Index 2005.

The organisation has a self-organised lesbian, gay, bisexual and transgender (LGBT) group called 'Pride in Nacro' which is funded by Nacro. Nacro canvasses staff attitudes in an annual equality and diversity audit. Staff asked for the organisation to start monitoring with respect to sexual orientation – this was one of the outcomes of the audit. In 2004 Nacro found that 8.1% of its staff defined themselves as lesbian, gay or bisexual: an increase from 6% the year before. The audit does not tell Nacro if the number of LGB staff has gone up or if the increase in numbers is more about the confidence of their employees in answering that particular question.

Pride in Nacro however does report that the last recruitment drive in Manchester resulted in half of those appointed identifying as LGB and that those people applied to work for Nacro because they felt comfortable to apply for a post with a company who is obviously an equal opportunities employer and sympathetic to LGBT issues. Nacro also organised a very successful conference on LGBT issues in November 2004 that was attended by 90 staff. The conference generated a lot of interest and received excellent feedback.

The monitoring information is collected anonymously and confidentially by the group's Race Equality Adviser whose position is located within the Chief Executives Office.

Checklist

- Make sure you are aware of discrimination legislation and what you need to do to comply
- Make reasonable adjustments so that disabled people can work in your organisation
- Draft a diversity and equality policy
- Develop a diversity and equality action plan. Start with steps you can achieve and review progress regularly
- Take practical steps to promote diversity – avoid institutional discrimination
- Monitor applicants for employment and (unless your organisation is very small) your workforce
- Keep checking how you are doing – implementing diversity is an ongoing process
- Investigate fully and promptly any allegations of discrimination, harassment or victimisation

Further information

The following organisations offer advice and resources about the subjects covered in this chapter to new and existing employers, often free of charge:

Acas
The following publications can be downloaded from the Acas website:

- Guidance on Age and the workplace: a guide for employers
- Guidance on Religion or belief and the workplace
- Guidance on Sexual orientation and the workplace
- Good practice guide – tackling discrimination and promoting equality

Acas also runs Equality Direct, which is a confidential advice service for small businesses on equality.
www.acas.org.uk

Age Positive
You can download the Code of Practice on Age Diversity in Employment from the Age Positive website
www.agepositive.gov.uk

Business Link
www.businesslink.gov.uk

Department for Business, Enterprise and Regulatory Reform (DBERR)
www.berr.gov.uk

Equality and Human Rights Commission (EHRC)
www.equalityhumanrights.com

HM Revenue and Customs
www.hmrc.gov.uk

Jobcentre Plus
www.jobcentreplus.gov.uk

National Centre for Diversity
www.nationalcentrefordiversity.com

National Council for Voluntary Organisations (NCVO)
www.ncvo-vol.org.uk

UK Workforce Hub
www.ukworkforcehub.org.uk

A listing of all the useful organisations referred to in this Good Guide can be found at the back of this book with full contact details.

Three
Recruitment

This chapter gives you good practice information about each step in the recruitment process. It covers:

- Defining what you need
- The job description
- The person specification
- Finding applicants
- The application process
- Short listing
- Arranging and preparing for interviews
- The interview
- Other selection methods
- Deciding who to appoint
- References
- Checks under the Immigration, Asylum and Nationality Act 2006
- Criminal Records Bureau checks ('Disclosures')
- Independent Safeguarding Authority
- Registration
- Recruitment of care staff in regulated social care services
- Monitoring recruitment
- Genuine occupational qualification/requirement

NCVO has a specific publication on recruitment, called 'Are you looking at me?' It is available for order from www.ncvo-vol.org.uk/publications, or by calling the NCVO helpdesk 0800 2 798 798.

'Before spending time and money on recruiting someone, take some time to consider what you actually need'

Defining what you need

Before spending time and money on recruiting someone, take some time to consider what you actually need. For example:

- Is your need long term or short term?
- Is it full time or part time?
- What hours are required and how constant is the work?
- Do you need a permanent employee, an employee for a fixed term, or perhaps a freelance consultant to complete a specific project?
- How will this role interact with the current responsibilities of your existing employees, trustees and volunteers?
- Who will manage the new employee?
- What is the salary level/grade of the post?
- If replacing a previous employee, are there any changes to make to the job role/description?

The job description

Once you have decided broadly what you need, you can draft a job description. The job description sets out the position to be filled and the responsibilities involved.

There is no one right way to draft a job description, but try and make it clear using straightforward language. Generally, you should need to specify no more than around eight key responsibilities. It is good practice to include a statement in the job description outlining the employee's equality and diversity responsibilities.

Example job description

JOB DESCRIPTION

Job Title: Personal Assistant
Responsible to: Director
Responsible for:
Office Administrator

Purpose of role
To be responsible for providing administrative support to the Director and for ensuring the smooth running of the office.

Key Responsibilities
1. To manage the Director's diary, including booking meetings and making travel arrangements.
2. To arrange Trustee meetings and take minutes.
3. To manage the information services (reference library, filing system, database and address lists).
4. To ensure input to (organisation's) database is consistent and accurate.
5. To manage the stationery supplies, ensuring that there is always adequate stationery and that costs are controlled.
6. To manage the photocopier contract.
7. To provide general administrative support to the Director.
8. To undertake all duties in a way that values others, does not discriminate and promotes equality.
9. To undertake any other duties as may be required from time to time.

Date drafted/updated: March 08

The person specification

The person specification sets out the knowledge, skills and experience that are required for the job. This is a really important document, because you will use it to decide who to shortlist for interview and who to appoint.

Make sure that all the criteria you use in the person specification are justified and necessary for the job, to avoid putting barriers in the way of applicants who may actually be suitable.

Consider the following:

- specify clearly which criteria are essential (the ones that applicants must have) and which criteria are desirable (these criteria could be acquired after appointment)
- avoid stating the number of years experience in a job that may be required, because people learn at different rates. It could also constitute discrimination on the grounds of age. Instead, define the specific experience required
- state that the required experience may have been gained from paid or voluntary work
- only ask for qualifications if they are necessary for the job. For example, 'A level standard or above' could be made more specific by explaining what you actually need. Your need might be, for example, an ability 'to analyse information and produce logical conclusions'
- if you do need a qualification, make sure you say 'or equivalent overseas qualification'
- avoid subjective words such as 'intelligent' or 'energetic'. Instead, describe what is required to do the job, for example, 'the ability to manage and organise several tasks at once'

- don't put in any age restrictions, such as 'age 18–30'. Not only is it irrelevant to the ability to do the job, it also is a strong indication that you will discriminate against candidates outside of this age range. Such discrimination is unlawful under the Age Discrimination Regulations 2006
- if you want 'good interpersonal skills', define what you mean by this. For example, do you mean 'able to deal with a wide range of people in a courteous and helpful manner' or: 'able to present proposals in a logical manner, argue a case and resolve conflict'?
- avoid requiring applicants to be able to drive, unless absolutely necessary. You might state instead: 'Must be able to travel around the xx area'. This allows for applicants who are unable to drive, for reason of disability or for another reason, to propose how they could do the job without driving a car
- state whatever flexibility you can in terms of working hours – job share or part time working, for example.

Example person specification

PERSON SPECIFICATION **Job title:** Personal Assistant		
Criteria	E or D	S or I
Knowledge Knowledge of Microsoft Word, Excel, PowerPoint, databases and electronic diary management	E	S/I
A knowledge of office procedures	E	I
Skills Able to prioritise and carry out administrative tasks independently.	E	I
Shows initiative and takes personal responsibility for completing tasks.	E	I
Able to communicate with others courteously on routine matters.	E	I
Adopts a positive attitude – willing to assist others even when busy.	E	I
Able to write clearly, with correct grammar and punctuation.	E	S/I
Able to work under pressure on occasions, to achieve administrative deadlines.	E	I
Able to type quickly (60wpm) and accurately	E	I
Able to pay attention to detail, ensuring that nothing is forgotten.	E	I
Experience Previous experience of administration (in paid or unpaid work), including: drafting correspondence independently; diary management; and dealing with a variety of administrative matters simultaneously.	E	S/I
Experience of taking minutes.	D	S/I
Experience of supervising others.	D	S/I
Qualifications No specific qualifications required.		
Circumstances This post is based at our Head Office in xxxx.		
The post is a full time job, but we will positively consider applications from part time workers and job sharers.		
Flexible working hours are available for this post.		
There is a very occasional requirement for evening/ weekend work in this job.		

E = essential criteria
D = desirable criteria
S = short listing criteria
I = interview criteria

Finding applicants

There are a number of ways of finding applicants for your job. The way you choose to advertise will depend on:

- how much you are willing and able to pay
- how fast you want to get a response
- how much time you have to administer the response
- the type of job to which you are recruiting.

Jobcentre Plus

The Jobcentre Plus service is similar to that offered by employment agencies, but is free of charge.

Within two hours of receipt Jobcentre Plus will post your vacancy on their website. Your vacancy will also be shown on the touchscreen 'jobpoints', where job applicants can browse for jobs in jobcentres.

Jobcentre Plus offices may also offer extra services, for example:

- use of interview rooms
- help with sifting applications
- job fairs
- government support for employers.

You can find out more about Jobcentre Plus on their website at www.jobcentreplus.gov.uk. Alternatively, you can find your nearest Jobcentre Plus in your local telephone directory.

Website recruitment

Recruitment via the internet can be relatively quick and lower cost than, for example, a newspaper advertisement.

There are several recruitment websites and the one you choose will depend on which job you are filling.

Here are four websites for the voluntary sector:

www.charitypeople.com

www.jobsincharities.co.uk

www.jobsincharity.co.uk

www.charityjob.co.uk

There are also general websites that include voluntary sector jobs. One of the largest is www.totaljobs.com

You can place details of your vacancy on the recruitment website you choose, for a fee. Once you have placed the information, applicants can contact you in one of the following ways:

- by following a weblink to your organisation's website (if you have one) and from there downloading an application pack and application form
- by contacting you via your phone number, address or email address to request an applicant pack
- by applying online by sending a CV to you or completing an online application form, which is then sent to you.

Try and give applicants as many ways of contacting you as possible to meet different needs.

Newspaper and magazine advertisements

Newspapers and magazines may help you target more accurately (you could use a fundraising magazine if you are looking for a fundraiser, for example) but may not be as quick or as cheap as using an internet site.

Here are some things that your newspaper or magazine advert should include:

- a brief summary of the job – enough information for applicants to decide whether to apply
- the skills and experience needed (base these on your person specification and beware of adding new words such as 'dynamic' or 'energetic')
- the location (be as specific as possible) and the pay
- how the applicant should apply: by sending a CV or requesting an application form. Include a variety of ways of contacting you, such as telephone, e-mail or via your website
- the closing date for applications.

'Newspapers and magazines may help you target more accurately but may not be as quick or as cheap as using an internet site'

The more you include in your advertisement, the more it will cost, but if possible, you could also include the following:

- a statement of commitment to equality and diversity
- a statement of commitment to flexible working including job share
- a statement offering the advertisement and other recruitment material in an alternative format if required
- a statement indicating that experience may have been gained from paid or voluntary work.

For ideas on drafting advertisements, have a look at some local and national papers. Alternatively, you could ask a recruitment advertising agency to draft and typeset your advertisement for you. Their artwork is likely to be better than most voluntary organisations could produce in house. This approach may be no more expensive than placing the advertisement yourself, because recruitment advertising agencies often have discounts with local and national newspapers.

Recruitment agencies
Recruitment agencies have a database of job applicants and will search the database to find suitable applicants for your job. They can also place an advertisement and short list on your behalf. This can save you time.

If you are recruiting to particular types of job, such as IT staff, you may wish to approach an agency that specialises in this field. Alternatively, you could approach an agency that deals in the not-for-profit sector. You can find a list of recruitment agencies which specialise in the not-for-profit sector at www.workingforacharity.org.uk.

If you decide to use an agency, make sure you have agreed fees, including any advertising costs, and other terms before you appoint them.

Internal advertisements
Make sure you always advertise your vacancy amongst your existing workforce. It can be very demoralising for an existing member of staff seeking promotion to learn about a vacancy only when it is filled.
Some organisations only advertise internally in the first instance, in order to give staff career development opportunities and to alert volunteers to vacancies. If no suitable applicant is found, only then is the post advertised externally.

Other organisations always advertise internally and externally at the same time. This will be particularly important if your current workforce is not very diverse, because an internal advert will just perpetuate the profile of your existing workforce. Some funders also require all new posts to be advertised externally. Please note, however, that there is no legal requirement to place an external advertisement.

Other sources of applicants
You could try a number of free ways of advertising, such as local colleges and schools or a notice outside your own premises.

'To avoid allegations of age discrimination it is recommended to have an age neutral application form'

Targeting specific sections of the community

You may find that your workforce is not representative of specific sections of the community. For example, you may find that you have few BME (Black and minority ethnic) staff at senior levels, or that you are not attracting older workers.

You can use advertising to target specific sections of the community. You could place your advertisement with Jobcentre Plus and discuss recruiting disabled people with the Jobcentre Plus Disability Employment Advisor. You could try the publications produced by the Ethnic Media Group, in order to attract more BME applicants. You can contact them via their website at www.ethnicmedia. co.uk or call 020 7650 2000.

You could simply advertise in the local or national media (which after all will be read by people with diverse backgrounds), but also include a welcoming statement in your advertisement, that you wish to attract people from all sections of the community, or that you are particularly keen for certain groups to apply.

Experiment with different approaches and monitor the result.

Example recruitment advertisement by the Westwich Association

Community Outreach Worker

15 hours per week (flexible working hours possible)

£20,000 pro-rata.

One year contract (may be extended subject to funding)

The Westwich Association exists to provide youth services in the local community. We are looking for an Outreach Worker to help us reach the local Bengali community.

You should have experience of working (on a paid or voluntary basis) in the Bengali community. Computer skills, ability to travel round the local area, ability to speak Bengali and to work independently are essential.

For an application pack, telephone 0103 666 345, write to Westwich Association, 12 Holly Hill, Westwich, WA2 6EN, or e-mail vacancies@ westwich.org.uk. If you would like to receive the application pack in an alternative format, please let us know.

Closing date: 15 July 2008
Interview date: 22 August 2008

We value diversity and welcome applicants from all parts of the community

The application process

You will need to make clear to applicants how you want them to apply.

You may find that for some types of job, applicants are more likely to apply if they can just send in their CV, rather than having to complete an application form. CVs may also be less work for you initially, because you do not need to send out an application form to prospective applicants. However, the short listing process may take you longer, as it can be more difficult to short list when applications do not come in a common format.

Application forms
This is generally considered better from an equal opportunities/diversity point of view, because information on each applicant is presented in a common format and there is therefore less possibility of bias creeping in.

If you want to use an application form, you can draft your own. You could look at examples of application forms from other employers to get ideas. Alternatively, you could use the model form available from the Acas website. Go to www.acas.org.uk and in the search box, type 'employment forms.'

To avoid allegations of age discrimination it is recommended to have an age-neutral application form. There is an example model form produced by the Employers' Forum on Age. It is designed so that the required information for a job is gained, but that any indication of the applicant's age or educational dates (which should be irrelevant to your considerations) are removed. You can access the form at www.efa.org.uk/policy/steps_recruitment.asp.

You could consider having an application form where the front page containing individuals' names, addresses and other personal details is removed from the rest of the application form before short listing, to avoid bias.

Application Pack
It is helpful to produce an application pack as well as an application form because it gives applicants additional information and is also your opportunity to sell your organisation. You could send or e-mail your pack to applicants with an application form or make it available on your website if you have one.
Below are some of the things you should consider including in the pack:

Covering letter
This should welcome the application and give details of: the closing date for applications; the date for interviews; and (if possible) a named person whom applicants can call to discuss the job. You could also include a statement of your organisation's willingness to cater for specific requirements, for example on grounds of religion or belief, disability or caring responsibilities. The letter could ask applicants what adjustments they may need to the selection process, such as larger print or an application on tape. You could also include a statement of your organisation's positive attitude towards ex-offenders and that criminal records will only be taken into account if relevant to the job.

In order to minimise administration, some voluntary organisations include a statement in the covering letter to say that if the applicant has not heard from the organisation by a certain date, the applicant should assume that they have not been short listed for interview.

Application form
and any guidance about completing the form.

Job description
See the earlier section in this chapter.

Person specification
See the earlier section in this chapter.

Your equality and diversity policy
See chapter 2 for further information.

Continued overleaf...

Short listing

Summary of the terms and conditions of employment for the job

You could produce a one-page document, giving details of the salary and any salary scale, annual leave, sick pay, pension and any flexible working arrangements. A word of caution here, though – when someone is appointed, they may be able to rely on information given in this summary or elsewhere in the application pack as a contractual term. Make sure this information is correct.

Equal opportunities monitoring form

This enables you to monitor the diversity of applicants. The information on this form should not be used in the short-listing process. The form should make clear why it is important for applicants to complete it. The section on monitoring later in this chapter provides an example form.

Some information about your organisation

A brief and positive overview of what your organisation does and about the part the job plays in the organisation can be helpful in encouraging applicants.

Short listing is the process of deciding who you will invite for interview.

After the closing date for applications and before short listing, the recruitment monitoring forms should be removed. They should be removed if possible by someone who is not involved in the short-listing and selection process.

Once removed, the monitoring forms should be set-aside until the end of the recruitment process. The section on monitoring recruitment, later in this chapter, explains what to do with the forms.

You can now consider which applicants you wish to invite to interview. You should look to short-list a manageable number of applicants. About seven or eight applicants is normally about the right number.

You should compare the knowledge, skills and experience of each applicant against the essential criteria outlined in your person specification. It can be helpful to list the criteria on a sheet of paper, then mark the candidates against these criteria, for example in terms of 'meets criterion', 'partly meets criterion' and 'does not meet criterion.' You could use a short-listing form for this process. For an example form, see the NCVO recruitment publication 'Are you looking at me?'.

If you still have a large number of applicants, you can then further reduce the number you will short list by assessing them against the desirable criteria in the person specification.

You could take a policy decision in your organisation that disabled applicants who meet the essential criteria for the post will be automatically interviewed, even if they do not meet the desirable criteria. This is one of the commitments that 'two ticks' (positive about disabled people) symbol users make. You can make this commitment whether or not you are a 'two ticks' symbol user (if you want to become a 'two ticks' symbol user, contact your local Jobcentre Plus, or see www.jobcentreplus.gov.uk

When short-listing, you should obviously not discriminate unlawfully against applicants, for example on the grounds of sex, race, disability, sexual orientation, religion or belief or age – see chapter 2 for further information.

'you should interview with at least one other person, to avoid bias and gain a rounded view of each applicant'

Arranging and preparing for interviews

Invite short-listed applicants to interview by letter or by telephone.

You should tell them:

- when, where and how long the interview will be
- how to get there – provide a map if necessary – and whether you will pay travel expenses
- what, if any, documents they should bring
- who they should ask for on arrival
- the names and job titles of the people conducting the interview
- details of any test or presentation they may be required to do
- your willingness to cater for specific requirements, for example due to disability or religious belief. You should ask applicants to tell you if they have any such requirements. For example, they may require wheelchair access or facilities to assist with sight or hearing impairments.

You should prepare for the interview in advance. The more preparation you do, the easier it will be for both you and the applicant.

Before the interview you should consider and prepare for the following:

- you should interview with at least one other person, to avoid bias and gain a rounded view of each applicant.
- use the criteria from the person specification to develop a set of questions. For example, if one of the requirements is to organise one's own workload, you could prepare a question about how applicants have gone about organising their workload in previous employment or voluntary work
- decide between yourself and other interviewers who will deal with which topics
- think about what information applicants may want about the job and your organisation
- make sure that the interview venue is as accessible as possible and that the interview room is properly prepared, with drinks available
- make the applicant feel comfortable physically in the interview to enable them to give a better performance at the interview. For example, it is best not to hold the interview sitting behind a desk, or to use a higher chair than the person being interviewed. Sitting around a low round table can be a good idea

- make sure you have made any requested adjustments for disabled applicants. A person with a learning disability may wish to bring a supporter, for example, or a hearing impaired person may wish to have a copy of the interview questions
- avoid holding the interview on the date of a major religious festival
- timing of the interviews should be flexible to help applicants with family commitments
- make sure there will be no interruptions and switch off mobile phones
- brief other members of staff, such as receptionists, to expect the applicant
- allow enough time for each interview so you don't have to rush. This may be particularly important if you need to accommodate an applicant with a disability.

'It is good practice to involve service users in the selection interview and often at the short-listing stage as well'

The interview

The following guidelines will be useful during the interview itself:

- start by welcoming the applicant and try to put them at their ease. Introduce yourself and the other interviewers. Explain the structure of the interview
- avoid making up your mind within a few minutes of meeting an applicant, not on the basis of their abilities, but rather on the basis of appearance, or interests, experiences and views which they may share with you
- use the questions you have prepared in advance, based on the criteria in the person specification
- depending on the answer each applicant gives, you may need to rephrase the question or ask follow up questions which are related to the criteria you are testing. It is quite acceptable for these follow up questions to be different for each applicant, because each applicant is also different
- make sure your questions are open-ended, requiring more than a "yes" or "no" answer
- ask additional questions that arise from the application form if relevant. For example, if a criminal conviction is declared, you should ask about the circumstances surrounding the conviction, to assess if it is relevant to the post. If there are gaps in employment, you will need to ask about these

- you should ask all applicants if they have any unspent criminal convictions.

An unspent conviction is one that all applicants should reveal if asked. Convictions which are spent (ie the individual has served a specific rehabilitation period) do not need to be revealed in most circumstances. However, for posts which involve working with children or vulnerable adults, an Exception Order to the Rehabilitation of Offenders Act 1976 allows you to ask about spent convictions as well as unspent ones.

- explain to applicants that if they do have a criminal conviction, your organisation takes a positive stance towards ex-offenders and that the conviction will be taken into account only if considered relevant to the job
- make sure that you don't ask irrelevant, possibly discriminatory questions such as asking how the applicant will cope with childcare. Applicants will have a variety of backgrounds and you should assume that they are all attending the interview on the basis that they are available to do the job
- keep control of the interview. If you feel the applicant is going off-track turn the conversation back to the information you need
- as the interview progresses, make notes on how well the applicant meets each criterion – based on their answers to questions

- at the end of the interview, ask the applicant if they have any questions
- if you give information about terms and conditions, make sure this is correct – if someone is later appointed, they may rely on this information as part of the employment contract
- inform the applicant of the next stage in the recruitment process, such as a second interview or a test. Let the applicant know when they can expect to hear whether their application has been successful
- thank the applicant for coming
- keep your interview notes. Only record what has been said in the interview and how you arrived at the selection decision. Be aware that applicants who later make a complaint to an employment tribunal have the right to ask for copies of any notes made during the interview, and that you may need them for defending any possible discrimination case relating to the process.

Other selection methods

Involving service users in the interview

It is good practice and increasingly common practice, to involve service users in the selection interview (as a panel member) and often at the short-listing stage as well.

One organisation, which has involved users of its mental health services in selection interviews, has the following good practice points to make:

- help the service users to prepare and make sure they have some interesting and challenging questions for the candidates
- make sure that the questions are prepared in advance
- provide training on recruitment and selection
- make sure the service users have a chance to read the application forms beforehand
- make sure that service users understand the seriousness of the task and that they are able to make their decisions without staff influence.

As well as interviewing, there are other ways of selecting the best applicant. Studies have indicated that interviewing on its own is not always the most reliable method of choosing the right person for the job, especially if interviewers are relatively inexperienced.

To find out more information about whether applicants possess the criteria you are looking for, you could consider the following:

Practical tests

A practical test might be a case study that the applicant needs to comment on.

Alternatively, you might simulate a typical in-tray which the applicant might need to deal with, if appointed.

Such practical tests can show the knowledge and skills the applicant may possess to undertake the job in reality.

Psychometric tests

Psychometric tests can be used to assess skills such as: problem solving; decision making; and thinking style.

You should bear in mind that these tests:

- are not always a good indicator of future performance – they are most helpful used alongside other selection methods
- should not be used unless there is a proven need and a suitably qualified person to administer them
- often require a fee when you use them.

Presentations

You could ask applicants to make a presentation on a specific topic. You would be able to assess from this the applicant's verbal communication skills or their knowledge of a specific subject.

Role plays

You could ask applicants to role-play a specific scenario. This can be helpful to assess how they act and co-operate with others.

Assessment centres

Assessment centres typically run over one or two days and may use all the above selection methods, including an interview. Assessment centres can give a thorough picture of applicants, but they can also be expensive and time consuming.

Deciding who to appoint

Deciding on a selection method

If you want to use any of the above selection methods, consider the following:

- make sure you know which criteria you are assessing from each test. For example, if you ask an applicant to undertake an in-tray exercise, are you testing their ability to communicate in writing, to plan and organise, their knowledge of their job or all three of these?
- don't use a test that is irrelevant. For example, if someone will rarely be required to make presentations in the job, then don't ask them to do one as part of the selection process
- make sure you make adjustments for disabled people. An applicant with a stammer may require more time for a verbal presentation. You may need to provide documents in a larger text size for a visually impaired applicant
- make sure that the subject matter of your tests does not disadvantage some people. If there is no need to have knowledge of the voluntary sector for a particular job, then don't give applicants a case study about a management committee. This might disadvantage very suitable applicants who may not be familiar with the voluntary sector
- If you want to use tests but are not sure how, you could take advice from a human resources specialist.

Once you have undertaken all interviews and other selection tests, you and other members of the selection panel should consider the suitability of each applicant against the requirements of the person specification. A good way of deciding which applicant is the most suitable is for members of the selection panel to jointly score the extent to which the applicant meets each criterion. For example, 3 would be "meets requirements", 2 would be "partly meets requirements" and 1 would be "does not meet requirements". Evidence should be cited to back up any scores.

Be cautious about simply adding up all the scores given to each applicant and offering the job to the applicant with the highest overall score. You need to consider the matter in more depth than this. If, for example, an applicant has scored extremely well on most criteria, but scored badly on ability to deal effectively with conflict in a non-confrontational manner, you may feel that this one criteria is sufficiently important that the applicant is not suitable, regardless of whether they were the highest scoring applicant overall.

Once you have chosen the most appropriate person for your job, you can send them a provisional offer of employment. This can be in the form of a letter, stating the position you are offering, the salary and when you hope the person will start. Make sure that the salary and any terms and conditions you mention are correct – they could be relied on later as part of the employment contract.

The letter should state clearly that the offer is provisional on receipt of satisfactory references; Immigration, Asylum and Nationality checks; confirmation that the employee has passed a medical examination (where relevant); registration (where relevant) and Criminal Records Bureau (CRB) clearance (where relevant).

Once the provisional offer of employment has been accepted, you should send a letter to those who were not successful at interview, thanking them for their time. If you can, it is good practice to offer these people feedback on their application.

A failure to give feedback following a request by an unsuccessful applicant can give rise to an implication that the reason for rejection is a discriminatory one. Therefore you should ensure that you respond to requests for feedback promptly. Feedback can be written or oral and should be provided in a sensitive manner, with any negative comments or criticisms relating directly to the applicant's failure to meet the requirements of the role or the person specification. A feedback response could prove to be a critical document in an employment tribunal claim.

'References should be used to support or deny the information gained about an applicant, not to choose between applicants'

References

References from previous employers should always be followed up. The present employer should not be contacted until the applicant has accepted your provisional offer of employment and has told their employer.

If there is only one previous employer, or none, academic references should be sought in preference to personal references.

References should be used to support or deny the information gained about an applicant, not to choose between applicants.

A reference request should cover the following areas:

- name of applicant
- post applied for
- who the reference is from, who it needs to be returned to and by when
- a request for confirmation of the role, the duties the applicant undertook with the referee, the dates of employment
- the reason for leaving (where applicable)
- whether there are any live disciplinary warnings on file
- a request for comments on the applicant's reliability, trustworthiness, attendance, performance in the job and relationships with others
- number of days of sickness absence in month period, and the number of occasions in the previous 12/24 months
- a request that the referee give any other information that they feel may be useful.

Someone named as a referee by an applicant is not under any legal obligation to provide a reference. However, a person who does provide a reference is under a legal obligation to ensure that the information given is accurate and truthful.

If a reference does not provide straightforward information in response to the initial request, you might want to follow up with a telephone conversation. Make notes of the telephone conversation for future reference.

Consider references in an impartial manner and be aware that on occasions, the referee may not be impartial – an applicant may have experienced prejudice in a previous organisation.

Checks under the Immigration, Asylum and Nationality Act 2006

The Immigration, Asylum and Nationality Act 2006, which came into force on 29 February 2008, sets out the current law on the prevention of illegal migrant working in the UK.

The key points are as follows:

- The Act puts an onus on you as an employer to undertake checks on anyone you propose to employ, to make sure they have the right to work in the UK.
- You could be liable to a civil penalty of up to £10,000 for each person you illegally employ.
- A proper checking process provides you with a legal 'excuse' from prosecution, if it were found that one of your employees were working illegally.
- If you were to knowingly hire someone who is not entitled to work in the UK, you could be subject to an unlimited fine and a prison sentence of up to two years.
- You should make sure you undertake the checks on everyone you propose to employ. It is not appropriate, for example, to only check the status of people whom you consider may not be entitled to work in the UK, because of their accent or ethnic origin. Such assumptions are inappropriate and could imply race discrimination.

- The process you need to go through involves checking and copying one, or a specified combination, of original documents before employment commences.
- There are two lists of documents for checking (see opposite). If the individual is not subject to immigration control, or has no restrictions on their stay in the UK, they should be able to produce a document, or a specified combination of documents, from List A. The most common document that a prospective employee will produce is a 'secure' document, such as a UK or European Economic Area (EEA) passport, a national ID card or a UK residence permit.
- Where the leave to enter or remain in the UK granted to an individual is time-limited, the document or documents provided will be specified in List B. If this is the case, you must repeat the checks every 12 months until the employee can produce documents indicating that they can remain permanently in the UK.
- If you acquire staff as a result of a TUPE transfer, you will have 28 days following the date of transfer to undertake the appropriate document checks.

- You must take reasonable steps to satisfy yourself that your prospective employee is the rightful holder of any documents presented to you, that the documents allow the employee to do the type of work offered and that the documents are valid.
- The documents must then be photocopied or scanned in their entirety, apart from passports and other travel documents where only the front cover and the pages giving personal details, including photograph, signature and any relevant endorsements, need be captured.
- If you are presented with a false travel document or visa, you will only be required to pay a civil penalty if the falsity is 'reasonably apparent'.
- A record of everything copied or scanned must be kept.
- You must 'take action' (that is, terminate someone's employment) if you become aware at any stage that a person is working illegally.

Lists A and B

Following are lists A and B, reproduced from the Border and Immigration Agency Summary Guidance for Employers on the Immigration, Asylum and Nationality Act. This guidance is available at http://www.bia.homeoffice.gov.uk/employers/ or by calling the BIA employers' helpline on 0845 010 6677.

LIST A
Documents which provide an ongoing excuse

1. A passport showing that the holder, or a person named in the passport, is a British citizen or a citizen of the United Kingdom and Colonies having the right of abode in the United Kingdom.

2. A passport or national identity card showing that the holder, or a person named in the passport as the child of the holder, is a national of the European Economic Area or Switzerland.

3. A residence permit, registration certificate or document certifying or indicating permanent residence issued by the Home Office or the Border and Immigration Agency to a national of a European Economic Area country or Switzerland.

4. A permanent residence card issued by the Home Office or the Border and Immigration Agency to the family member of a national of a European Economic Area country or Switzerland.

5. A Biometric Immigration Document issued by the Border and Immigration Agency to the holder which indicates that the person named in it is allowed to stay indefinitely in the United Kingdom, or has no time limit on their stay in the United Kingdom.

6. A passport or other travel document endorsed to show that the holder is exempt from immigration control, is allowed to stay indefinitely in the United Kingdom, has the right of abode in the United Kingdom, or has no time limit on their stay in the United Kingdom.

7. An Immigration Status Document issued by the Home Office or the Border and Immigration Agency to the holder with an endorsement indicating that the person named in it is allowed to stay indefinitely in the United Kingdom or has no time limit on their stay in the United Kingdom, when produced in combination with an official document giving the person's permanent National Insurance Number and their name issued by a Government agency or a previous employer.

8. A full birth certificate issued in the United Kingdom which includes the name(s) of at least one of the holder's parents, when produced in combination with an official document giving the person's permanent National Insurance Number and their name issued by a Government agency or a previous employer.

9. A full adoption certificate issued in the United Kingdom which includes the name(s) of at least one of the holder's adoptive parents when produced in combination with an official document giving the person's permanent National Insurance Number and their name issued by a Government agency or a previous employer.

Continued overleaf...

LIST A continued

10. A birth certificate issued in the Channel Islands, the Isle of Man or Ireland, when produced in combination with an official document giving the person's permanent National Insurance Number and their name issued by a Government agency or a previous employer.

11. An adoption certificate issued in the Channel Islands, the Isle of Man or Ireland, when produced in combination with an official document giving the person's permanent National Insurance Number and their name issued by a Government agency or a previous employer.

12. A certificate of registration or naturalisation as a British citizen, when produced in combination with an official document giving the person's permanent National Insurance Number and their name issued by a Government agency or a previous employer.

13. A letter issued by the Home Office or the Border and Immigration Agency to the holder which indicates that the person named in it is allowed to stay indefinitely in the United Kingdom when produced in combination with an official document giving the person's permanent National Insurance Number and their name issued by a Government agency or a previous employer.

List B

Documents which provide an excuse for up to 12 months

1. A passport or travel document endorsed to show that the holder is allowed to stay in the United Kingdom and is allowed to do the type of work in question, provided that it does not require the issue of a work permit.

2. A Biometric Immigration Document issued by the Border and Immigration Agency to the holder which indicates that the person named in it can stay in the United Kingdom and is allowed to do the work in question.

3. A work permit or other approval to take employment issued by the Home Office or the Border and Immigration Agency when produced in combination with either a passport or another travel document endorsed to show the holder is allowed to stay in the United Kingdom and is allowed to do the work in question, or a letter issued by the Home Office or the Border and Immigration Agency to the holder or the employer or prospective employer confirming the same.

4. A certificate of application issued by the Home Office or the Border and Immigration Agency to or for a family member of a national of a European Economic Area country or Switzerland stating that the holder is permitted to take employment which is less than 6 months old when produced in combination with evidence of verification by the Border and Immigration Agency Employer Checking Service.

5. A residence card or document issued by the Home Office or the Border and Immigration Agency to a family member of a national of a European Economic Area country or Switzerland.

6. An Application Registration Card issued by the Home Office or the Border and Immigration Agency stating that the holder is permitted to take employment, when produced in combination with evidence of verification by the Border and Immigration Agency Employer Checking Service.

7. An Immigration Status Document issued by the Home Office or the Border and Immigration Agency to the holder with an endorsement indicating that the person named in it can stay in the United Kingdom, and is allowed to do the type of work in question, when produced in combination with an official document giving the person's permanent National Insurance Number and their name issued by a Government agency or a previous employer.

8. A letter issued by the Home Office or the Border and Immigration Agency to the holder or the employer or prospective employer, which indicates that the person named in it can stay in the United Kingdom and is allowed to do the work in question when produced in combination with an official document giving the person's permanent National Insurance Number and their name issued by a Government agency or a previous employer.

'You are responsible for ensuring that the worker has a registration certificate within the first month of starting work with you'

Workers from the latest EU accession states

You must carry out the standard checks outlined above for nationals of the latest EU accession states. These are all the countries that joined the EEA on 1 May 2004 and 1 January 2007.

You also need to undertake the following:

- In respect of a national of the Czech Republic, Estonia, Hungary, Latvia, Lithuania, Poland, Slovakia or Slovenia, you should ensure that the prospective employee (subject to some exemptions) registers with the Border & Immigration Agency under the 'Worker Registration Scheme' within one month of starting employment. You can find out more information about the Worker Registration Scheme at http://www.bia.homeoffice.gov.uk/workingintheuk/wrs/.
- For a national of Bulgaria or Romania, you should check and copy the prospective employee's authorisation document which allows them to work, (or any document establishing that the person is exempt) before their employment commences.

The Employer Checking Service

In some cases, the documents of prospective employees will be with the Border and Immigration Agency in connection with an outstanding application or appeal. You may contact the Employer Checking Service for information about these documents.

You can find out more information about the Employer Checking Service from the Border and Immigration Agency website, or call the employers helpline on 0845 010 6677.

Applying for a work permit

If you know that an applicant does not have the right to live and work in the UK, you can consider applying for a work permit for them. There is a points system with five tiers (tier 1 being for highly skilled individuals, tier 5 being for low skilled individuals to fill temporary shortages in specific industries). The points system is being phased in during 2008/2009.

You can find out how to apply for a work permit on the Government website http://www.workingintheuk.gov.uk.

You should be aware that it appears that the Home Office is unlikely to provide a work permit unless you can show that the skills required are scarce such that you cannot recruit appropriate individuals in the UK, or in the EC.

Criminal Records Bureau checks (Disclosures)

A Disclosure is a document containing information held by the police and government departments. You can use it to make safer recruitment decisions. Disclosures are provided by the Criminal Records Bureau (CRB), an executive agency of the Home Office. They are available for England and Wales.

Disclosures can be obtained for both paid employees and volunteers. There is a charge for obtaining a Disclosure for paid employees, but no charge for volunteers. It is good practice, and indeed common practice, to pay the charge for the prospective employee.

When to seek a Disclosure

In some circumstances, you are under a legal obligation to obtain a Disclosure. If your employees or volunteers may have regular or substantial contact with children in a childcare organisation regulated by the Protection of Children Act; or vulnerable adults in a body regulated by the Commission for Social Care Inspection (under the Care Standards Act), you must seek CRB checks (Disclosures) on them.

Other organisations involving employees or volunteers in work with children or vulnerable adults should be aware that they have a duty of care towards their service users. This means that you should take all reasonable steps open to you to lower risk of harm to them. A CRB Disclosure is likely to be one step that you take to meet your duty.

Please note that only certain roles are eligible for Disclosures. Organisations blanket checking all employees and/ or volunteers, even where they are not directly working with vulnerable groups, are likely to be breaking the CRB Code of Practice and the Police Act 1997.

You should only seek a Disclosure on the person to whom you have actually offered the post, not to all applicants.

Levels of Disclosure

There are two levels of Disclosure, as follows:

Standard Disclosures

Standard Disclosures are primarily for posts that involve working with children or vulnerable adults.

The Standard Disclosure contains details of all convictions held on the Police National Computer including current and spent convictions as well as details of any cautions, reprimands or final warnings.

If a position involves working with children, the Disclosure will indicate whether information is held on certain government department lists, of those who are banned from working with children.

If a position involves working with vulnerable adults, the Disclosure will indicate whether information is held on a government department list of those who are banned from working with vulnerable adults. This is called the PoVA (Protection of Vulnerable Adults) list.

Enhanced Disclosures

Enhanced Disclosures are for posts involving a far greater degree of contact with children or vulnerable adults.

In general the type of work will involve regularly caring for, supervising, training or being in sole charge of such people. Examples include a Care Worker/Support Worker, Scout or Guide leader or Sunday School volunteer.

This level of Disclosure involves an additional level of check to those carried out for the Standard Disclosure. An Enhanced Disclosure includes a check on local police records. Where local police records contain additional information that might be relevant to the post the applicant is being considered for, the Chief Officer of Police may release information for inclusion in an Enhanced Disclosure. Exceptionally, and in a very small number of circumstances (typically to protect the integrity of current police investigations), additional information may be sent under separate cover and should not be revealed to the applicant.

'If the Disclosure indicates that the applicant has a criminal record, you should consider whether it is relevant to the post for which they are applying'

Registration with the CRB

The Disclosure service is only available to organisations that have registered with the CRB.

If you are likely to submit less than the minimum 100 applications per year, your organisation cannot become a registered organisation. Instead, you can gain CRB Disclosures via an Umbrella Body. An Umbrella Body is a Registered Body that acts on behalf of other organisations.

Even if you are likely to submit more than 100 applications per year, you may prefer to use an umbrella body, rather than register your organisation if, for example, you do not have the necessary administrative resources.

Some Councils for Voluntary Services (CVSs) offer Umbrella Body services, or they may know of a local organisation that acts as an Umbrella Body. Alternatively, you can find an Umbrella Body by calling the CRB information line on 0870 90 90 811 or by searching for a relevant Umbrella Body on the Disclosure website: www.crb.gov.uk.

Application process

The prospective employee is responsible for making the Disclosure application. You can hand the employee a paper application to complete, but the most frequent approach is via telephone application.

You should ask the prospective employee to telephone the Disclosure application line on 0870 90 90 844, to start the application process. Give them your 11-digit Registered Body number (of your own organisation or of the Umbrella Body which processes Disclosures for your organisation) – they will need this when they call. They should be advised to make the phone call as soon as possible, so that their start date with you is not delayed.

The CRB will then send the prospective employee a Disclosure application form to complete. The employee must sign this, and then send it to a registered counter signatory, with the originals of a number of identity documents. The registered counter signatory is a person in the Registered Body who is authorised by the CRB to check and sign Disclosures. The registered counter signatory will check the form and the documents then sign the form and send it to the CRB.

The completed Disclosure should then be sent to the prospective employee within a few weeks, with a copy to you, or to your Umbrella Body if you are using one.

If the Disclosure indicates that the applicant has a criminal record, you should consider whether it is relevant to the post for which they are applying. If you consider it is, and if you are considering withdrawing your offer of employment, you should meet with the individual to ask them about any convictions and give them the opportunity to explain the circumstances surrounding the conviction(s). You can then take a decision as to whether or not to proceed with appointing the applicant.

The prospective employee can refuse to apply for a Disclosure, but if this is the case, you may withdraw the job offer. Thus it is particularly important that an offer made states that it is dependent on receiving an acceptable Disclosure from the CRB.

'The Criminal Records Bureau has access only to information held on the Police National Computer, so cannot provide information from foreign countries'

Starting an employee before a Disclosure has been received

If you are recruiting a care worker for vulnerable adults or a childcare worker, you must make sure you have received a Disclosure, before allowing the individual to start work (unless you use the PoVAFirst service, see below). This is because it is a legal offence to knowingly employ someone in these positions, if they may be on the lists of people barred from working with children or vulnerable adults.

In other circumstances, you may allow the applicant to start work, provided that you ensure that the employee is fully supervised in his or her work, whilst you are waiting for the Disclosure to come through.

For vulnerable adults only, there is a service which is available in England only called the PoVAFirst check. This allows registered bodies to check an individual against the list of people barred from working with vulnerable adults (the PoVA list) and get a response normally within 48 hours, with the full Disclosure following later.

It means that you can start the employee (under supervision) once an acceptable PoVAFirst check has been received, even if you are still awaiting the full Disclosure.

PoVAFirst checks are available in only very exceptional circumstances, such as where there is otherwise a real danger that staffing levels will fall below numbers required to meet statutory obligations. PoVAFirst checks are mainly available for those staff working in care homes and domiciliary care.

You can find out further information about the PoVAFirst checks by going to www.crb.gov.uk, then typing 'PoVAFirst' in the search box. The cost of the PoVAFirst check, as at July 2007, was £6.

Portability

In some cases, if an employee already has a recent Disclosure from a post in a different organisation, you may wish to consider accepting it rather than seek a fresh Disclosure. This is called portability.

The CRB does not support portability, and points out that organisations which choose to accept a previously issued Disclosure do so at their own risk. However, sometimes, for example if you are appointing a worker on a very short-term basis you may feel that it is a pragmatic approach to accept a Disclosure sought by another organisation.

In this case, it is suggested that you follow the CRB guidelines below:

- ask the individual to show their copy of the CRB check

Contact the Countersignatory named on the front of the CRB check and confirm that the reference number and identity details match

- ask if the Countersignatory received any additional information from police records – the Countersignatory can only confirm or otherwise the existence of such information – but not the content of the information

- if there is no additional information, carry out a formal risk assessment to decide whether to accept the CRB check

- the CRB strongly advises that if there was additional information, you should ask the individual to apply for a fresh check.

In respect of the formal risk assessment, the CRB sets out the steps you can take. To find out about the risk assessment steps. go to the CRB website www.crb.gov.uk and type 'disclosure' in the search box.

Independent Safeguarding Authority

Confidentiality

Disclosure information must be treated with the utmost confidentiality. Under Section 124 of the Police Act 1997, it is an offence to pass Disclosure information to persons not authorised to receive it. Those authorised to receive Disclosure information are those who have a need to know, ie those responsible for the recruitment decision or for advising on it. Records must be kept securely and destroyed after use.

If your organisation is a Registered Body, you will need to comply fully with the CRB Code of Practice regarding the correct handling, use, storage, retention and disposal of Disclosure information. The Code is available from the CRB website www.crb.gov.uk.

If you are using an Umbrella Body, they will be able to advise you further on the process and any matters that may arise.

Criminal records information from abroad

The Criminal Records Bureau has access only to information held on the Police National Computer, so cannot provide information from foreign countries. You can find out about how to obtain information from foreign countries at www.crb.gov.uk.

A new registration scheme, run by the Independent Safeguarding Authority (ISA), is expected to start coming into force in stages during 2008.

The scheme introduces new, more effective and streamlined processes for checking people who should not work with children and vulnerable adults. Only applicants who are judged not to pose a risk to vulnerable people can be ISA registered. If data indicates that an individual might pose a risk to vulnerable people, they will be put on one of the ISA Barred Lists. Employers who work with vulnerable children or adults will only be allowed to recruit people who are ISA registered.

Please note that organisations may still wish to apply for CRB Enhanced Disclosure as well, to obtain an applicant's full criminal record. In some circumstances, it will be mandatory to do this.

You are advised to keep abreast of any information about the scheme and its implementation, and then revise your recruitment, screening and child/vulnerable adult policies where necessary.

For further information go to www.isa-gov.org.

Registration

You should check that the person you are appointing is appropriately registered, where relevant. For example, The General Social Care Council currently registers Social Workers. It is intended that later in 2007, domiciliary care workers will also need to be registered. Further information is available from the General Social Care Council at www.gscc.org.uk.

The above applies only to England; different provisions apply in Wales, Scotland and Northern Ireland.

Recruitment of care staff in regulated social care services

The National Minimum Standards (NMS) in Social Care set standards on the recruitment of the social care workforce. These NMS are not legally enforceable but they do identify what a care service needs to do in order to meet its legal obligations under the Care Standards Act 2000.

There are NMS for:

- older people's care homes
- younger adults' care homes (for people with learning disabilities, mental ill health and physical/sensory disabilities)
- domiciliary care agencies
- children's homes
- fostering services
- adoption agencies.

The relevant National Minimum Standards include the following references to the recruitment of staff:

- a written, robust policy and procedure is in place for the recruitment, selection and vetting of staff
- all candidates for employment complete an application form
- satisfactory Criminal Records Bureau (CRB) disclosure
- satisfactory Protection of Vulnerable Adults (PoVA) and/or Protection of Children Act (PoCA) checks
- where appropriate, visitors and volunteers are subject to CRB and PoVA/PoCA Disclosures
- checks on registration, for example that nursing and midwifery registration
- managers are qualified to the required level
- the care service makes detailed records of the information provided at interview. Any gaps in employment histories are fully explored and evidenced. The records are signed and dated
- two written references, one from the current or most recent employer
- all documentation required by the NMS and regulations, for example proof of identity documents, is collated on the staff files
- there is evidence that all staff are provided with a copy of terms and conditions of employment and a copy of the General Social Care Council's Code of Practice.

Full details of each National Minimum Standard can be found at www.csci.org.uk.

Monitoring recruitment

It is good practice to monitor each recruitment exercise, in order to assess whether you are attracting applicants from a range of backgrounds, and how different applicants fare in the selection process. Your funders may also expect this of you.

You should consider monitoring recruitment by gender, ethnic group, age and disability. You may also wish to monitor by sexual orientation and religion, although some applicants may be less keen to tell you about these.

To the right, is an example monitoring form. The ethnic origin categories used are those used in the most recent national Census (2001). The Equality and Human Rights Commission advises that organisations should use these categories. This enables organisations to make comparisons with census output data.

Example equality monitoring form

Westwich Association

Equality monitoring form

The Westwich Association wishes to be representative of the community it serves. To do this, we monitor applicants for employment, so that we can check whether we are attracting and recruiting a diverse group of people.

Please complete this form. It will be separated from your application form on receipt and will not be taken into account when we shortlist applicants or choose who we appoint to the job.

Post applied for:

I would describe myself as:

White
- [ ] British
- [ ] Irish
- Other white background, please state:

Black or Black British
- [ ] African-Caribbean
- [ ] African
- Other black background, please state:

Mixed
- [ ] White and Black Caribbean
- [ ] White and Black African
- [ ] White and Asian
- Other mixed background, please state:

Chinese or other Ethnic group
- [ ] Chinese
- Any other ethnic group, please state:

Asian or Asian British
- [ ] Indian
- [ ] Pakistani
- [ ] Bangladeshi
- Other Asian background, please state:

Your date of birth
■ ■ ■ ■ ■ ■

Your gender
- [ ] Female
- [ ] Male

If you wish, you may tell us about your religion or faith and sexual orientation below.

How would you describe your religion or other belief?
My faith is:
- [ ] I do not have a faith

How would you describe your sexual orientation?
- [ ] Towards persons of the same sex
- [ ] Towards persons of the opposite sex
- [ ] Towards persons of the same and the opposite sex

- [ ] I consider myself to have a disability
- [ ] I do not consider myself to have a disability

Where did you see this job advertised?

For office use only.
Applicant reference number

You could monitor at the following stages:

- applications received and source of applications
- short-listed
- offered post
- accepted post

You can use this information to consider any action needed if the profile of applicants does not reflect the population profile within your organisation's area of remit.

For further information about how to monitor, and how to use the results, see the Acas good practice guide 'Tackling discrimination and promoting equality', which you can download from the Acas website at www.acas.org.uk, or order from the Acas publications order line: 08702 42 90 90.

There is also additional information about monitoring in chapter 2 of this guide.

Genuine occupational qualification/ requirement

A genuine occupational qualification/ requirement is an exception in law. In most circumstances, it is unlawful to say, for example, that you want to recruit a woman or a man, a person from a particular ethnic group or a person from a particular religion.

However, if the job requires a particular type of person for reasons of decency, privacy, or authenticity in dramatic performances, then the advertisement may be selective on the grounds that the job requires a genuine occupational qualification or requirement. An example might be where the job requires a woman rather than a man to be a care assistant at a women's refuge.

For further information about genuine occupational qualifications/ requirements, see chapter 2.

Checklist

	Establish exactly what tasks need to be done and whether there is a budget to recruit someone to do the tasks
	Write a job description and person specification
	Draft your advertisement. Always advertise internally. When choosing the best place to advertise externally, think about where your potential recruits might look for jobs
	Produce an application form. Include an equal opportunities monitoring form with it, and ideally put together an application pack
	Establish a panel of interviewers
	After the closing date, select applicants for interview based on the person specification
	Interview applicants based on the person specification. Consider involving service users in the interview process
	Design other selection tests as required
	Focus only on the requirements of the job when selecting – remember that discrimination on grounds of race, sex, age, marital status, disability, sexual orientation and religion/belief are unlawful
	Select the most suitable applicant taking account of interview scores and offer them the position
	Inform unsuccessful applicants once the position has been provisionally accepted and provide feedback if requested

	Review references; undertake immigration, asylum and nationality, CRB and any other checks (if required for the post)
	Maintain records for at least 6 months, so that you can explain why you chose one applicant over another. Remember that applicants can now request to see any interview notes
	Ensure all papers relating to the successful applicant are transferred to their personnel file
	Go through the Equal Opportunities monitoring forms to see if your organisation is attracting and selecting a cross-section of applicants. If it is not, consider reviewing your advertising and recruitment processes

Further information

The following organisations offer advice and resources about the subjects covered in this chapter to new and existing employers, often free of charge:

Acas
Acas has an advisory booklet on recruitment and induction.
www.acas.org.uk

Business link
www.businesslink.gov.uk

Care Standards Commission
www.csci.org.uk/professional

Criminal Records Bureau (CRB)
www.crb.gov.uk

Equality Direct
www.equalitydirect.org.uk

Border and Immigration Agency
www.workingintheuk.gov.uk

Independent Safeguarding Authority
www.isa-gov.org

Jobcentre Plus
www.jobcentreplus.gov.uk

NCVO
A listing of all the useful organisations referred to in this Good Guide can be found at the back of this book with full contact details.
www.ncvo-vol.org.uk

Four
Types of contract ('written statement')

This chapter gives information about the contractual relationship between employer and employee, and explains what documentation has to be provided.

'You are advised to always put in writing any discussions with employees which might be deemed to be of a contractual nature'

The written statement

The written statement of terms and conditions of employment is the principal document that gives written evidence of the contractual agreement between an employer and an employee. It is often called the contract of employment.

Whilst the written statement is the main evidence of the contract of employment, contractual agreements can be entered into in other ways. A verbal promise of a pay rise in 6 months time could be considered to be part of an employee's contract, even if that promise was given by a manager or Trustee unauthorised to give it. That employee could then apply to an employment tribunal claiming breach of contract, if the pay rise did not materialise. You are therefore advised to always put in writing any discussions with employees which might be deemed to be of a contractual nature.

The Employment Rights Act 1996 Section 1 says that a written statement must be given to all employees who will be employed for more than 1 month. The written statement must be given within 2 months of the employee joining the organisation. In practice, it makes sense to provide the statement when offering the job, or at the latest, on the person's first day at work. This helps avoid confusion and misunderstanding.

Minimum clauses in a written statement

The Employment Rights Act 1996 (ERA) says that the written statement must contain certain clauses. These clauses are listed in the model written statement which follows.

In addition, the ERA says that some information may be given by reference in the written statement to some other document. For example, you must make a reference in the written statement to your disciplinary procedure, but you do not need to include the whole procedure in your written statement. Where the law allows you to make a reference, this is indicated by a * in the model written statement.

Using the model written statement

The model written statement on the following pages can be adopted for different types of contractual arrangements, such as full time, part time, permanent, temporary or fixed term.

Please note that the model is for your guidance. You can use it as a basis for producing a written statement for your organisation. However, since the written statement is such a key employment document, and since employment law may change after this guide is published, you are advised to seek Human Resources or legal advice before finalising your written statement.

Model written statement

This written statement replaces any previous agreements and arrangements, whether verbal or written, relating to your employment with (employer).

1. Name of employer and employee

Name of employer

_____

_____

(state full name and address of organisation)

Name of employee

_____

_____

(state full name)

2. Date the employment and continuous employment began

Your employment with (employer) begins/began on (date).

No employment with a previous employer counts towards your service with (employer)

OR your employment with (previous employer, state name) counts towards your service with (employer). Your continuous employment started on (date).

Note: in most cases, the date of employment and date of continuous employment will be the same. In a minority of cases, for example in the case of a merger, the date of continuous employment may be an earlier date.

3. Remuneration and the intervals at which it is to be paid

Your salary will be £xx,xxx per year. You will be paid on or near to the last working day of each month by direct credit into your bank account.

Salaries are normally reviewed, and may be increased, each April. The Employer is under no obligation to increase them.

Note: you must pay at least the minimum wage. For further information, see chapter 6.

4. Working hours
EITHER

You are employed on a full time basis, that is xx hours per week. Your normal working hours will be (for example) 9.30am to 5.00pm Monday to Friday. Overtime is paid at a rate of xxx/is not paid. Time off in lieu is/is not given.

You should also state here any flexibility in working hours, such as evening or weekend work, that may be required.

OR

You are employed on a part time basis, for xx hours per week. Your normal working hours will be (state hours). You should also state here any flexibility in working hours, such as evening or weekend work, that may be required.

Note: the Working Time Regulations 1998 limit, for health and safety reasons, the maximum working hours for most employees. For further information see chapter 11.

5. Holiday entitlement

Your annual holiday entitlement is xx days per year (this is pro-rata for part time staff). The dates of your leave must be agreed with your line manager

In addition, you are entitled to paid leave for the eight normal bank and public holidays (NB there are 10 bank/public holidays in Northern Ireland each year). This entitlement is pro-rata for part time staff. If you need to work on these days, you will be entitled to equivalent time off in lieu at a time to be agreed with your line manager.

Note: the Working Time (Amendment) Regulations 2007 state that a minimum of 24 days (4.8 weeks) per employee (rising to 28 days (5.6 weeks) in April 2009) must be given each year. The minimum statutory leave can include bank and public holidays. For further information, see chapter 6.

On leaving, any accrued leave not taken will be calculated to the nearest day and given to you as pay in lieu of holiday. If you have taken more leave than you have accrued, payment for the excess leave will be deducted from your final salary.

6. Place of work

Your normal place of work is (state place and address). However, if needed by (employer), you may be required to change your work location.

Note: the above clause gives flexibility, but must be implemented reasonably, taking into account: the distance of the move; the ease/difficulty of travel; and the employee's personal circumstances.

7. Job description or job title

You are employed as a

_____

Your manager will give you a copy of your job description.

Your job description does not form a part of your contract of employment and may change from time to time.

It is preferable only to give the job title, rather than the full job description, in the written statement. This makes the written statement more manageable.

8. Collective agreements that affect employment

EITHER:

There are the following collective agreements that affect your employment:...

OR:

There are no collective agreements in force that affect your employment.

Note: a collective agreement is an agreement entered into between an employer and a trade union. Its effect is that the terms and conditions of individual employees can be changed via agreements between the employer and the union. If you are a new or small employer, it is unlikely that you will have entered into a collective agreement with a union, but you still need to indicate in the written statement whether or not there is such an agreement.

*9. Entitlement to sick leave and pay

If you are not able to come into work, you must inform your manager by (time) on your first date of absence. You must state the reason for your absence and its likely duration.

EITHER

If you are off sick, and adhere to notification and certification procedures, you will normally be entitled to statutory sick pay for up to 28 weeks, subject to the scheme rules.

OR

If you are off sick, and adhere to notification and certification procedures, you will be entitled to full pay for a short period, followed by half pay for a further period. Your exact entitlement depends on your length of service.

Note: there is no requirement on an employer to provide anything more than statutory sick pay for absent employees.

For further information, please see the sickness absence procedure, available from.... This procedure does not form a part of your contract of employment and may be changed from time to time.

*10. Pension scheme and pensions contracting-out certificate

(Employer) offers a stakeholder pension scheme. You may contribute up to x% of your salary to the scheme each month.

OPTION

(Employer) will also contribute x% of your salary to the scheme.

A pensions contracting out certificate is/is not in force in respect of this scheme.

For further information on the pension scheme, please contact....

(Employer's) contribution levels and the scheme administrator may change in the future.

Note: if you have five or more employees, you must provide access to a stakeholder pension scheme. For further information, see chapter 6.

*This information may be given by reference to another document

*11. The entitlement of employer and employee to notice and termination

EITHER

For information about the notice you are required to give and entitled to receive, please see (document).

OR

You are required to give the following notice if you leave (employer):

During the probationary period: one week

After the probationary period: 2 months

(Employer) will give you the following notice:

During the probationary period: one week

After the probationary period: 2 months or the statutory minimum, whichever is higher.

Note: the above notice periods are examples only. You can determine different notice periods if you wish. However, the law says that as a minimum, one week's notice of termination of employment must be given by the employer after the employee has completed 1 month's service. This notice increase to 2 weeks after 2 years' service and then by a further week for each year served up to a maximum of 12 weeks' notice after 12 years' service.

*12. Duration of employment

EITHER

Your employment is intended to be permanent, although is subject to funding.

Include the reference to the employment being subject to funding if you wish, and if relevant. You would need to follow your redundancy procedure, or the guidelines in chapter 13 (if you do not have a redundancy procedure), if the funding ran out.

OR

Your employment is temporary and will terminate at the end of your temporary assignment, with notice in accordance with clause 11 above.

OR

Your employment is for a fixed term. The fixed term will end on (date) and prior notice will be given in accordance with clause 11 above.

Any termination of employment will take place in accordance with the statutory minimum dismissal procedure.

*13. Disciplinary procedure and rules

(Employer's) disciplinary procedure and rules are attached to this written statement/are available from xxx.

The disciplinary procedure does not form a part of your contract of employment and may be changed from time to time.

*14. Disciplinary appeal

If you are unhappy with any disciplinary decision relating to you, you should apply in writing to (name, eg the Director or the Chair of the Trustees), within the timescales indicated in the disciplinary procedure.

*15. Grievances

If you have a grievance relating to your employment and the matter cannot be addressed informally, you should apply in writing to your line manager in the first instance.

The grievance procedure is attached to this written statement/is available from...

The grievance procedure does not form a part of your contract of employment and may be changed from time to time.

*This information may be given by reference to another document

Other clauses in a written statement

Whilst there is no legal obligation to include the following clauses, they can be useful to include in the written statement:

16. Probationary period

You will be on probation for the first xx months (eg 6 months) of your employment with (employer). Your probationary period may be extended if more time is needed to assess your suitability for the job.

If your performance or conduct is not considered to be satisfactory either during or at the end of the probationary period or during any period of extension, your employment may be terminated with 1 week's notice, in accordance with the statutory minimum dismissal procedure.

17. Retirement age

The normal retirement age of (employer) is (state age). If you want to keep working after your normal retirement age, you may make a formal request to do so, in accordance with statutory procedures.

Note: Under the Age Discrimination Regulations, the retirement age must be age 65 or over. You do not need to set a retirement age if you do not want to. See chapter 16 for the statutory retirement procedure.

18. Health and Safety

(Employer) sets great importance by health and safety. You are required to adhere to (employer's) Health and Safety Policy, which is displayed on xxxx. Failure to do so will render you subject to (employer's) disciplinary procedures.

19. Employer's property

You must take good care of (employer's) property at all times. On leaving (employer), you must return all (employer's) property in your possession to (employer) in the same condition as it was provided to you, subject to normal wear and tear. Failure to do so will render you subject to (employer's) disciplinary procedures.

20. Other work

You must not engage in any paid or voluntary work with another employer/organisation without first seeking written permission from (name). Permission will not be unreasonably withheld.

21. Copyright and inventions

You must promptly disclose to (employer) all copyright works, inventions, discoveries or designs originated, conceived, written or made by you alone or with others. The only exception is if they are conceived, written or made by you outside your normal working hours and wholly unconnected with your employment.

You will at the request and expense of (employer) do all things necessary or desirable to enable (employer) or its nominee to obtain the benefit of the (employer) invention and to secure patent or other appropriate forms of protection for it throughout the world.

You assign to (employer) all copyright design right and other proprietary rights, if any, throughout the World in respect of all (employer) Inventions during the period of your employment.

22. Confidential information

During and after the termination of your employment you must not disclose any confidential information about the work of (employer), its service users, staff or volunteers, without prior authorisation. If you are unsure about whether something is confidential, you must check with your manager.

23. Criminal records checks

If you may be working directly with children or vulnerable adults, you must have a criminal records check (via the Criminal Records Bureau) which must be satisfactory to (employer), before joining (employer). It is a condition of your employment that you consent to periodic criminal records checks during the course of your employment.

24. Parental rights
EITHER

Maternity, paternity, adoption and parental leave and provided in accordance with legal requirements. For further information, please refer to/see....

OR

We offer some enhancements to maternity, paternity, adoption and parental leave. For further information, please refer to/see....

Note: There is no legal requirement to include information on parental rights in the written statement. If you are simply offering parental rights at statutory levels (see chapter 8), then there is really no need to mention them here. Keeping things brief means that you don't need to update written statements every time the law changes.

25. Equal opportunities
(Employer) is an equal opportunities employer and will not treat any job applicant or employee less favourably on grounds of their sex, sexual orientation, age, disability, marital status, creed, colour, race, religion or philosophical beliefs or ethnic origin, nor will any job applicant or employee be disadvantaged by conditions or requirements which cannot be shown to be justifiable. It is the duty of all employees to ensure that this policy is observed at all times.

(Employer) will seek to ensure that individuals are selected and promoted on the basis of their aptitude, skills and ability.

26. Expenses
Reasonable expenses, incurred solely as a result of your work with (employer), will be reimbursed. You must provide receipts or other proof of expenditure and you must not make an expense claim if you have claimed or intend to claim the expense from elsewhere.

Please check with your manager before incurring expenses, so that you know what is considered to be a reasonable expense.

27. Deductions from salary
If at any time you owe (employer) money, you hereby authorise (employer) to deduct money from your salary. This includes but is not limited to overpayment of wages and any loan provided to you by (employer).

If, on termination of your employment, you owe (employer) money, this sum will be deducted from your final salary.

28. Ability to alter the written statement
(Employer) may change the terms and conditions of this written statement in certain circumstances. Minor changes will be made and notified to you in writing. You will be formally consulted in respect of more significant changes.

Note – you cannot unilaterally change significant terms (such as someone's working hours), unless they agree to this. You must therefore consult with them. The length of the consultation will depend on the number of employees that will be affected by the variation. If they disagree to any change and there is a strong business reason why you must implement the change, one option (not to be taken lightly!) is to terminate the existing contract of employment and offer a new contract on revised terms. If you are considering such a step, you are strongly advised to take advice from an employment lawyer or Human Resources specialist. This may potentially constitute a fair dismissal but requires that a fair process is also followed.

29. Data Protection

You accept and understand that (employer) will keep personnel records during your employment here and for a period of time after you leave which will be dependant on business needs taking into account professional guidelines and statutory requirements. You understand that the information contained in these records may be used for monitoring the effectiveness of (employer's) equal opportunities programmes, for personnel administrative tasks and for business management purposes. Information known as 'sensitive personal data' will also be processed as part of your personnel records which includes details of any medical condition, and you agree to the (employer) processing such data. You understand that where this is the case, processing will take place in accordance with the provisions of the Data Protection Act 1998. (You further understand that data may be sent to [country]). By signing this document you acknowledge that you will be providing (employer) with your consent to these uses.

30. Lay-offs and short-time working

(Employer) reserves the right to lay you off without pay, or to reduce your pay and hours of work, for a period of up to two weeks, should there be a case of extreme financial difficulty and/or where no work is available. Such a step would not be taken without consultation with staff and would be a measure to avoid or minimise the need for redundancies.

Note:

Employees can be laid off without pay only where there is a specific term in their contract allowing the employer to do so.

When employees are laid off, they may be entitled to a statutory guarantee payment from the employer.

On days on which a guarantee payment is not payable, employees may be able to claim Jobseekers Allowance and should contact their local Jobcentre about eligibility.

31. Third party liability

If you shall become entitled to receive any payments from a third party (including your own Insurance Company) in respect of damages for absence from employment due to incapacity, then you agree that you will follow up payment of such entitlement. If you receive any such payments from a third party, any sums paid by (employer) to you in excess of its obligations under Statutory Sick Pay regulations and in respect of the same period of absence shall be recoverable by (employer) out of such damages as money due to (employer).

32. Acknowledgement (signature)

This document is agreed to cover the terms and conditions of employment for (name).

Signed:

_____

(for the employer)

Job title:

_____

Signed:

_____

(employee)

Different types of employment contracts

The traditional employment relationship has historically been permanent and full time. However, this is changing, with an increasing number of staff working on a variety of part time contracts (such as job sharing and term time working) as well as contracts which are fixed term or temporary.

This section identifies a number of different employment contracts, and highlights some points of note about each.

Fixed term contracts

A fixed term contract is a contract that ceases when a specific date is reached. You might decide to issue an employee with a fixed term contract in circumstances such as:

- where the appointment is made to cover the activities of another member of staff eg to cover sickness, maternity, sabbatical etc
- here there is no reasonably foreseeable prospect of short-term funding being renewed nor other external or internal funding being available or becoming available
- where the post has been created to satisfy a short term need eg the implementation of a specific time limited project.

No less favourable treatment

The Fixed-term Employees (Prevention of Less Favourable Treatment) Regulations 2002 state that workers on fixed term contracts should be treated no less favourably than workers on comparable permanent contracts. So, for example, if you have two project workers, one on a permanent contract and one on a fixed term contract, their terms and conditions should be equally favourable overall.

You should tell employees on fixed term contracts about permanent vacancies that may be available and you should give them access to training.

Legal rights of employees on fixed term contracts

- if an employee has two years' service or more at the date of termination of the contract, they will be entitled to a redundancy payment (at the minimum statutory rate of £330 per week (as at 1 February 2008), for each year of service)
- if the employee has one year's service or more at the date of termination of the contract, they have the right to claim that they were unfairly dismissed
- there is no longer the facility to include waiver clauses in fixed-term contracts, which in the past were used to take away employee rights to a redundancy payment or any claim to unfair dismissal
- after a fixed term contract has run for four years, it automatically becomes permanent
- even where a fixed term contract is due to expire, there must still be a potentially fair reason for dismissal. The most likely potentially fair reasons for dismissal are redundancy or what is termed as 'Some other Substantial Reason'
- a fair procedure for the dismissal must also be followed. This is outlined below.

'You should be aware that the government intends to revoke the current procedures for termination of a contract'

Minimum procedures for terminating a contract

The Employment Act 2002 brought into force new minimum procedures for the termination of employment. These procedures came into force on 1 October 2004. If the minimum procedures are not followed, a dismissal will be found to be automatically unfair by an employment tribunal. These minimum procedures should be used for terminating all contracts and are also outlined in the chapters in this Good Guide on probation, discipline and redundancy. There is a different procedure for retirement dismissals, which is outlined in chapter 16. You should be aware that the government intends to revoke the current procedures for termination of a contract but the minimum procedures will remain in force until at least 2009. Please take advice as to the latest situation.

Below are the current minimum procedures to terminate a fixed term contract:

1 You must set down in writing the reasons why you are contemplating terminating the contract (this will normally be that a specific project has ceased, that someone has returned from maternity leave, or that funding has stopped). This statement must be sent or given to the employee.

2 You must arrange a meeting in order to discuss the proposed termination of employment and your reasons. This meeting should be held at a reasonable time and place and the employee should have reasonable notice of the meeting ie a minimum of 48 hours. The employee should take reasonable steps to attend and may be accompanied by a colleague or trade union representative.

3 After the meeting you should inform the employee in writing of the decision and offer them the right of appeal.

4 The employee must inform you if they wish to appeal. It is advisable to ask the employee to put their appeal in writing. You should then invite the employee to a hearing which should be chaired, where possible, by a more senior manager or by a Trustee. Afterwards, the outcome of the hearing should be communicated in writing to the employee. The employee is entitled to be accompanied by a colleague or trade union representative at the meeting.

5 If the appeal confirms that the employment should be terminated prior to the end of the agreed fixed term, the employee will be entitled to the notice outlined in their written statement of terms and conditions of employment or the statutory notice (if longer). If the termination is as a result of the natural end of the original fixed term, there may be no entitlement to notice.

Case study – terminating a fixed term contract

The following case study illustrates how a worker on a fixed-term contract should (or should not) be treated.

Joe is a caretaker/handyman at Westwich Association (the WA).

At the time Joe was taken on, it was felt that the WA would move to new premises within the next 3 years and that after the move, a caretaker/handyman would not be needed.

Joe was therefore given a fixed term contract of 2.5 years.

In actual fact, by the time Joe's contract was due to end, it was clear that the WA would not be moving premises.

However, the WA General Manager is not keen to keep Joe on, because his work performance is poor and his time-keeping erratic.

The General Manager has never addressed these problems, because she has only been in post for a year and knew that Joe's fixed term contract was due to expire.

After consultation with the Management Committee, the General Manager therefore informs Joe that it has been decided that his fixed term contract will not be renewed when it expires at the end of next month.

Joe is totally surprised – he thought that as the Westwich Association were not moving to new premises, his employment was safe.

Joe has been to the Citizens Advice Bureau to check his rights. He has now asked for written reasons for his dismissal.

Some points to consider:

Joe is entitled to have written reasons for his dismissal. The WA must provide them.

In order to prove that Joe's dismissal is fair, the WA must first show that the dismissal was for one of the reasons which are potentially fair under the law. The three main ones are conduct, capability and redundancy.

If the dismissal was for misconduct, then the WA will have problems proving that it was reasonable – Joe was never warned that his conduct was below standard and was not given the chance to improve. Nor was a disciplinary procedure followed.

If the dismissal was for capability (poor work performance), then the WA will have similar problems – Joe was never warned nor given the chance to improve, and no capability procedure was followed.

The WA could try and argue that the dismissal was for redundancy. But to prove this, they must show that the requirement for Joe's work has ceased or diminished, and as far as we know, this is not the case. In addition, they have not consulted Joe about redundancy or tried to redeploy him. They would also need to give him redundancy pay.

If the WA had followed the statutory minimum procedures when contemplating dismissal, they could have discussed Joe's concerns and their concerns at an earlier stage, and hopefully come to a more considered decision about Joe's employment. As it is, the termination of Joe's employment will be found by an employment tribunal to be automatically unfair, because the statutory minimum procedures were not followed and Joe had over 12 months service.

In addition, it would be a wrongful dismissal, because the appropriate notice was not given. Joe should have been given a minimum of two weeks' notice (one for each full year of service) prior to the termination of his contract or alternatively he could have received payment in lieu of his two-week notice period.

Part-time contracts

The Part Time Workers (Prevention of Less Favourable Treatment) Regulations 2000 state that part time employees should enjoy terms and conditions pro-rata to full time employees. Two examples of part time contracts are job sharing and term-time only contracts.

Job sharing contracts

Job sharing contracts are a type of part time contract. Job sharing is where one job is shared between two people. It is different from two part-time jobs, because the two parties should work together to ensure that the job runs smoothly and that there is continuity throughout the week.

You are still employing two individuals and each should receive their own written statement of terms and conditions of employment. If one resigns or is dismissed, the other still has the right to remain employed. You could then seek a job sharer for the other half of the job.

If you are employing a job sharer, you may wish to include the following clauses in the written statement:

'You are employed on a job share basis. You are expected to work with your job share partner to ensure that the work of the full job is covered during the working week. You are expected to agree how you will plan and complete work with your job share partner and in discussion with your manager.'

'You are employed for your own skills and abilities and your performance will be assessed using (employer's) normal procedures. Should your job share partner leave, any decision about appointing a new job share partner will be taken by (employer) in line with its normal recruitment procedures.'

More information is given about job sharing in chapter 8.

Term-time only contracts

A term-time only contract is a further type of part-time contract.

Under a term-time only contract, an employee works only during school term times. The salary is normally paid in equal monthly instalments during the year.

If an employee on a term-time only contract leaves an organisation, a reckoning needs to be made as to the salary paid compared with the hours worked up to the date of leaving. This may mean that additional salary needs to be paid, or that some salary needs to be deducted.

You could include the following clauses in your written statement for term-time only working:

'You are required to work during term-time only. You will not be required to work during the following times: for two weeks over the Christmas/New Year period; for two weeks over the Easter period; for six weeks from late July and during August; and for one week during each of the three school half terms. You are therefore required to work during 39 weeks of the year and not to work during 13 weeks of the year. You must agree your non-working weeks with your manager each January, for the following 12 months.'

'Your annual leave will be calculated pro-rata according to your working time. You will also receive paid leave, pro rata, for bank and public holidays.'

'Your salary will be spread evenly over the year. If you leave (employer) having been paid for more hours than you have worked, the amount of excess pay will be deducted from your final salary, or if this is not possible, you will be required to pay the amount back to (employer). If you leave (employer) having worked more hours than you have been paid for, the additional hours worked will be paid with your final salary.'

Annual hours contracts

An annual hours contract states the number of hours that must be worked over the year, rather than over a week. It can be a full-time or a part-time contract. It can give flexibility for employers where work is seasonal, or can offer flexibility to employees who wish to work more at certain times of the year and less at other times of the year.

Generally, the salary for an annual hours contract is paid evenly throughout the year.

It is important to have an effective system for recording hours, so that employer and employee can keep track over the year.

As with term-time only contracts, if an employee on an annual hours contract leaves an organisation, a reckoning needs to be made as to the salary paid compared with the hours worked up to the date of leaving. This may mean that additional salary needs to be paid, or that some salary needs to be deducted.

You could use the following clauses in your written statement:

'You are employed on an annual hours contract, that is on the basis of 1924 hours per year, over a period from 1 January to 31 December each year. This is an average of 37 hours per week, but you may be required to work more hours in some weeks and less in others, depending on the requirements of (employer). You may also request to work fewer or more hours in a particular week. Your request will be met where possible and taking into account the hours you have already worked in the year.'

'If you leave (employer) having been paid for more hours than you have worked, the amount of excess pay will be deducted from your final salary, or if this is not possible, you will be required to pay the amount back to (employer). If you leave (employer) having worked more hours than you have been paid for, the additional hours worked will be paid with your final salary.'

Consultancy and worker contracts

Sometimes, you may have a specific and short-term job that needs doing, such as the setting up of a new computer network or specific advice on an employment matter.

For such cases, you will probably need a self-employed person rather than an employee.

A self-employed person does not have any ongoing obligation to work with you, beyond the specific piece of work they arecontracted for. A self-employed person is responsible for their tax and national insurance, so you do not need to pay them via your payroll.

The arrangements you have agreed should be put into a written contract. This could be drawn up by you, by the consultant, or jointly.

The contract covers both the work that will be done, and the conditions under which it will be done.

The contract might include:

- purpose of the agreement
- a specific brief – what must be delivered and when
- how the consultancy will be managed
- the length of the consultancy
- confidentiality
- who owns rights to intellectual property arising from the consultancy work
- who must pay for expenses incurred, eg travel costs
- how the contract can be terminated
- charges and payment arrangements

A contract between you and your consultant is likely be one of two types:

- time and materials (T&M) contracts
- fixed-price contracts

In a time and materials contract, you will assume most risk, whereas in a fixed price contract, the consultant assumes most risk.

Below is an example agreement for engaging a self-employed consultant:

Example consultants agreement

Consultants Agreement

1. Introduction and Definitions
This Agreement is between _____
(organisation's name and address) (herein after called _____)
and (_____) (herein after called 'the Consultant').

The Agreement will be in accordance with the following Terms and Conditions unless and until an alternative is specifically agreed between the Parties.

2. Purpose of the Agreement
The purpose of the Agreement is:

Further details of the Agreement are set out in the attached Schedule of work.

The Consultant shall provide regular contact and activity reports to the Organisation's Project Manager, (name).

3. Commencement date and duration of the Agreement
This Agreement will commence on (_____) and is to be carried out in accordance with the following conditions:
It may be terminated by either party giving one month's notice in writing.
_____ may terminate the agreement immediately in the event that the Consultant commits any material breach of the terms of this Agreement, or is guilty of gross misconduct.

4. Fees and expenses
Fees for the Agreement will be as follows:

Where necessary, VAT will be added at the appropriate rate.
Where appropriate, travel, subsistence and other expenses will be paid at cost and in accordance with arrangements specifically agreed, in advance, with the Consultant.

5. Invoices and payment
Unless specifically agreed otherwise, invoices will be submitted monthly by the Consultant and payment made within 30 days.

6. Taxation

The Consultant is a self-employed person responsible for taxation and National Insurance or similar liabilities or contributions in respect of the fees and the Consultant will indemnify [organisation] against all liability for the same and any costs, claims or expenses including interest and penalties.

7. Confidentiality

The Consultant will not divulge to third parties matters confidential to   (_____) (whether or not covered by this Agreement) without

(_____) explicit written permission.

Except where specifically agreed otherwise, all material, data, information etc. collected during the course of the Agreement will remain in the possession of (_____) and not used without their permission.

8. Publication of material

Where the Agreement provides for the publication of material, the following specific conditions shall apply:

(a) _____ will retain the right to edit the final draft prior to publication subject, in the case of joint publications, to amendments proposed being agreed with the author(s).

(b) prior to publication, the Consultant and/or others associated with the publication shall not disclose any material obtained or produced for the purposes of the project to any other party unless _____ have given prior approval in writing.

(c) the Consultant will provide to _____ copies of all material, data etcetera collected specifically for the project and indicate the source of other material used.

(d) _____ will, except where specifically agreed otherwise, hold copyright to the publication.

Other matters relating to the use of the material shall be covered as an Appendix to this Agreement. Where other uses are agreed, all material and publications based on the project shall acknowledge _____ .

9. Restrictions

The Consultant shall not whilst this Agreement is in force be engaged or concerned directly or indirectly in the provision of services to any other party in the same or similar field of business or activity to _____ without the prior written consent of _____ .

10. Resources

The Consultant shall be responsible for obtaining whatever equipment, materials and/or additional persons that may be required to adequately provide the services.

11. Other conditions

Any other conditions, including variations to the terms set out above, shall be included as an Appendix to this Agreement.

For (Organisation) _____

Signed: _____

Date: _____

Name: _____

Designation: _____

For the Consultant

Signed: _____

Date: _____

Name: _____

Designation: _____

Name: _____

Designation: _____

It is important that you are clear when you may need a consultancy agreement/contract for services and when you may need a contract of employment. Don't be tempted to take someone on as a consultant, when really they are doing the job of an employee for you. There are the following possible danger areas:

- someone you thought was not an employee claims employment rights (eg claims you have dismissed them unfairly, claims a redundancy payment or claims holiday pay)
- HM Revenue and Customs declares that someone you thought was self-employed should have been paid on the payroll, with tax and national insurance deducted. In this case, you may be liable to pay the employee's tax as well as employer's and employee's National Insurance

There is no single test of employed/self-employed status and indeed an employment tribunal and HM Revenue and Customs could come to a different conclusion about the same case. However, in general terms, an individual is likely to be an employee if they meet all or most of the following criteria:

- they work standard hours for you under your control
- they are part and parcel of your organisation (they are integrated into the organisation)
- there is a mutuality of obligation – you are expected to offer ongoing work and they are expected to do it
- they are not in business on their own account, ie they do not bear the financial risks of failure to perform and they use your equipment rather than their own.

An individual is likely to be self-employed if they meet all or most of the following criteria:

- they have a lot of control over their work (for example, over hours and place of work)
- they are separate from your organisation
- they do not expect ongoing work and are not under an obligation to perform it
- they provide the main items of equipment needed to do their job
- they are free to hire other people to do the work they have taken on
- they are responsible for correcting unsatisfactory work in their own time and at their own expense.

Case study – self-employed or employed

Zoe was initially taken on as a gardener for the grounds at the Westwich Association (the WA). When unable to attend (either because of illness or because she was doing something else), Zoe would ask a friend to do the work instead. The WA did not have any gardening tools; Zoe would supply these.

The WA assumed Zoe to be self-employed, although nothing was in writing. She was paid £16 in cash each week and worked until the job was done – generally for 1.5 – 2 hours per week. She had several other jobs and would carry her equipment from job to job.

After a while, the WA found difficulties with the arrangement. Firstly, Zoe would come at different times in the week. Sometimes the children from the toddler group were in the garden when Zoe was working. There were concerns about the safety of having gardening tools in the garden at the same time as the children. Secondly, the General Manager felt that the standard of gardening of Zoe's friend was low. Thirdly, Zoe's lawnmower was becoming unreliable.

By this stage, Zoe was spending more time caring for her elderly father and had stopped all other gardening jobs apart from the WA. She was therefore reluctant to purchase a new lawnmower. The General Manager agreed that the WA would purchase a lawnmower for its grounds. It was also agreed that Zoe would come regularly on Monday morning between 10.00am and 12.00pm and that she would no longer ask anyone else to do the work.

The General Manager realised that Zoe's employment status had changed. She came at regular times, used the WA's equipment, did not have lots of other jobs and could no longer send a substitute. Taken as a whole, Zoe's status was more that of employee than self-employed person.

Having talked the situation through with Zoe, an agreement was reached and Zoe became an employee of the WA. Although her hourly rate was lower than her self-employed hourly rate, she felt that generally she was better off, as she could receive paid annual leave, sick pay and could join the WA pension scheme.

'Workers have some rights under employment law, but not as many as those who are also employees'

Workers

There is one further category of contract that you may wish to use.

In some cases, you may require someone to work on a flexible and casual basis. In this circumstance, you could employ someone as a worker.

Workers adopt a middle ground between employees and the self-employed. The Department for Business, Enterprise and Regulatory Reform (formerly the Department of Trade and Industry) describes workers as: 'essentially individuals who do not have a contract of employment, but who have some other contract to perform personally any work or services to another person although they are not genuinely in business on their own account.'

If you wish to use workers, the most likely use is for casual work. Casual workers:

- generally supply a short-term or specific need
- typically, will have periods of work with breaks in between where no work is performed
- are offered and accept work 'as and when required'
- are not under an obligation to accept the work
- have no agreement on the particular number of hours of work

Such an arrangement may suit individuals who want the flexibility to take work as and when it suits them. The arrangement may suit employers, to fill short term needs, such as to cover shifts in a care home or to deal with occasional peaks in administrative workload.

Workers have some rights under employment law, but not as many as those who are also employees. For example, they do not have the right to claim unfair dismissal, notice pay or redundancy pay.

Workers do, however, have the following core employment rights:

- to receive the national minimum wage
- not to suffer unlawful deductions from wages
- to receive paid holiday at Working Time Regulations levels of 4.8 weeks per year (as of 1 April 2009 this is due to increase to 5.6 weeks per year).

As workers are not considered to be genuinely self-employed, in most cases, they should be paid via the payroll. You still need to take references on them, check their right to live and work in the UK (under the Asylum and Immigration Act) and, if they work with children or vulnerable adults, you will need to seek a Disclosure (criminal record check) on them from the CRB. You can find out more about all these checks in chapter three.

You do not need to make a contractual written agreement with a casual worker, but it is good practice and it avoids misunderstandings if you do. This is not the same as a written statement of terms and conditions that you will issue to an employee.

You could include clauses such as:

- the intention that they are a worker not an employee
- the hourly rate of pay
- the fact that there is no obligation on either side to accept or to offer work
- that if work is accepted, they must do the work
- their entitlement to annual leave and how it will be paid
- that they may join your stakeholder pension scheme if they wish.

Checklist

	Make sure all your employees, whether permanent or temporary, full-time or part-time, have a written statement of terms and conditions of employment
	Remember that the written statement is the fundamental basis of the employment relationship. It is important to get it right. Use the information in this chapter to create a written statement appropriate to your organisation, but you are advised to seek advice before finalising it
	Do not provide less favourable terms and conditions to part-time employees or employees on fixed-term contracts – it could be unlawful
	If you are engaging a self-employed person, use the information in this chapter, legal and human resources advice to check that they really do count as self-employed
	If you need casual work to be undertaken, you may need a worker. It is good practice to enter into a written agreement with the worker. You are also advised to seek legal or Human Resources advice to ensure the individual is a worker and not an employee

Further information

The following organisations offer advice and resources about the subjects covered in this chapter to new and existing employers, often free of charge:

Acas
The following documents can be downloaded from the Acas website:

- A self-help guide on producing a written statement
- An example of a written statement
- An e-learning self-help guide to producing a written statement

www.acas.org.uk

Business Link
The Business Link website also has information on written statements. They have an excellent online tool that you can complete and which helps you create a written statement for employees.
www.businesslink.gov.uk

HM Revenue and Customs
The HMRC website has useful information to help you to determine employment status
www.hmrc.gov.uk

NCVO
www.ncvo-vol.org.uk
A listing of all the useful organisations referred to in this Good Guide can be found at the back of this book with full contact details.

Five

Induction and probation

Good induction and probation programmes can lead to more settled employees, better work performance, lower labour turnover and improved employee relations.

Employees who may need special attention

Induction is the process of familiarising the employee with the organisation over the first few days and weeks of employment.

Probation is a period of time during which the employee and employer can assess whether the job and the employee are suitable. Typically, probation lasts for around 6 months. The employee is normally confirmed in post at the end of the probationary period, although if the employee and job are not suited to each other, termination of employment may occur during or at the end of the probationary period. If your recruitment processes are working well, termination of employment at the probationary stage should only occur occasionally.

New employees who have done the same sort of work before, have been in the workplace for several years and are of similar background to existing employees, may have very different needs during their induction and probationary period, compared with new employees who, for example:

- have just left school or college
- have been out of the workplace for some time
- will be in a minority in the workplace
- are disabled.

Induction and probation processes should be flexible to meet individual needs. New employees should gain the impression that yours is an organisation which celebrates diversity and differences in people, not an organisation that finds such differences a problem. See chapter 2 for information about the Diversity Hub, which provides induction training on diversity very early on in the new recruit's employment.

School and college leavers
The Acas advice on inducting school and college leavers is reproduced opposite.

For school or college leavers, who may be nervous but excited at their first job, it is particularly important for the employer to encourage a positive attitude to work, and to allay any fears the new recruit may have. They need to be sure of their position in the company, and of the opportunities they will have to train and develop their skills.

Health and safety is a particularly important area to stress. Young people often have no feel for workplace hazards, and may be vulnerable to accidents. A group of young people together may get high-spirited and, without proper guidance on safety, be unaware of the potential dangers.

Continued overleaf...

Young workers are seen as being particularly at risk, and employers are required to:

- assess risks to young people under 18, before they start work
- take into account their inexperience, lack of awareness of existing or potential risks, and immaturity
- address specific factors in the risk assessment. Employers are required to make a suitable and sufficient assessment of the risks to the health and safety of employees and identify groups of workers who might be particularly at risk.

People who have been out of the workplace for some time
Acas advises the following:

Men or women returning to work after some years caring for children or other relatives may feel apprehensive about the new job – even when they may have worked for the company in the past. They may feel out of touch with developments, and in need of re-establishing themselves. Their induction programme needs to take this into account, offering training and extra help to settle in and become valuable members of the organisation.

This is also true of those who might have been living/working abroad, or who are changing their career focus.

'Studies have shown that people who are in minorities in organisations tend to take longer to be inducted and socialised'

Minorities

Some research has indicated that managers may not be used to dealing with particular minority groups or be aware of the issues that might affect them. They may have stereotypical views of the capabilities of certain groups (reference – Bauer and Green 1994).

People who are a minority in an organisation should have the same induction programme as any other new starter, but make sure you pay attention to any specific requirements. Be aware of cultural and religious customs. For example, a Jewish person may feel uncomfortable being invited to socialise with other staff after sunset on a Friday, a Muslim may feel embarrassed at being offered alcohol. However, individuals will vary in the extent to which they adhere to their religion, so be wary of making assumptions.

Try and create an environment where staff know that they can ask for religious or cultural commitments to be accommodated and do not feel embarrassed to do so. The same applies to individuals with caring commitments – ask them what they need and try and accommodate them if needed. Most people will be pleased that yours is a flexible place to work and will not abuse any flexibility you give them. If you can, find a buddy (see below) who can support the individual to settle into the work environment. You could also consider diversity/equal opportunities awareness training for your employees, so that they have a better awareness of differences.

Disabled employees

If an employee has a disability which puts them at a substantial disadvantage compared to others, you must, under the Disability Discrimination Act 1995, consult with the employee about making reasonable adjustments to their work or working environment. Where appropriate, you might also arrange awareness training for existing staff.

Acas has the following advice about disabled employees:

Careful pre-planning can reduce the problems which may arise for employees with disabilities, whether in terms of access, equipment or dealing with colleagues. Specialist advice is available from the Disability Employment Adviser and the Disability Service Teams of the Department for Work and Pensions. The Department for Work and Pensions also operates the Access to Work Scheme, whereby assistance may be available in meeting the cost of any aids and adaptations required. These services can be contacted via the JobCentre network.

Induction period

A good induction programme should make new employees feel welcome and ready/able to contribute fully.

When they have completed their induction, each employee should have an understanding of:

- what your organisation does and the jobs people do
- their role – how they will undertake the duties outlined in their job description
- how what they do fits in with the wider aims of the organisation.

Preparing for the new employee

Provide the following information for the new employee before their first day:

- start time
- who and where to report to
- brief details of what will happen on the first day
- the employee's written statement of terms and conditions
- your staff handbook (if you have one)
- your health and safety procedure
- your equal opportunities/diversity policy or statement of intent.

Information about the new employee can also be provided to other staff in advance – their name, their start date and what they will be doing. The information could be accompanied by a request for support to help the new person settle in.

The first few days

It may seem obvious, but make sure the employee's line manager is available on the first day. There will be documentation to complete, introductions to be made and essential information such as where to get a cup of tea or coffee. It is also good to give the new employee some (but not too much) work on the first day, so that they feel that they have started in the organisation.

You will find that during the first few days, your new employee will be able to take in only so much information and should not be overloaded.

Managers' responsibilities

Managers should be clear on their responsibilities to ensure that the employees they manage are fully inducted into the organisation. Managers should ensure that:

- new employees are given time to absorb new information. Information is best given in small digestible chunks
- sufficient time is set aside to meet induction needs
- the induction needs of internal promotees are not overlooked
- the needs of existing employees are still met during induction, ie that the novelty factor does not override ongoing work.

Buddying system

Some organisations have a buddy system, whereby a member of staff who is not the line manager is assigned to the new employee, to help them settle and to answer any questions, especially those questions that the employee may not want to bother the manager with. Such a system can help the new employee to feel settled more quickly.

Induction checklist

Acas suggests that induction should follow a systematic plan, and be written down so that nothing is overlooked. Each stage should be ticked off as it is completed. Not only does this give some structure to the induction but it also ensures that both the new starter and the manager know what has or has not been covered at any given time. Both manager and employee should have a copy of the list. It should be their joint responsibility to ensure that everything is covered.

The following checklist is adapted for the voluntary sector, from the Acas checklist which is contained in their Good Practice Guide to Recruitment and Induction. You can find the booklet at www.acas.org.uk. Enter 'recruitment and induction booklet' in the website search box.

Example induction checklist

Name:	Date of starting:		
	Carried out by	Date	Comments
Reception			
Received by			
Security/identity card issued (where relevant)			
Introduction to the organisation			
Who's who			
History			
Activities and services			
Future plans and developments			
Terms and conditions of employment			
Signed written statement of terms and conditions received			
Written statement of terms and conditions reviewed			
Hours, breaks, method of payment			
Holidays			
Flexitime			
Probationary period and procedure			
Notice period			
Sickness provisions			
Pension provisions and retirement procedure			
Parental leave provisions			

Example induction checklist continued

Name:	Date of starting:		
	Carried out by	Date	Comments
Equal opportunities policy and employee development			
Equal opportunities policy			
Measures to prevent bullying/ harassment			
Training needs and objectives			
Training provision			
Further education/training policies			
Performance appraisal			
Promotion avenues			
Employee/employer relations			
Trade union membership			
Other employee representation			
Employee communications and consultation			
Grievance and disciplinary procedure			
Appeals procedure			
Organisation rules			
Smoking policy			
General behaviour/dress code			
Telephone calls			
Canteen/break facilities			
Cloakroom/toilets			

Example induction checklist continued

Name:	Date of starting:		
	Carried out by	Date	Comments
Health and safety			
Risk assessment			
Preventative and protective measures			
Pregnant women and new mothers			
Emergency procedures			
Awareness of hazards – any particular to type of work			
Safety rules			
Clear gangways/exits			
Location of exits			
Dangerous substances or processes			
Reporting of accidents			
First aid			
Employee benefits			
Parking facilities/arrangements			
Discounts available to the organisation			
The job			
Discussions with manager/supervisor			
Requirements of new job			
Standards expected			
Co-workers			
Supervision arrangements			

Reviewing your induction procedures

You could gain feedback from each new employee, after around 6 months, on what they felt about the induction process – the good points and areas to improve. Make changes to your induction procedures if needed.

Case study – Induction

The Westwich Association (the WA) has been successful in recruiting a Bengali speaking outreach worker, Rakin. Rakin is a Muslim and there are no other Muslim staff at the WA.

Rakin started five weeks ago now and the General Manager is concerned. Rakin does not seem to be settling into the job quickly and does not seem very enthusiastic about the role. The General Manager has been on leave for a couple of weeks and on her return, the WA Administrator says that Rakin seems withdrawn, does not mix with other employees, doesn't eat lunch with them and doesn't join in tea or coffee breaks. Indeed, he appears not to be eating anything during the working day at all.

The General Manager realises that it is currently Ramadan, during which Muslims fast between dawn and sunset. She realises that she has not discussed this with Rakin or the other employees. She is also conscious that by his gender, race and religion, Rakin is in a minority in the organisation.

As an immediate first step, the General Manager finds out more about Rakin's religion. She downloads the Acas guide Religion or Belief and the workplace from their website: www.acas.org.uk.

This tells her the following:

Islam (Muslims)
Observant Muslims are required to pray five times a day. Each prayer time takes about 15 minutes and can take place anywhere clean and quiet. Prayer times are:
At dawn (Fajr)
At mid-day (Zuhr) in winter sometime between 1200–1300hrs and in summer
Between 1300–1600hrs.
Late afternoon (Asr) in Winter 1430–1530
After sunset (Maghrib)
Late evening (Isha)

Friday mid-day prayers are particularly important to Muslims and may take a little longer than other prayer times. Friday prayers must be said in congregation and may require Muslims to travel to the nearest mosque or prayer gathering.

Before prayers, observant Muslims undertake a ritual act of purification. This involves the use of running water to wash hands, face, mouth, nose, arms up to the elbows and feet up to the ankles, although often the washing of the feet will be performed symbolically.

Ramadan, which takes place in the 9th month of the Muslim lunar calendar, is a particularly significant time for Muslims. Fasting is required between dawn and sunset. Most Muslims will attend work in the normal way but in the winter they may wish to break fast with other Muslims at sunset. This could be seen as a delayed lunch break. For those working evening or night shifts, the opportunity to heat food at sunset and/or sunrise will be appreciated.

Food

Muslims are forbidden to eat any food which is derived from the pig, this includes lard which may be present in bread or even ice cream. In addition they are forbidden to eat any food which is derived from a carnivorous animal.

Meat that may be consumed must be slaughtered by the Halal method. Islam also forbids the consumption of alcohol which includes its presence in dishes such as risotto or fruit salad.

Other

Observant Muslims are required to wash following use of the toilet and will therefore appreciate access to water in the toilet cubicle. Often Muslims will carry a small container of water into the cubicle for this purpose. By agreement with other staff and cleaners, these containers could be kept in the cubicle.

Physical contact between the sexes is discouraged and some Muslims may politely refuse to shake hands with the opposite sex. This should not be viewed negatively.

The General Manager now feels that she has more information about Rakin's religion and culture, which she wishes she had known before he started. She arranges to meet with Rakin, not to make assumptions about how he practices his religion, but to discuss how he is getting on and what accommodation he may require. She asks about any specific requirements he may have and expresses her willingness to accommodate him.

Mindful that the majority of employees at the WA are female, the General Manager assigns to Rakin, with his agreement, a male colleague as a buddy with whom he can discuss any issues he wants to.

The General Manager arranges to meet with Rakin again in a week's time to discuss work progress and any further specific requirements.

'If you have concerns about the employee's performance, you should say so. Be specific and tell the employee what good performance looks like'

Probationary period

When an employee starts work, their manager must ensure that the employee is clear on how their performance and progress will be reviewed and assessed during the probationary period.

Probation terms

Check the term on probation, set out in the written statement of terms and conditions, issued to the employee on joining. For example, a term might read: 'you will be on probation for the first 6 months of your employment with (employer). Your probationary period may be extended if more time is needed to assess your suitability for the job.'

This means that you must have a system in place to ensure that the new employee's performance is assessed regularly during the first six months. You should meet regularly to discuss progress, but it is recommended that you also have formal review meetings:

- when the employee has been in post for three months
- when the employee has been in post for just under six months.

At the six-month stage, you should confirm the employee in post, extend their probationary period or terminate their employment.

The probationary period does not, however, have to run for the full period in all circumstances. On some occasions, if you are certain that the employee is performing at an appropriate standard, you may wish to confirm the employee in post prior to the end of the probationary period.

On other occasions, you may feel that the employee will never reach the required standard and you may wish to terminate employment prior to the end of the probationary period. If you want to take this step, though, it is advisable that you follow the statutory dismissal procedures outlined in this chapter. You should also make sure that you have been totally fair to the employee and given them sufficient time to demonstrate that they could do the job.

Formal review meetings

A formal review meeting is an opportunity for the employee and the manager to jointly discuss the employee's performance and identify any needs for training or guidance. The three-month review meeting should cover a review of the employee's performance against the job description and against any specific targets that have been set.

If the employee is performing satisfactorily, say so. Arrange a date for the further formal review meeting just prior to the end of the 6 months probation. Don't ignore the employee for the next three months, though – keep a track on their work and meet to discuss it as required.

If you have concerns about the employee's performance, you should say so. Be specific and tell the employee what good performance looks like. It is important that the employee understands clearly what they should do to improve and also that they understand that if improvement does not occur, the probationary period may be extended or their contract may be terminated.

Ask the employee if there are specific barriers preventing them from achieving their best. If there are, work with the employee to remove these barriers. Provide additional training or coaching if needed.

Give the employee a clear note confirming your discussions. Arrange to meet regularly with the employee to help them improve their performance and to review progress. How regularly you meet will depend on the specific circumstance, but a brief meeting each week to keep the employee on track is often better than a longer meeting each month.

Terminating employment during or at the end of the probationary period

A further formal review meeting should be held shortly before the employee has completed six months' service.

If at this stage, you feel that the employee's performance and progress are satisfactory, you can confirm the employee in post.

If you feel that the employee's performance is still unsatisfactory, but could reach a satisfactory standard given a bit more time, you could extend the probationary period, say by a further three months. You should make it clear to the employee that if improvement does not occur during the period of extension, termination of the employee's contract may occur. Details of the decision should be recorded in writing and a copy given to the employee.

If you feel that the employee will not reach the required standard and you are contemplating terminating the employee's contract, you must set out your concerns in writing in advance of the meeting, in order to comply with the law on dismissal. The statutory procedure that you must follow is set out below.

If your disciplinary procedure is a part of the employee's contract of employment, you should follow this procedure if you are looking to terminate an employee's contract. Otherwise, as a minimum, it is advisable that you do the following:

Step one – written statement
You should set out in writing your concerns (conduct, capability or other circumstances) and state that these may result in dismissal or disciplinary action. You should give or send this statement to the employee, give the employee the opportunity to consider their response, and invite the employee to a meeting at a reasonable time and place to discuss the matter. It is recommended that the employee receives a minimum of 2 days notice prior to the meeting. You should remind the employee of their right to be accompanied at the meeting.

Step two – meeting
The employee must take all reasonable steps to attend the meeting. Both you and the employee should have the opportunity to give your points of view. You should fully consider what the employee has to say about their work performance.

Keep an open mind and don't take a final decision on whether to terminate the employee's contract until you have heard everything that has been said and until you have had a chance to consider it. After the meeting, adjourn and consider what has been said. You should inform the employee about your decision, which could be to dismiss the employee, extend their probationary period or to confirm them in post. You should offer the employee the right of appeal.

Step three – appeal
If the employee wants to appeal, they must inform you in writing. You should give the employee a timescale by which to appeal. Acas advises a timescale of 5 working days.

You should then invite the employee to a further meeting, which should be arranged without unreasonable delay and should be at a reasonable time and place. The employee must take all reasonable steps to attend. You should arrange for a more senior manager to chair the meeting, where possible. If this is not possible, a Trustee may chair the meeting.

After the meeting, you should communicate the final decision to the employee.

Continued overleaf...

You should give the employee the notice period outlined in his or her written statement of terms and conditions of employment, except if the employee is summarily dismissed for gross misconduct.

Please note that at both the stage 2 meeting and the stage 3 meeting, the employee has the right to be accompanied by a colleague or trade union representative. If you wish, you may allow the employee to be accompanied by a friend or family member instead. You should inform the employee of their right to be accompanied prior to the meeting, so that the employee has the time to make arrangements.

Review of procedures for terminating employment
At the time or writing, the government had just completed consultation on a major review of the procedures for dealing with disputes, including the termination of employment. The current statutory procedures will be abolished and replaced but any change is unlikely to take effect until 2009.

Checklist

	Make sure you tailor your induction and probation procedures to employees' specific needs
	Think carefully about how you will structure the new employee's first day
	Use an induction checklist, to ensure you don't forget anything
	Monitor the employee's progress and performance carefully during probation and meet regularly
	If there are areas where performance is below standard, be honest and say so. Support the employee by being specific about what good performance 'looks like' and by providing additional coaching/training if needed
	Confirm the employee in post at the end of the probationary period, if appropriate
	In exceptional cases and if the employee's performance is not satisfactory, either extend the probationary period or terminate employment
	If you terminate employment, remember to follow the 3 step statutory dismissal procedures

Further information

The following organisations offer advice and resources about the subjects covered in this chapter to new and existing employers, often free of charge:

Acas
You can download an advisory booklet on recruitment and induction from the Acas website.
www.acas.org.uk

Business Link
The Business Link website has a very useful section on induction.
www.businesslink.gov.uk

NCVO
www.ncvo-vol.org.uk
A listing of all the useful organisations referred to in this Good Guide can be found at the back of this book with full contact details.

Six
Pay and benefits

Whilst organisations in the voluntary sector may not be able to pay the highest salaries, you still need to make sure you adhere to the law and that your pay system is fair – and seen to be fair by your employees. Staff should understand how their pay is determined and where possible should be paid reasonably relative to similar jobs in other organisations.

The Minimum Wage

The National Minimum Wage Act 1998 says that you must pay at least the national minimum wage. This is an hourly rate set by the government. It is reviewed each October. There are three rates of the national minimum wage:

- a rate for employees aged 22 and over(adult rate)
- a development rate applicable to 18 to 21-year-olds
- a young workers' rate for 16 to 17-year-olds.

The rates are reviewed each October. The adult rate as at October 2007 is £5.52 per hour.

You can find out the current rates by calling the National Minimum Wage helpline on 0845 6000 678.

The minimum wage covers almost all workers in the UK. Not all the money you pay a worker counts as pay for the purposes of the minimum wage. For example, allowances, such as London or regional allowances or shift allowances do not count, unless they are consolidated into an employee's basic pay.

The only benefit in kind which can be counted towards the minimum wage is accommodation. There are special rules for calculating the value of the accommodation provided which counts towards the minimum wage.

Making sure you are paying the National Minimum Wage

There are different ways of calculating the hours that count towards the National Minimum Wage, depending on the type of work. This means that if the salaries you pay are relatively low, you may need to undertake some calculations to make sure you are paying the National Minimum Wage.

You can find out how to make the calculations by reviewing the 'detailed guide to the national minimum wage', available for download from the website of the Department for Business, Enterprise and Regulatory Reform (formerly the Department of Trade and Industry) at www.berr.gov.uk[1]

Alternatively, you can call the minimum wage information line on 0845 8450 360 and ask them to send you a copy.

The National Minimum Wage helpline 0845 6000 678 can also provide general advice and assistance.

Equal Pay/fair pay

The Equal Pay Act 1970 (amended by the Equal Pay Regulations 1983) says that men and women are entitled to equal pay for work of equal value. Equal pay includes basic pay as well as other contractual conditions of employment, such as hours of work, bonuses and pension contributions.

The Act requires that employers must pay men and women an equal wage when the work they do is:

- the same or like work
- of equal value
- rated as equivalent via a job evaluation scheme.

Claims for equal pay are applicable only when comparing rates of pay with one or more workers of the opposite gender. So the employee has to identify an actual person of the opposite sex doing equal work in the same employment in order to bring a claim in the employment tribunal.

Employees have the right to issue an equal pay questionnaire to their employer, asking for information to help them work out whether they have received equal pay, and if not, why.

Employees who believe they haven't received equal pay may take the case to an employment tribunal, which may use the information in the questionnaire.

Continued overleaf...

An employer may be able to justify differences in pay, if there is a 'genuine material factor' or reason for the difference which is not the individual's gender – location may be such a genuine material factor. For instance, a female employee based in London could be doing identical work to a male employee based elsewhere, but might receive a higher wage as a result of a London allowance.

An employer may also be able to justify differences in pay, if the difference came about because of a TUPE transfer (see chapter 14).

If an Employment Tribunal decides an employer is at fault, the employer may have to pay compensation and the rate of pay claimed may be backdated for up to six years (and in certain circumstances, further than this).

If you carry out regular reviews of your pay system, you can build and maintain a robust, fair pay system that stands up to scrutiny and is less susceptible to claims for equal pay. It is also more likely to be fair not only in terms of gender, but also in terms of matters such as race, disability and age. If you do not review your pay system regularly, you may find that anomalies have crept in over the years and that some differences in pay are no longer justifiable.

The Equality and Human Rights Commission (EHRC) has an equal pay toolkit called 'a small business guide to effective pay practices'. You can download the toolkit from the EHRC website at www.equalityhumanrights.com

There is an accompanying CD Rom, which you can obtain free of charge, by calling the helpline of the Commission (see Resources).

Setting and reviewing salary levels in smaller organisations

The level of formality in your salary system is likely to depend on the size of your organisation.

If you are a small voluntary organisation, with, say, under 10 employees, you may be able to set salary levels in the following way:

- determine a reasonable rate you can afford and that allows you to attract external recruits. You can determine this rate by looking at local advertisements for similar jobs and by checking with local contacts
- keep job descriptions up to date and review them regularly, so that you can make sure that they reflect the actual jobs done and responsibilities held
- review salary levels each year, to ensure they continue to reflect responsibility levels and external market rates.

'Review salary levels each year, to ensure they continue to reflect responsibility levels and external market rates.'

Job evaluation

Once your organisation grows, you may start to need more formal systems, because it may become more difficult to determine relative levels of responsibility of jobs in an objective way. At this stage, you may wish to implement some form of job evaluation.

Job evaluation is the method by which jobs are assessed to determine their level of responsibility relative to each other. The principle is that those jobs which are more responsible will be rated higher in the job evaluation. Job evaluation does not determine pay and it does not assess the ability of the job holder, but it produces a hierarchy of jobs against which to set pay levels.

Job evaluation schemes fall into two types: analytical and non-analytical.

Analytical job evaluation

Analytical schemes are based on the analysis and scoring of elements (factors) within jobs, as follows:

- a number of factors are selected and defined, such as technical knowledge and skills, freedom to act, interpersonal skills or decision making
- each of these factors is described at different levels. These levels are called factor definitions (see example)
- each of the levels has a points score assigned to it
- each job is analysed against each factor and assigned to a level and points score
- from the above analysis, a total points score for the job is produced
- all jobs are ranked in terms of their total points score
- jobs are then graded according to their ranking
- rates of pay are allocated to the grade.

Example
Factor definitions – interpersonal skills

Level 1 of a 5 level factor definition on 'interpersonal skills' might be: 'the job requires the ability to deal courteously with others on the phone and in person, responding to their requests.'

The level 5 definition would require greater interpersonal skills and might be described as 'the job requires the ability to deal with complex negotiations with influential external bodies on behalf of the organisation; and to reconcile often differing priorities, resolving situations of conflict.'

Case study – analytical job evaluation

Carers Unite started off as a local self-help group of carers. Over the years, it has grown to around 100 employees, with 20 different job titles.

Carers Unite has found it increasingly difficult to ensure that jobs are paid fairly relative to each other. It therefore enlisted the assistance of a consultant to help it develop a job evaluation scheme.

The consultant worked with Carers Unite to manage the project. The first step was to set up a working group, comprising staff from different parts of the organisation and doing different jobs.

The working group agreed the factors that were felt to determine job size within Carers Unite. These were: interpersonal skills, management of budgets, people management, decision-making and job knowledge.

Once the factors were agreed, the consultant produced five statements for each factor, level 5 describing the greatest job requirement (eg advanced decisions being made) and level 1 describing least job requirement (eg only simple decisions need to be made). Points were then allocated to levels 5 to 1 as follows: 100, 80, 60, 40 and 20 points.

Jobs were then analysed against each factor in turn. Some jobs scored highly for some factors, and less high for other factors. The post of Project Worker, for example, scored high on interpersonal skills (80 points), but lower on budgets and people management (20 points). Once each job had been analysed, a total points score was allocated to each job.

Once all jobs were scored, the jobs were put in order of points score. The jobs were then grouped into grades, for the purposes of allocating a pay range.

The outcome of the work was that Carers Unite had a hierarchy of jobs, which could form the basis of a logical and defensible pay structure.

Analytical job evaluation is a robust approach which should enable employers to defend an equal pay claim. However, it can be more time–consuming than non-analytical job evaluation and may be more appropriate to organisations which feel that they are of a size that needs a more rigorous approach to evaluating jobs.

If you wish to implement an analytical job evaluation scheme, you are advised to seek assistance from an external consultant.

Non-analytical job evaluation
Non-analytical schemes compare whole jobs with one another – there is no attempt to distinguish between the factors within the jobs which may differentiate them. Non-analytical job evaluation is more suited to smaller organisations. Examples of non-analytical schemes are job ranking, paired comparison and job classification.

Job ranking
In this form of non-analytical job evaluation all jobs are placed in rank order, based on a review of the responsibilities of each job. It is considered the simplest method, since there is no attempt to break down or analyse the whole job in any way. It is therefore easy to understand and implement, particularly with a small number of jobs.

'Job classification is relatively easy to understand but it can be difficult to classify very different jobs... and some jobs may straddle grade definitions... '

Example
Job ranking/non-analytical job evaluation

A female office manager and a male supervisor in production may both be involved in allocating and checking work, providing technical advice and assistance, motivating staff, and making sure standards, such as timekeeping and attendance, are met. Even though they work in different areas, an analysis from a job ranking exercise may reveal that their jobs require similar levels of effort, skills, knowledge and responsibility.

Example from the Equal Opportunities Commission small business guide to effective pay practices.

Here is an approach to a job ranking exercise:

Step 1 – Planning
- include all jobs in your organisation in the review, both full time and part time
- talk to your employees – tell them that you are undertaking the review. They may have comments on how pay arrangements actually operate, that you may not be aware of
- decide a good time to start and decide will do the work – some time will need to be set aside.

Step 2 – Analysing jobs
- update all existing job descriptions
- produce job descriptions in a common format
- update the person specifications to go with each job description
- produce the person specifications in a common format, so that for each, the level of effort, skills, knowledge and responsibility are clearly defined
- agree the job descriptions and person specifications with your staff and their immediate managers
- assess all jobs. Come up with a rank order.

Paired comparisons

This is a statistical technique used to compare each job with others. It is based on the premise that it is easier to compare one job with one other rather than one job with several. Using a ranking form, points are allocated to the job:

• two points if it is considered to be of higher value
• one point if it is regarded as equal worth
• no points if it is less important.

Paired comparisons gives greater consistency, but takes longer than job ranking as each job is considered separately.

Job classification

This is another whole job evaluation technique. With job classification, the number of grades is decided first and detailed grade definitions are then produced. Jobs are then slotted into the grades, by matching the job descriptions against the grade definitions. The grade definitions should be suited to and drafted for the jobs in your organisation. You can seek external support in achieving this, if you need to.

Job classification is relatively easy to understand but it can be difficult to classify very different jobs (eg a fundraising job compared with a project worker job) and some jobs may straddle grade definitions.

Example job ranking form – paired comparisons

Job ref	A	B	C	D	E	F	Total score	ranking
A	–	0	0	0	1	0	1	=5
B	2	–	2	2	2	0	8	2
C	2	0	–	2	2	0	6	3
D	2	0	0	–	2	0	4	4
E	1	0	0	0	–	0	1	=5
F	2	2	2	2	2	–	10	1

'When setting salaries, you should also take into account market rates of pay, because if you are paying well below market rates, it may be difficult to recruit and retain staff...'

Example job classification system

Levels	Definitions
Foundation skill and knowledge (Equivalent to NVQ/SVQ Level 1)	The job involves a range of routine and predictable tasks, carried out under supervision.
Intermediate skill and knowledge (Equivalent to NVQ/SVQ Level 2)	The job involves a range of tasks, carried out with limited supervision in a variety of contexts. Some tasks are complex or non-routine and there is some personal responsibility or autonomy. Working in a group or team may often be a requirement.
Advanced skill and knowledge (Equivalent to NVQ/SVQ Level 3)	The job involves a defined occupation or a range of jobs where there is a broad range of varied tasks carried out in a wide variety of contexts. Most tasks are complex and non-routine, and there is considerable personal responsibility and autonomy. Supervision or guidance of others is often required.
High skill and knowledge (Equivalent to NVQ/SVQ Level 4)	The job involves a broad range of complex, technical, or professional work tasks, carried out in a variety of contexts. There is a substantial degree of personal responsibility and autonomy. Responsibility for the work of others and the allocation of resources is often required.
Very high skill and knowledge (Equivalent to NVQ/SVQ Level 5)	The job involves work at a professional level or equivalent, requiring the mastery of a range of relevant knowledge and the ability to apply it at this level. There is very substantial personal autonomy. Significant responsibility for the work of others and for the allocation of substantial resources is often required, as are personal accountabilities for analysis and diagnosis, design, planning, execution and evaluation.

Determining pay levels against the outcome of job evaluation

Once you have evaluated your jobs and put them in a rank order, you will need to determine pay levels.

You will need to review existing annual salaries. You can plot annual salaries onto a spreadsheet if this assists you. The Equal Opportunities Commission advises that you should put down on the spreadsheet whether the employee is male or female. This helps you to assess for equal pay. You can plot on the spreadsheet current pay and then compare this with job evaluation rankings.

Assessing the reason for any differences

If there are any differences in pay levels compared with job evaluation ranking, you will need to consider the reason for the differences. It is possible that the differences may have come about for reasons which are no longer valid.

If you find any unfairness, for example that part-time workers are paid less, pro rata, for a job that requires a similar level of effort, skills, knowledge and responsibility, or that staff with shorter service (who may be predominantly women) are paid less, then you should look to address the anomalies as soon as you can.

If you find an employee is being paid above the level determined by the job evaluation, you need to approach the situation with caution.

The employee may find themselves above the top of the grade the evaluation has placed their job role in, and therefore they may be being paid more than an employee at the same point of the same grade – this could be a case of inequality in pay. Your salary policy should state that as a result of any job evaluation undertaken an employee's salary will be protected, but not subject to any pay increments until it is brought into line with other jobs at the same level.

Setting new salaries

You can set new salaries that reflect the outcome of your job evaluation.

When setting salaries, you should also take into account market rates of pay, because if you are paying well below market rates, it may be difficult to recruit and retain staff.

Sometimes, you may find that you need to pay a particular job more than others, on account of market rates, even though job evaluation indicates that it is not such a responsible job as the other jobs.

If this is the case, one approach is to pay a basic salary, plus a separate market supplement. This sends a clear message as to why additional pay is being made and will remind you to review the payment against the market at a later date.

Salary surveys

In order to be able to assess market rates, you can use salary surveys.

You can undertake your own salary survey. Here are the steps you would need to take:

- draft clear job descriptions for your jobs
- decide which organisations you wish to approach to exchange salary data. These organisations will be those who have similar jobs to yours
- approach the organisations, to see if they would be willing to participate in a salary survey
- send them, on a confidential basis, details of your job descriptions, salaries and benefits
- gain information from the participant organisations on the salaries and benefits payable for similar jobs in their organisations
- summarise the data and give participant organisations a copy.

It is important to gain appropriate job matches and take into account factors such as the date salaries were last reviewed, any allowances and benefits. Salary data is also sensitive. For these reasons, organisations may prefer to ask an external consultant to conduct the salary survey on their behalf. A consultant will collect the salary data and will summarise the results, so that confidentiality of individual salaries is maintained.

As an alternative to conducting your own salary survey, you could participate in an existing commercial survey. Two significant salary surveys in the voluntary sector are those run by Croner Reward and CELRE. Contact details for these two organisations are given in the Resources section at the back of the book.

If you participate in a survey, you will normally be given a copy of the survey results at reduced or no cost. If you do not participate, you may be able to purchase the survey (if it is not a members only survey), but normally at a higher cost.

The market rate

There is a temptation to believe that there is a market rate for each job. In fact, this is not the case. There will be a variety of pay rates and benefits in the external market for any one job. As a result of this, salary surveys do not always give consistent data. Where possible, you should use more than one survey and consider the information from each.

Setting salaries based on the market rate

Some organisations choose to set salaries based entirely on market rate information, rather than any form of job evaluation. However, as mentioned above, market rates are not always consistent. In addition, salary survey data may simply replicate any pay discrimination that exists in the wider employment market. It is therefore advisable to pay attention both to market rates and to internal relativities.

Salary progression

Once you have set broad pay rates, you will need to decide whether you wish to allow for salary progression and if so, in what form (eg based on length of service or performance). Consider all options and choose the most appropriate for your organisation.

If you are thinking of making a change to the way staff salaries may progress, make sure you consult with staff first and involve them in the development of any new system. You should also check your employees' written statements of terms and conditions (employment contract) to check the contractual flexibility you may have to change terms. If, for example, your written statements give your employees the right to automatic incremental progression according to length of service, you will only be able to change this in respect of each individual employee, if you have that employee's agreement to do so.

'Having very long salary scales...may have a disproportionate adverse effect on women, who tend to have more career breaks and job changes...'

Job evaluation

Incremental salary scales

Some voluntary organisations link salaries to local authority salary scales. They may not link pay rates to specific local authority jobs, but simply place their salaries on the NJC (National Joint Council) pay spine. They may do this on the basis of a spot rate (ie no increments are guaranteed), on the basis of automatic annual incremental progression (with a progression range, of, say 3–4 points) or on the basis of progression based on individual contribution/performance.

The advantages of using NJC scales are:

- NJC scales are familiar to many staff, so they can understand their spinal point and compare it with other jobs externally
- NJC scales are familiar to funders, so it may be easier to obtain funding increases if pay rates are linked to NJC.

The disadvantages of using NJC scales may be:

- NJC scales increase by a certain percentage cost of living amount each year. If voluntary organisations follow these scales, then flexibility to pay what the organisation itself can afford may be limited
- if voluntary organisations do not link their cost of living awards to NJC scales in any one year, but still maintain a pay structure based on NJC rates, then it may give the impression to staff that they have missed out on a pay increase.

If you decide to use the NJC scales, it is recommended that it be made clear to staff that incremental salary progression each year is not guaranteed, but dependent on affordability and is at Trustee discretion.

Graded structure
– not using NJC scales

As an alternative, you could develop a pay spine specific to your organisation. You can do this relatively simply on a spreadsheet, with increments of an agreed percentage eg 2% or 3%. Grades of, for example, 3 or 5 increments could simply be plotted onto the spreadsheet.

Example
Long salary scales
One matter to consider, if you want to introduce an incremental salary structure, is that long salary scales based on length of service may not be appropriate. Think about how many years it may take your employees to be fully competent (eg 3 or 5 years?) and set your maximum increments accordingly. Having very long salary scales (eg 10 increments) may have a disproportionate adverse effect on women, who tend to have more career breaks and job changes; and younger workers. It is best to keep the number of increments relatively short (eg up to 5 increments) to avoid or minimise any adverse effect on particular groups.

Example pay spines with 3% and 2% increments

Grade	Spine point	3% Increments	2% Increments	Grade	Spine point	3% Increments	2% Increments
A	1	£11,564	£11,340	C etc	18	£19,113	£15,879
	2	£11,911	£11,567		19	£19,687	£16,197
	3	£12,268	£11,799		20	£20,277	£16,521
	4	£12,636	£12,034		21	£20,886	£16,851
					22	£21,512	£17,188
B	5	£13,015	£12,275		23	£22,157	£17,532
	6	£13,406	£12,521		24	£22,822	£17,883
	7	£13,808	£12,771		25	£23,507	£18,240
	8	£14,222	£13,027		26	£24,212	£18,605
					27	£24,938	£18,977
C etc	9	£14,649	£13,287		28	£25,687	£19,357
	10	£15,088	£13,553		29	£26,457	£19,744
	11	£15,541	£13,824		30	£27,251	£20,139
	12	£16,007	£14,100		31	£28,068	£20,541
	13	£16,487	£14,382		32	£28,910	£20,952
	14	£16,982	£14,670		33	£29,778	£21,371
	15	£17,491	£14,963		34	£30,671	£21,799
	16	£18,016	£15,263		35	£31,591	£22,235
	17	£18,557	£15,568		36	£32,539	£22,679

'Paying employees differently according to performance can be divisive and demotivate those who are solid performers but who get no additional pay award...'

Spot rate structure

Some voluntary organisations have a spot rate structure, rather than salary scales.

A spot rate structure can be cheaper than an incremental structure, because there are no annual increments to be paid in addition to a cost of living award.

The disadvantage of a spot rate structure is that it can be relatively inflexible.

An individual may be recruited on a different spot rate (for example, due to experience) compared with those already in the same type of post. This can cause the spot rate structure to erode. Over time, the rationale for the pay difference may be forgotten or may be no longer relevant.

Sometimes organisations combine a spot rate system with a system of bonuses paid on the basis of individual performance. However, be aware that in a small voluntary organisation, the payment of bonuses to some staff and not others could be divisive.

Linking pay to performance

Some organisations link salary increases directly to performance or competencies, as assessed in the performance appraisal. In these cases, the employee will be awarded higher pay when they have met pre-agreed targets.

Such targets may include concrete achievements – such as achieving certain fundraising targets – or may involve demonstrating competence in a new area, such as the use of information technology or the display of specific behaviours such as good team working, communication skills or planning/organising.

Whilst there may be an attraction in the inherent logic of paying for individual performance ('if an individual is performing better, they should be paid more'), the reality of linking pay to individual performance or contribution can be difficult. Paying employees differently according to performance can be divisive and demotivate those who are solid performers but who get no additional pay award.

Managers can be reluctant to implement such systems. The annual appraisal system would need to be sufficiently robust in design and implementation to enable judgements to be made about performance awards.

You should also note that linking pay and performance is likely to change the focus of the appraisal meeting, because a member of staff will be conscious that the outcome of the appraisal will determine their pay. Some organisations decide to have a separate review of performance, mid-way in the appraisal year. This review, rather than the annual appraisal, is then used as the basis for the pay review. The advantage of this approach is that if concerns are identified in the annual appraisal, the individual has six months to rectify them before the pay review.

Acas makes the following points in its publication about appraisal-related pay (APR), which can be downloaded from the Acas website at www.acas.org.uk:

- there must be commitment to ARP from senior managers
- the role of managers is critical
- adequate resources and suitable training should be provided
- employers should consult with managers, employees and their representatives before ARP is introduced
- all employees involved must receive full and clear information about how the scheme will operate
- ARP should be fair and open and based on a formal system of performance assessment
- the scheme should be carefully designed, simple to operate and should encourage consistency and objectivity
- there should be an appeals procedure and the scheme should be regularly evaluated.

You should also remember that factors other than pay can motivate workers and may lead to better retention rates. These factors might include regular feedback, supervision, training, consultation and work-life balance.

Linking pay to qualifications

Some organisations link pay increase to qualifications. These can be less subjective than linking pay to performance (as you either have a qualification or you have not). Consider, though, which qualifications you wish your employees to attain in order to progress their salaries. Think also about whether you can link pay increases to qualifications for all employees, or whether the system may in fact only be relevant to some.

As an alternative to linking pay increases to qualifications, you could consider making a small lump sum bonus payment, when an individual achieves a qualification.

Developing a salary policy

You should consider developing a salary policy, so that all staff and managers are clear about how pay is reviewed.

Your salary policy could include the following:

- a statement of intent, explaining the organisation's commitment to an open and fair pay system, paying within its resources
- the normal pay review date
- a statement that rates of pay are reviewed annually without any obligation on the Employer to increase them
- how jobs are evaluated
- what salary progression, if any, exists
- the criteria for pay increases
- the process that staff can follow if they feel that their pay is unfair.

The following case study shows how one organisation aimed to have a fair and open pay system and developed a salary policy. What suits one organisation will not necessarily suit the next, so make sure what you do fits the requirements of your organisation.

Pensions

From the point at which you employ your fifth employee, you must, within three months, provide your employees with access to a stakeholder pension scheme. A stakeholder pension is a low cost personal pension regulated by the government and provided through a pension company.

You may be exempt from the requirement to provide a stakeholder pension if you:

- offer all employees aged 18 or over a personal pension scheme through which you contribute an amount equal to at least 3 per cent of the employees' basic pay
- offer an occupational pension scheme that all your staff can join within a year of starting to work for you.

If you have an occupational scheme or an arrangement with a personal pension provider (often called a group personal pension scheme), you should check with the provider of the scheme to find out if it meets the conditions for being exempt.

Case study – salary policy

When the Westwich Association (the WA) recruited its first employee it set pay by reviewing salaries of similar jobs in the local area, and considering what it could afford.

As it took on more employees over the years, these employees were recruited on a similar basis, but also taking into account the salaries of employees already in post.

By the time the WA employed its 10th employee, the Trustees decided to review pay. Some jobs had grown in scope, whilst others had stayed the same or grown smaller. Salaries had not changed with these changes in job size. The salaries of new recruits were not always consistent with the salaries of existing staff.

As a first step, the WA decided to implement a salary policy. The development of the salary policy helped the Trustees to agree between themselves how salaries should be reviewed, when they should be reviewed, who should be responsible for reviewing them, what criteria should be taken into account if increasing pay and what employees should do if they were unhappy about their pay.

The Trustees consulted with employees about the policy, made some amendments as a result and then produced the final version.

With the involvement of employees, job descriptions were reviewed and jobs assessed on a 'whole job' basis, taking into account the level of effort, skills, knowledge and responsibility required for each job.

As a result of the review, it was clear that there was a need to review some salaries that had fallen behind compared with the level of responsibility of the jobs.

The Trustees used the annual pay increase budget to give each employee a small cost of living award, with the remainder of the budget being used to deal with the salary adjustments.

'If employees transfer into your organisation from another organisation, in some circumstances you may need to match employee pension contributions up to 6% of basic salary'

Even if you are exempt you can still give your employees access to a stakeholder pension scheme if you want to.

Stakeholder pension schemes must satisfy certain criteria:

- currently the pension scheme provider cannot charge more than 1 per cent a year of the individual's fund
- members must be able to transfer into and out of a stakeholder pension scheme, or stop paying into one, without facing additional charges
- all stakeholder schemes must accept minimum contributions of as little as £20, which can be paid each week, each month or at less regular intervals. Some offer an even lower limit
- the schemes must be run in the interest of members. They are either run by trustees or by the scheme manager.

Your obligations include:

- consulting the employees or their representatives as to the choice of scheme
- supplying all employees with information about the scheme
- affording representatives of the scheme reasonable access to employees to provide information about the scheme
- agreeing, on request, to collect employees contributions from their pay and remit them to the scheme.

You do not have to make contributions to your employees' stakeholder pension. They are not obliged to make contributions either.

There is no charge for employees changing their contribution amounts. They cannot change the amount more than once every six months, unless you as the employer agree to it.

Employee access

You do not have to provide access to a stakeholder pension for any employee:

- who has worked for you for less than three months in a row
- who is a member of your occupational pension scheme
- who cannot join your occupational scheme because they are under 18 or they are within five years of the scheme's normal pension age
- who decided not to join your occupational pension scheme
- whose earnings have fallen below the National Insurance lower earnings limit (£90 per week as at April 2008) for one or more weeks within the last 3 months
- who cannot join a stakeholder pension scheme because of HM Revenue and Customs restrictions (for example, the employee does not normally live in the UK).

Annual leave

Selecting and implementing your stakeholder pension

You can choose a stakeholder pension scheme from the list of providers registered with the Pensions Regulator. You can see the Pensions Regulator's register of approved stakeholder pension schemes at www.thepensionsregulator.gov.uk or you can write to them to request a copy. Their full contact details can be found in the resources section at the back of the book.

Once you have compared some different stakeholder pension schemes and you have made your choice, you then need to do the following:

- discuss your choice of scheme with your eligible employees
- designate (formally choose) your stakeholder pension scheme
- give your employees the name and address of the stakeholder pension scheme
- tell your employees about your payroll deduction arrangements
- make the payroll deductions if an employee wants you to
- send your employee contributions (and any employer contributions) to the stakeholder pension scheme provider within the given time limits
- record the payments you make to the stakeholder pension scheme provider.

For further information about stakeholder pensions, you can go to the government website www.thepensionservice.gov.uk

Pensions and TUPE
Transfer of Undertakings Regulations

If employees transfer into your organisation from another organisation, in some circumstances you may need to match employee pension contributions up to 6% of basic salary. For further information about the implications of TUPE, please see chapter 14.

Pensions and age discrimination
Please see section on 'benefits and age discrimination' on page 122.

The legal minimum entitlement to annual leave increased on 1 October 2007 from 20 days to 24 days (4.8 weeks). The legal minimum entitlement will increase again to 28 days (5.6 weeks), with effect from 1 April 2009. These minimum entitlements are inclusive of the eight bank and public holidays and are pro-rata for part-time staff.

You cannot pay the minimum entitlement in lieu (except when the employee is leaving), because the legal minimum annual leave is considered to be a health and safety measure – your employees should take the leave.

However, please note that until 1 April 2009, there is an exception: the additional holiday entitlement of 4 days from 1 October 2007 may be paid in lieu, rather than taken, if it suits you and the employee.

If you currently pay your employees the legal minimum level of annual leave, then the increased leave from October 2007 and April 2009 can be calculated proportionally depending on when an employee's leave year starts. Here is an example of how it works:

Setting annual leave
Whilst voluntary organisations cannot pay the highest salaries, annual leave is an area where it may be possible to be more generous.

'Whilst voluntary organisations cannot pay the highest salaries, annual leave is an area where it may be possible to be more generous'

Consider what annual leave provision you can afford above the statutory minimum. You might want to benchmark your annual leave against the levels of leave of other similar voluntary sector organisations.

'Rolling up' holiday pay

If you have workers or employees who work on a casual or irregular, part time basis, it may be complicated to work out their entitlement to paid annual leave.

Some employers have got round this by adding a monetary amount of holiday pay to each hour worked. This is referred to as 'rolling up' holiday pay.

There has been debate for some time as to whether rolling up is lawful. Following a series of inconsistent decisions in the UK, the European Court of Justice handed down its decision in Robinson Steel v RF Retail Services Ltd on 16 March 2006. In essence, it said that rolling up the statutory annual leave element of holiday pay is unlawful, and the employer must pay at least the statutory element of holiday pay during the period while the employee is actually on leave. The background to this is that the Regulations were designed as a health and safety measure – and if individuals receive rolled up holiday pay, they may not actually take the time off to rest from work.

This is a case law decision, not a change of statute, so contracts of employment which include a right to rolled-up pay are not automatically changed. If you roll up holiday pay for some or all employees in your organisation, you are advised to consider when and how best to change from rolled up holiday pay to payment for statutory annual leave at the time when leave is taken. You may wish to take legal or HR advice on this matter.

Holiday pay on leaving

When an employee leaves, you should pay them for any annual leave earned but not taken.

Annual leave requests

Unless the individual's contract of employment states otherwise, the default legal requirement is that an employee must provide notice of twice as many days as the length of leave that is to be taken, in advance of the first day of leave requested. For example, if an employee requests 2 week's annual leave, they must give 4 week's notice prior to the first day on which the leave was due to start.

If you can't agree to the request for leave, you must inform the employee of this a period of time in advance that is equal to the amount of leave requested. So if 2 weeks is requested, you must tell the employee at least 2 weeks in advance if you intend to reject the request for leave.

Example
Minimum leave entitlement

Employee X's leave year starts in April. She works a 5-day week and she currently receives 20 days' leave including bank and public holidays. As half of her leave year is remaining, when the statutory minimum leave increases to 24 days, she will be entitled to 2 additional days in the period from October 2007 to March 2008.

Sick pay

You have an obligation to provide employees who fall ill and cannot work with a minimum level of sick pay. This is known as Statutory Sick Pay (SSP).

Employees are normally entitled to SSP if they are unable to work for four or more consecutive days. It is not payable for the first three days in any period of entitlement but thereafter SSP can be paid for up to 28 weeks for a single period of illness.

SSP is liable to tax and National Insurance Contributions. You can find out about keeping records for SSP and about the current rate, from the HM Revenue and Customs website www.hmrc.gov.uk.

You may be able to reclaim a proportion of any SSP you pay. For this to happen, the total SSP payments in any tax month must exceed 13% of the overall gross Class 1 National Insurance Contributions for the entire business. You can then recover the difference between the two. In other words, the recoverable SSP is the amount above 13% of the total NIC liability. Contact HM Revenue and Customs for more information.

You are free to have a contractual sick pay agreement with your employees above the minimum payment. The contractual sick pay should include SSP payments. In setting contractual sick pay, consider what other similar employers pay and also consider what you could afford to pay, should someone be on long-term sick leave.

For information about managing absence, please see chapter 10.

Other benefits

Flexitime
Many voluntary sector employers offer flexibility in working times and arrangements. For more information about flexitime, see chapter 8.

Parental benefits
For more information on parental benefits, see chapter 8.

Counselling
You could consider offering access to employee counselling, where needed. This could be provided via an Employee Assistance Programme (EAP). You can obtain a list of EAP providers, and obtain quotes, from www.employeeassistance programme.com.

'There are lots of benefits you could offer your employees, at low cost or no cost'

Low cost or no cost benefits

There are lots of benefits you could offer your employees, at low cost or no cost. Some examples are listed below:

Childcare vouchers

Employers can provide childcare vouchers up to a value of £55 per week (as at July 2007) free from tax and national insurance contributions.

To take advantage of this tax beneficial offer, the employee makes a contractual agreement to give up part of their salary in exchange for the vouchers. This is known as salary sacrifice. Their employer also needs to have negotiated and implemented a voucher scheme with an appropriate provider. You must make sure that an employee does not take a salary sacrifice such that their new salary falls below the National Minimum Wage.

An employee can save up to £850 per year by not paying 11% national insurance contribution and standard rate tax on the vouchers. Employees paying higher rate tax could save over £1000 per year.

There is no cost to the employer apart from the administration costs and the management fee to the voucher company. However, the savings a company makes in terms of reduced National Insurance contributions usually exceeds the management fee charged by the voucher company.

Any scheme that is implemented needs to be open to all employees not just to specific groups of staff. Both parents who are working can claim the benefit on the same child.

For more information on providing childcare vouchers, including information on voucher providers, see the Daycare Trust website at www.daycaretrust.org.uk. Full contact details for the Daycare Trust are shown in the resources section at the back of the book.

Staff discounts

There are several discounts you may be able to negotiate locally. For example, you might be able to negotiate a staff discount at your local gym.

You may wish to contact a benefits company to help you to source staff discounts, in areas such as holidays, car rental, theme parks, hotels and cinema tickets. The Personal Group is one such benefits company. It is not necessarily expensive to use such a company, as they will receive income from the organisations whose products they are promoting. You can see information about the Personal Group at www.personal-group.com.

Buying and selling annual leave

Some staff may wish for more annual leave than the standard provision in your organisation. You could allow staff to take, say, an additional 5 days unpaid leave per year (buying leave). Some staff may prefer less annual leave and to be paid for the days they do not take, again up to a maximum of 5 days (selling leave). Make sure, though, that employees still take the minimum statutory annual leave (see earlier in this chapter).

Interest free travel loans

You could offer interest free travel loans, for staff to purchase season tickets.

Workplace facilities

You could offer a variety of workplace facilities at low cost, such as:

- access to the internet for personal use in lunchtimes and before/after work
- online ordering of groceries and delivery to workplace
- prayer room/quiet room (or a meeting room/office set aside at certain times of the day)
- access to local independent financial consultation on site
- microwave, grill and fridge facilities
- free tea and coffee.

'If you are reviewing the benefits you offer,
it is a good idea to consult with your staff about
what they would most value'

Example
Effects of Age Discrimination Regulations

Employer A has the following annual leave entitlement for its staff:

On joining – 24 days
After 3 years' service – 25 days
After 5 years' service – 26 days

Employer A's annual leave entitlement is within the five year qualification period, so is permitted under the Age Discrimination Regulations.

Employer B has the following annual leave entitlement for its staff:

On joining – 24 days
After 3 years' service – 25 days
After 5 years' service – 26 days
After 10 years' service – 30 days

Employer B must be able to show, if challenged, that the additional annual leave after 10 years' service is a reasonable way of fulfilling a business need, eg to reward loyalty or to maintain motivation. The employer might need to evidence this from monitoring or staff attitude surveys, for example.

Benefits and your workforce
Think about the benefits you are offering or considering offering. Are these benefits that suit the profile of your workforce? If you are reviewing the benefits you offer, it is a good idea to consult with your staff about what they would most value.

Benefits and age discrimination
The Age Discrimination Regulations are designed to ensure that workers, regardless of their age, are treated fairly.

The Regulations provide that using length of service to calculate an employment benefit (pay or non-pay) will be lawful if a qualification period of five years or less is used. The employer can choose whether to calculate the five years by reference to total length of service, or length of service in a role at or above a particular level.

If a qualification period of more than five years is used, to be lawful it must reasonably appear to the employer that adopting the length of service criterion fulfils a business need of the undertaking (such as encouraging loyalty or motivation).

In practice, the Age Discrimination Regulations are new and we don't yet know how the courts will interpret this provision. However, if you do have benefits which increase by service after five years, you should review whether they do really fulfil a business need. If not, you may wish to change this practice for any new employees. You could only withdraw the benefit from existing employees with their agreement – which may not be forthcoming!

Pensions exception
Please note that pension schemes are largely unaffected by the age discrimination regulations. For example, the following are all still permitted: the use of age criteria in actuarial calculations; the setting of pension contribution levels by reference to age; and the setting of pension benefit levels by reference to length of service.

For further information, go to www.berr.gov.uk/employment and search for 'Age legislation fact sheet number 8'.

One thing you will not longer be able to do is to set a maximum age for contributions to a pension scheme. However, you will be able to set a maximum number of years of pensionable service. The following case study explains how this will work in practice.

Age discrimination and redundancy payments
For information on age discrimination and redundancy pay, please see chapter 13.

Case study – pensions scheme membership and age discrimination

The Westwich Association provides a defined benefit pension scheme for all of its employees. One employee, Judy Snow, is 64 and has requested to continue working after the default retirement age of 65. The General Manager has agreed to this request.

Judy wants to know whether she can remain in the pension scheme and continue building up pension until she retires.

The Westwich Association can't stop contributing to Judy's pension scheme, unless she has already built up the maximum number of years' service under the scheme, which is set at 40 years. Judy only joined the Westwich Association in 1996, so she can carry on being a member of the scheme and receiving contributions from the Westwich Association.

Had Judy been a member of the scheme for 40 years, the Westwich Association would not have needed to keep contributing to her pension scheme or provide her with an alternative pension scheme, unless they wanted to. This is because she would have reached the maximum number of years' service under the rules of the scheme.

Provided the pension scheme rules permitted, Judy could alternatively draw all or part of her pension while continuing to work, if she wishes. Whether the Westwich Association would continue to make contributions would depend on the rules of the pension scheme.

Administering pay

Salaries are normally paid weekly or monthly by cheque or credit transfer. Under the Wages Act 1986 an employee can no longer insist on being paid in cash.

Issuing pay statements

As an employer you are legally obliged to give each employee a written itemised pay statement, usually known as a payslip or wage slip. You must issue it at, or before, the time you pay your employee. You do not need to give such a pay statement to people you pay who are non-employees, such as consultants and contractors.

The itemised pay statement must show:

- the gross amount of the wages or salary before deductions
- the amounts of – and reasons for – any fixed deductions that you make every pay period and any variable deductions that are not the same every pay period
- the net amount of wages or salary payable after deductions
- a breakdown of each part-payment – such as part by cheque, part in cash.

The pay statement does not have to include the amount and purpose of every separate fixed deduction every time, but if you don't issue a payslip that does this, you must give the employee a standing statement of fixed deductions at least every 12 months.

If there is any change to an employee's fixed deductions, you must give them either:

- notification in writing of the details of the change
- an amended standing statement of fixed deductions, which is then valid for up to 12 months.

Making deductions from pay

Ensure that any deductions you make from a worker's pay are allowed for in their contract. Otherwise, you could be in breach of their contract.

A deduction is unlawful unless:

- it is legally authorised, eg PAYE income tax and National Insurance contributions
- it is allowed by the worker's contract. If this is the case, the worker must have been shown the term or notified in writing of its effect before the deduction is made
- workers have agreed in writing before you deduct pay for other reasons, eg as loan repayments or pension contributions.

Payments on leaving

When an employee leaves your organisation, you will need to give them:

- any outstanding pay to the date of leaving
- holiday pay for holiday earned but not taken
- pay in lieu of notice, if you dismissed

them (apart from for gross misconduct) and did not give them their full notice period
- any bonus payments, if earned
- statutory sick pay, if entitled
- statutory maternity pay, if entitled.

You will need to deduct:
- tax and national insurance as normal
- any money for outstanding loans, such as a season ticket loan.

Your payroll system

As an employer, you are under an obligation to set up a payroll system, to ensure you deduct the correct tax and national insurance from your employees' pay and submit the deductions to HM Revenue and Customs.

When you become an employer for the first time, HM Revenue and Customs will send you a new employer's starter pack, with all the tables, forms and information you will need to operate your payroll. Chapter 1 gives some information about this.

For further information on your tax and national insurance responsibilities, you can contact HM Revenue and Customs Employers Helpline on 08457 143 143.

Checklist

Outsourcing your payroll function

Calculating tax and national insurance can be time-consuming and complicated. You may also need to deal with tax credits, maternity pay and pensions.

Many small organisations choose to outsource their payroll functions, so that they can concentrate on their main business.

If you are considering outsourcing your payroll, you could do this either via an accountant's services, or via a specialist payroll service company.

When assessing a possible supplier, consider the following:

- whether they are experienced with your type and size of organisation
- whether they can supply monthly payslips, and provide monthly and annual returns
- the charge for setting up the payroll system
- the charge for administering the system
- whether the fees include making all the types of deductions
- whether they charge any additional fees
- what software they use, whether it is HM Revenue and Customs accredited, and if it is compatible with your own.

☐	Consider the basis of your pay system. Is it fair, open and understood by your employees?
☐	Make sure you pay the national minimum wage
☐	Audit your pay system regularly to ensure you are paying equal pay for work of equal value and that your pay system is fair
☐	Decide on a systematic way of setting and reviewing salary levels, commensurate with the size of your organisation
☐	Consider forms of salary progression – but be wary of giving guaranteed annual increments unless you are sure you will be able to afford them in the future
☐	Consider developing a salary policy, so that all staff know how pay is set and reviewed
☐	Provide a stakeholder pension for your employees, from the point at which you employ your 5th employee (unless an exemption applies)
☐	Provide other benefits such as paid annual leave and sick pay, which comply with the law and are as competitive and generous as you can afford
☐	Investigate low/no cost benefits and implement any that may be suitable for your organisation

Further information

The following organisations offer advice and resources about the subjects covered in this chapter to new and existing employers, often free of charge:

Acas

The following publications can be downloaded from the Acas website:

- Advisory Booklet – Job Evaluation (under revision at time of publication)
- Advisory Booklet – Pay Systems
- Advisory Booklet – Appraisal Related Pay
- Advice leaflet – Holidays and Holiday Pay (under revision at time of publication)

www.acas.org.uk

Business Link

The Business Link website contains information on all aspects of pay and benefits, including the minimum wage, equal pay and pensions.
www.businesslink.gov.uk

CELRE

CELRE produces an annual voluntary sector salary survey, in association with NCVO.
www.celre.co.uk

Croner Reward

Croner Reward produces an annual survey of salaries and benefits in the not-for-profit sector.
www.croner-reward.co.uk

Daycare Trust

The Daycare Trust has some useful information about childcare voucher schemes
www.daycaretrust.org.uk

Department for Business, Enterprise and Regulatory Reform (DBERR)

You can access a detailed guide to the national minimum wage and information about statutory annual leave entitlements from the DBERR website.
www.berr.gov.uk

Equality and Human Rights Commission

The commission has an equal pay toolkit called A Small Business Guide to Effective Pay Practices' specifically for small businesses. This is also available as a CD ROM.
www.equalityhumanrights.com

National Council for Voluntary Organisations (NCVO)

www.ncvo-vol.org.uk

Pensions Regulator

The Pensions Regulator has information about stakeholder pension schemes, as well as a register of approved stakeholder pension schemes.
www.thepensionsregulator.gov.uk

A listing of all the useful organisations referred to in this Good Guide can be found at the back of this book with full contact details.

Seven

Managing employee development and performance

This chapter contains information about how to develop your staff and manage their performance.

The legal position

There are the following legal rights and obligations concerning employee development:

- The Health and Safety at Work Act 1974 states that an employer must provide adequate health and safety training for its employees
- The Offices, Shops and Railway Premises Act 1963 requires an employer to provide training to employees on escape routes and the fire drill
- Young persons aged 16 or 17 who are not qualified to NVQ level 2 and in full-time work are entitled to a reasonable amount of paid time off for study or training
- Employers must allow reasonable time off for representatives of independent trade unions for training, where the union is represented for collective bargaining purposes
- Employers must give reasonable time off for training to Union Learning Representatives for training and to carry out their duties.

Producing a learning and development policy

It can be useful to produce a learning and development policy, for the following reasons:

- it makes clear to your staff your stance on employee development
- the process of drafting the policy will help you to clarify what staff development you want to do and why
- you will be able to refer to it in the future as a prompt as to what you should be doing.

Example

Policy statement – learning and development

(Organisation) recognises that its most important resource is its employees. We are committed to employee learning and development, in line with available resources.

Appropriately trained and skilled employees will be able to assist (organisation) to achieve our objective of providing specialised, high quality care and rehabilitation to vulnerable people.

Individual learning and development needs will be identified mainly through the staff supervision and appraisal process. Once identified, these needs will form a part of (organisation's) annual learning and development plan.

The learning and development needs identified will be met through a variety of activities. These activities may include:

- shadowing another member of staff
- planned reading
- working through a computer based package
- off the job training
- a qualification or an NVQ
- mentoring
- coaching

All internal training provided will be of no cost to the employee. External courses and professional qualifications may be fully or partly funded, depending on the following criteria:

- the relevance to the job
- the funds available
- whether the learning need can be met in another way

Employees are asked to provide feedback on the value and effectiveness of the learning and development activity they undertake, so that it can be further improved for the future.

This policy applies to all employees.

Developing an annual learning and development plan

Whilst some learning and development activities will occur on an ad hoc basis, it can be helpful to plan ahead and develop an annual plan, for the following reasons:

- it sets out how you are going to achieve your policy
- it helps you to take a strategic approach to learning and development. You can think about what your organisation is planning to achieve and consider whether the skills your staff have are sufficient and relevant to meet the needs of your organisation
- you can budget for planned activities – it is more difficult to budget for unplanned ones
- if you collate learning and development needs across the organisation, you can see which staff members have the same need, and plan a learning activity for all of them.

Example annual learning and development plan

LEARNING NEED IDENTIFIED FROM ANNUAL APPRAISAL	*Eg writing bids for funds*
LINK WITH ORGANISATIONAL STRATEGY	*We will need to raise £30,000 from external bids over the next financial year.*
STAFF WHO NEED THE LEARNING AND DEVELOPMENT	*John, Reema*
SUGGESTED ACTIVITY	*Frances is already experienced at this – she will work through a bid with them.*
LIKELY COST	*Staff time only*
PROPOSED DATE	*By April 2009 at the latest*

'Because of the sensitivity of 360-degree feedback, some organisations use an external organisation to collate feedback confidentially.'

Evaluating learning and development

It is important to evaluate the effectiveness of learning and development activities, so that you can plan for future activities and follow up on any learning needs that have not been met.

Prior to any planned learning, such as a training course or computer-based learning, clarify with the employee the objectives of the learning.

After the planned learning, discuss with the employee the extent to which the objectives were met. You could also ask the employee to complete a brief evaluation form immediately after the event.

At the annual appraisal, you could look back at the planned learning and assess the extent to which the learning has been applied in the workplace.

Supervision and appraisal

Staff supervision
Staff supervision is the process of regular one to one meetings with your employees to discuss:

- progress in achieving work plans
- any problems
- the next steps

Regular staff supervision meetings can help employees to feel that their work is noticed and valued and can help them keep on track for future work.

Supervision meetings can be held at a frequency that suits your organisation and the experience of the job holders. For example, you may wish to meet fortnightly with a new employee and monthly or even quarterly with more experienced employees.

Appraisal
The annual appraisal is a yearly review of the individual's work progress and performance. It should be a round up of what has been achieved over the past 12 months, and also an opportunity to plan work, set objectives and identify training needs for the next 12 months. If you have been holding regular supervision meetings and discussions with your employee, the annual appraisal should hold no surprises.

It can be useful to gain feedback from a variety of sources when undertaking an individual's appraisal. You could ask for comments (where relevant) from service users, volunteers, colleagues and staff managed. This process is called 360-degree feedback and can give a broad view of the individual's performance. However, if you intend to seek feedback in this way, discuss it with your staff first and gain their agreement. Be clear exactly how it will operate and think about how you will preserve anonymity with sensitive or difficult feedback. Because of the sensitivity of 360-degree feedback, some organisations use an external organisation to collate feedback confidentially.

It is worth training all supervisors and managers in supervision and appraisal. This could cover matters such as the importance of the scheme, giving feedback, setting objectives and dealing with poor performance. It is particularly important that all managers are committed to supervision and appraisal. If they are not, the system will soon fall into disuse and become discredited. You could consider including in managers' own appraisals an assessment of how well they supervise and appraise their staff.

Structuring your appraisal and supervision meetings

The annual appraisal meeting will probably be a longer meeting than your regular supervision meetings. You may not need to cover all the areas outlined below at each supervision meeting. However, the principles and format for each are similar.

Preparation
Have available prior to the meeting:

- a copy of the notes of the employee's last supervision or appraisal meeting
- their job description.

Hold the meeting in a room where you will not have interruptions and set aside sufficient time for the meeting.

Consider the key points you want to raise and make a note of them.

Give the employee at least a few days' notice of the meeting so that they have the time to prepare too. Ask the employee to look at their previous supervision or appraisal forms and to consider work undertaken since the last review.

Format for the meeting
Having an appraisal or supervision form will help you to format the meeting and provide a useful structure for the meeting. See later in the this chapter for example forms.

A useful format for the meeting is the **WASP** format:

Welcome
Ask
Supply
Plan and part

Welcome the employee. Try and put them at ease if needed. Offer a drink and explain the format of the meeting. Try and create an unhurried atmosphere, so that the employee does not feel that you are trying to rush things in order to get to something more important.

Ask the employee to give their views on work progress since the last appraisal or supervision meeting – what they are proud of as well as anything they feel could have gone better. You could ask them to consider what they think their main contribution has been to the work of the organisation.

If you are concerned about any aspect of the employee's performance, it may well be that the employee is too! It is easier for the employee to accept feedback and easier for you to give it, if the employee is able to state the concerns first.

Use phrases that encourage the employee to talk about their work, such as:

- Tell me a bit more about that
- I can see there is a problem, but what do you think might help?
- What support do you think you need to become more familiar with...?

Avoid phrases which may discourage the employee from talking:

- Its really quite easy when you get the hang of it, it won't take long
- If I were you...
- You'll be OK, don't worry
- Everything's going fine, I expect?

If the employee has had specific objectives/targets to achieve over the past year (this information should be on their last appraisal form), ask them the extent to which these were achieved, to standard and to deadline.

'If you feel that there are work performance problems that the employee has not mentioned, raise these with the employee'

Once you have given the employee full opportunity to talk, supply your comments.

Confirm anything you think went particularly well. Explain what you think the employee did that made things go well. This can help reinforce good performance for the future.

Discuss with the employee the areas they have identified that could have gone better. If you feel that there are work performance problems that the employee has not mentioned, raise these with the employee now. Give specific examples of your concerns. Jointly consider the possible reasons for problems and consider how the situation could be improved in the future. Make clear how you want their performance to change – what good performance looks like.

Explore reasons beyond the employee's control why things may have gone less well than planned. However, ensure that neither of you uses this as a means of avoiding a discussion on any work performance problems that the employee may have.

You might, particularly in the annual appraisal, also discuss the following areas with your employee:

- whether they are clear about all the responsibilities of their role – you could use the job description as a basis for these discussions
- if they feel that any aspects of their role should be changed
- whether they feel that there is adequate opportunity to discuss the work they are doing with you
- what they feel that you as a manager could do to further assist them in their role
- training and development activities they have undertaken since the last appraisal or supervision meeting
- benefits they gained from the activities
- any further need for training and development
- whether the employee has particular skills and knowledge that your organisation could perhaps use and is not currently using.

The next stage of the meeting is to plan for the short and the long term. Jointly agree what follow-up actions should be taken, by whom and by when. If you are holding a supervision meeting, you can discuss what work tasks the employee needs to achieve by the next meeting. If you are holding an annual appraisal, discuss the targets for the forthcoming year. It is a good idea to make the targets **SMART**, that is:

Specific
Measurable
Achievable
Relevant
Time-bound

Before you close the meeting, check with the employee if they have any other comments or matters they wish to raise. Thank the employee for their time. Inform them of the next steps:

- that you will write up the key points from the discussion
- that you will give them a copy to sign and keep; and that a copy will be put on their personal file
- when they can expect to receive the written document.

Supervision and appraisal forms

The forms you use can be less important than the actual discussion itself. However, it is very useful to capture the main points of your discussions.

You could draft a simple form which covers the main areas for discussion.

Supervision form
The form could cover the following headings:

- progress with work since last meeting
- particular achievements
- any difficulties discussed and measures to overcome them
- progress with learning and development
- tasks for the period until next supervision meeting
- any other matters arising
- a section for the employee to add their views.

Here is an example supervision form from a Council for Voluntary Service, Community Links Bromley.

Example record of staff supervision meeting

Employee name:		Date:	
Position:		Line Manager:	

Progress with work programme since last supervision meeting

Targets	Work completed	Next steps

Progress with other targets/objectives since last supervision meeting

Targets	Work completed	Next steps

Achievements since last supervision meeting

Difficulties or problems since last meeting.
Agreed actions to overcome them.

Progress with learning plans and any other matters agreed
at annual staff review

Other matters

Any other matters discussed

Signed (employee)   Signed (line manager)

Appraisal form

The appraisal form might follow a similar format but is likely to be more detailed. It could cover the following areas:

- review of objectives from over the past year
- review of job description
- learning and development completed over the past year
- objectives for the forthcoming year
- amendments to job description if needed
- learning and development plans of the forthcoming year
- a section for the employee to add their views.

Some appraisal forms include competencies – the behaviours and capabilities that indicate good performance in the job.

To the right is a chart showing some example competencies, used by a Council for Voluntary Service, Community Links Bromley:

Example competencies

Managing deadlines	Takes responsibility to ensure deadlines are met, works quickly and systematically, keeps people informed on progress of key tasks.
Initiative	Works to find a solution to problems, comes up with new ideas.
Managing change	Understands the need to change things, willing to learn and to be flexible.
Communicating with others	Takes account of different cultural styles and values when dealing with others. Show respect and courtesy to others at all times and listens attentively. Use language appropriately and not in a way that may offend, alienate or patronise others.
Personal development	Seeks opportunities to develop own skills.
Working as a team	Willing to assist and support other team members when required.
Approach to the job	Keeps good time. Maintains a positive attitude. Keeps word and does what says will do.

Example appraisal form

Following is an example appraisal form,
courtesy of Community Links Bromley.

Employee name:	Date:
Position:	Line Manager:

Employee's understanding of the plans of the organisation and how he/she can contribute to the organisation's success.

Achievements since last annual review – tasks, work programme and objectives.

TASK/OBJECTIVE	COMMENTS ON ACHIEVEMENTS AND ANY CHALLENGES/PROBLEMS Indicate if required standards reached, partly reached or not reached.

Continued overleaf...

Key elements of job description	
KEY ELEMENT	COMMENTS ON ACHIEVEMENTS AND ANY CHALLENGES/PROBLEMS

Agreement on any support/management to be put in place, including addressing any specific requirements the employee may have to help him/her work at his/her best.

Agreed changes in the way the manager and employee will work together

COMPETENCIES		
Competency	Examples of how the competency has been demonstrated over the year	Examples of how the competency should be demonstrated over the coming year
Managing deadlines		
Initiative		
Dealing with change		
Communicating with others		
Personal development		
Working as a team		
Approach to the job		

Continued overleaf...

Record of learning and development activities (courses, conferences, on-the-job training, shadowing, etc).		
Specific activities	How this has helped the individual carry out their tasks	How has this been of benefit to service users

Further training/development required		
Specific activities	How this would assist the employee to carry out tasks	How this would be of benefit to service users

Future plans

Any issues raised by colleagues, services users or volunteers which need to be considered with the future work plan

Are changes to be made to: Employee's job description? Employee's work plan?

Key tasks and objectives for the forthcoming year (NB these must relate to the priorities identified in the annual strategic plan)	
TASK/OBJECTIVE	TO BE ACHIEVED BY (date)

Other issues or comments

Manager's overall comments (this should include a summary of achievements over the year)	Signature and date

Employee's overall comments	Signature and date

Continued overleaf...

It is good practice for both you and the employee to sign the appraisal and supervision forms, once completed. Give the employee the opportunity to make comments if they feel that you have misrepresented anything in your write-up, or if there is anything else they want to record in writing.

If the employee strongly objects to your perception of their performance and refuses to sign the appraisal form, you should try and resolve the matter with them. If they remain dissatisfied, it is open to them to use your grievance procedure (see chapter 9). However, if ultimately there is no agreement, you have the right to expect that the employee will adhere to any reasonable management expectation of them.

Avoiding bias in appraisals

Sometimes, appraisers may allow one aspect of an individual to influence their opinion of the individual's whole performance.

Ensure you are not influenced by matters that may irritate you or affect your thinking, but may have no bearing on job performance. If they do have a bearing on job performance, keep them in context and avoid letting them cloud your whole view of the individual's performance.

As well as matters covered by law, such as gender, age, disability, race, sexual orientation and religion/belief, make sure you keep in context matters such as:

- a particular significant event or characteristic, good or bad
- scruffy appearance or alternatively very formal dress
- laid-back manner
- body piercing

You should also beware of belittling the work to yourself and hence to the employee. Just because you may feel their work is dull, it does not follow that they can't really enjoy it and be fully committed.

Dealing with performance problems

The most difficult appraisal and supervision meetings tend to be those where you feel that an employee is not performing satisfactorily in their job.

Hopefully, there should be no surprises for the employee in the meeting – you should have been addressing problems with the employee as they have arisen.

Below are some ideas on how you might handle these meetings.

Preparation
You'll need to do your normal preparation, but in addition, it may help to:

- list the main areas of concern and prioritise them
- think of examples of when the employee's performance has caused concern and why
- think about some positive aspects of the employee's performance – it is easier to receive criticism if it is balanced by some positive feedback.

'Think about some positive aspects of the employee's performance – it is easier to receive criticism if it is balanced by some positive feedback'

Welcome

Try something like: 'I think this has been quite a difficult period with a number of challenges. The purpose of the meeting today is to look at what has gone well, what not so well and how we can deal with any difficulties.'

Try and keep the meeting supportive and not adversarial – you are trying to look for ways to improve the employee's performance and you will achieve this best if the discussion remains constructive.

Ask

You should ask the employee to give feedback (self-appraise) on their own performance. However, sometimes when an employee is not performing well, they may be defensive and unwilling to give a view on their performance. Give the employee the opportunity to self-appraise, but be prepared to be more directive in giving feedback if needed.

You should also give the employee the opportunity to explain any reasons for difficulties in doing their job – there may be personal circumstances of which you are not aware, for example.

Supply

Give specific instances of concern and concentrate on the employee's performance, not personality. For example, 'you take a slapdash approach to your work' is not only likely to invoke a defensive response of 'no I don't!', but is also unspecific.

It is much better to give examples, such as: 'I am concerned that on (date), you didn't send out all the documentation to the conference delegates. As a result, they had less than a week to register for the conference. We spoke about this at the time and I want to discuss how things have gone since then.' This then gives you the opportunity either to confirm that improvements have occurred, or that the same behaviour is being displayed. Either way, you should continue to give specific examples for discussion.

Think about what the employee can cope with – if your point has been accepted, it may be inappropriate to give further examples of poor performance.

Targets for the future

Be specific about what you want the employee to do next. Sometimes, there are particular behaviours that are causing the poor performance. You might therefore want to include some objectives about behaviour (competencies), as well as about specific tasks to be achieved. For example, if communication is a problem, you might have targets of: 'show respect and courtesy to others at all times and listen attentively', or: 'keep manager informed on a weekly basis about progress with updating the contacts database.'

Writing up the notes of the meeting

You need to be very careful about writing the supervision notes or appraisal. It needs to be specific as to the concerns, what will be done by each of you to address them, the timescale for improvement and when you will meet again.

If the situation later reaches the stage where you have to pursue the disciplinary procedure on the grounds of continued poor performance (see below), it is not helpful if supervision and performance appraisal notes give a glowing picture of the employee when this is not in fact the case.

Case study – dealing with a performance problem

The General Manager of the Westwich Association has received some complaints regarding a member of staff who has been working at the Association for some time.

The complaints concern the employee's behaviour towards others. According to the complainants, the individual has adopted a manner which can be rude, abrupt and critical. This is upsetting for anyone dealing with this person. The General Manager has personally experienced such behaviour from the employee of late. This behaviour is, as far as the General Manager knows, relatively new; there were no complaints up until relatively recently.

The General Manager plans to raise the matter at the employee's supervision meeting the following week. She is anxious about raising the matter, because she has found the employee to be touchy about feedback in the past. However, she reminds herself that this is a difficult, not impossible employee.

She plans to undertake the supervision meeting as follows:

She will start by asking the employee about how her work is progressing, her achievements and any problems. The General Manager intends to listen, to give the employee the chance to talk. She wants to try and keep the meeting positive, whilst also making her concerns clear.

If the employee raises any concerns about working relationships, the General Manager will use this opportunity to raise the matter with her. She intends to start with praise (commenting on how efficient the employee is), but then ask the employee about how she deals with others.

She will then give specific instances of when the employee appears to have been impatient with others. She will ask the employee for her views. She intends to concentrate on behaviour, not on personality. The General Manager intends to use some examples of the inappropriate behaviour that she herself has witnessed, so that she does not need to mention the individuals who have complained.

The General Manager intends to encourage self-appraisal – asking the employee if there is anything she might approach in a different manner in future.

The General Manager will also ask the employee if there is anything worrying her that is causing her to behave differently. If the employee says there is, the General Manager will treat this confidentially and provide support where appropriate, whilst still explaining that the behaviour is not appropriate.

Finally, the General Manager intends to end by asking the employee to summarise the areas of her performance that are going well and what can be done to ensure the employee's whole performance is at this standard.

The General Manager knows that she will need to be flexible in the meeting and that it may go a little differently from her plan. However, by planning in advance, she feels more confident about what she wants to achieve and how she will do it.

Dealing with continuing poor performance

If you have followed through informal action with an employee, and their performance has not improved, you may get to the stage where you need to follow your formal disciplinary procedure, on the grounds of poor performance (see chapter 9 for further information about the disciplinary procedure).

You must first send or give the employee a statement of your specific concerns about their performance. You should invite the employee to a meeting to discuss the concerns. The employee has the right to be accompanied by a work colleague or trade union representative at the meeting.

At the meeting, you should discuss your ongoing concerns about the employee's performance.

After the meeting and after considering the employee's views, you may decide to issue a performance improvement note. This would be the first stage of your disciplinary procedure.

The performance improvement note should set out:

- the performance problem
- the improvement that is required
- the timescale for achieving this improvement
- a review date
- any support you will provide to assist the employee.

The employee should be informed that the note represents the first stage of the formal disciplinary procedure, on account of poor performance, and that failure to improve could lead to a final written warning and, ultimately, dismissal. A copy of the note should be kept and used as the basis for monitoring and reviewing performance over a specified period (eg, six months).

Example

How to deal with poor performance

A member of your accounts staff makes a number of mistakes on invoices. In an informal meeting, you bring specific mistakes to his attention. Your tone is supportive to the employee, but firm and honest about the difference between the employee's performance and your expectations. You listen to reasons the employee gives and discuss how to deal with any problems, whilst still being clear that current performance is not acceptable.

You gain the employee's agreement that there is a problem (ie a gap between his performance and the required performance). You ask the employee what support he needs to improve and agree to put in place the 1-1 coaching from his supervisor he suggests. In a calm but firm tone, you make sure that the employee understands that if the accuracy does not improve, you will proceed to the disciplinary procedure, on the grounds of poor performance. You confirm the meeting in writing and give the employee a copy, so that everything is a clear as possible.

The mistakes continue. You therefore send a written statement to the employee, explaining your concerns. You invite the employee to a disciplinary meeting and inform him of his right to be accompanied by a work colleague or employee representative. At the meeting, you remind the employee of your earlier informal discussion and that he and you agreed at this stage that there was a problem with his performance. You give further examples of the specific mistakes.

The employee does not give a satisfactory explanation for the mistakes, so after the meeting, you decide to issue an improvement note setting out: the problem, the improvement required, the timescale for improvement, the support available and a review date. You inform the employee that a failure to improve may lead to a final written warning, but emphasise also that agreed support will be provided to the employee to help him achieve the required standard.

If, ultimately and after warnings, the employee's performance does not improve and there is no possibility to redeploy the employee, or they do not agree to this, you can dismiss the employee on the grounds of capability. Please note that dismissal without prior warnings under your procedure is unlikely to be found to be fair. You also need to comply with the requirement set down by the statutory disciplinary procedure ie step1 letter, step 2 meeting and appeal (see chapter 9), otherwise the dismissal will be automatically unfair.

As an alternative, you might consider whether the job content has changed so significantly that you are actually dealing with a situation of redundancy (ie the requirement for work of a particular type has diminished or disappeared) rather than a matter of capability. In this case, discuss with the employee treating this situation as a redundancy matter.

'Poor performance is frequently a matter of inability, rather than unwillingness, to undertake the required work.'

Difficult situations in matters of poor performance

One of the difficulties managers may feel is discomfort in using the disciplinary process for a matter of poor performance – since discipline has connotations for many people of misconduct. Poor performance is frequently a matter of inability, rather than unwillingness, to undertake the required work.

To deal with this, some organisations call their procedure a 'disciplinary and capability procedure', or other organisations (particularly larger organisations) have a separate capability procedure. The steps taken in any of these procedures are the same, so it is a matter of preference for your organisation as to whether you combine capability matters into your disciplinary procedure or not.

Developing yourself as a manager

In the business of running a voluntary organisation, it may be easy to forget the need to develop your own skills.

Think about what development you might need. If you are a Chief Executive of a voluntary organisation, discuss with your Chair of Trustees your learning and development needs.

Think also about how you might prefer to learn. For example:

• self-directed learning
• action learning
• coaching or mentoring
• a short course or a longer course of study

Information about these different learning methods follow on the next page.

'By its very nature, a senior leadership role in the voluntary sector is a relatively isolated one, and action learning can help to reduce the isolation'

Self-directed learning

There is a wealth of information about management and leadership, which you can read, reflect on, and put into practice in your work.

A really useful source of information is the Third Sector Leadership Centre. The centre aims to be a catalyst to raise the profile of leadership and leadership development across the third sector.

The centre, a project within the UK Workforce Hub, has been set up to support leaders within the third sector, and to help them move forward.

You can find out about the Third Sector Leadership Centre at www.thirdsectorleadership.org.uk Once you register on-line (for free), you can access a range of written resources on leadership, as well as find out about events.

Another source of information is the UK Workforce Hub itself. Go to the publications section of www.ukworforcehub.org.uk and download the document 'Leading Managers – a Guide to Management Development in the Voluntary Sector'. The guide includes a checklist of essential management skills/competencies, covering areas such as:

- personal and communication skills – the way you relate to people from different communities and backgrounds and how you address conflict
- managing paid staff and teams – the way you supervise and appraise your staff and work with your volunteers
- resources management – the way you plan your annual budget and monitor financial expenditure.

You could also review the National Management Standards. These have been developed by the Management Standards Centre (MSC). The standards describe the level of performance expected for a range of management and leadership functions.

The standard overall has 6 sub sections, which are: managing self and personal skills; providing direction; facilitating change; working with people; using resources; and achieving results.

The standards can be read in full at www.management-standards.org.

Action learning

By its very nature, a senior leadership role in the voluntary sector is a relatively isolated one, and action learning can help to reduce the isolation.

Action learning involves working as part of a small group of peers to consider real-life problems. The action learning set will meet regularly and each participant will have the opportunity to explain a work problem. Other members of the set, plus sometimes also a facilitator, use questioning to help the individual consider their problem in a new way and to learn skills to solve problems in the future.

Coaching or mentoring

You may wish to consider whether coaching or mentoring may assist you. The terms coaching and mentoring are sometimes used interchangeably as both are about thinking things through with the help of another person.

Coaching tends to be about gaining the skills to deal with specific tasks in the short to medium term to meet organisation requirements. It is more goal-oriented and time-limiting than mentoring. Particularly at a senior level, coaching on a specific area may be of more assistance than a training programme. A coach may not necessarily have the same management/leadership experience as the person they are coaching.

Mentoring focuses more on the longer term, enabling individuals to develop the capability to think and act strategically. It is also about career development so may also be about thinking outside the organisational context.

A mentor will normally be a more experienced leader with the capacity to act as a sounding board to help you think through your ideas.

The mentoring relationship may be informal or formal.

You can find out more information on coaching and mentoring on the UK Workforce Hub website at www.ukworkforcehub.org.uk.

Training courses

Another way for managers in the voluntary sector to develop themselves is by undertaking a course, such as one provided by Working For A Charity (WFAC). WFAC provides training courses as well as an on-line course of study called Effective Voluntary Sector Management. See www.workingforacharity.org.uk for further information.

Investors in People

The Investors in People (IiP) Standard is a government quality award given to organisations that can demonstrate to an assessor that they invest in the development of all their employees.

IiP sets out best practice for the training and development of staff to achieve business goals. Employers who hold the IiP standard are able to send a positive message about their investment in employees to the outside world.

The aim of IiP is to help organisations to improve their performance by careful planning of the skills required to achieve their organisational objectives.

If you want to work towards the Investors in People standard, you can contact an accredited IiP assessor. They will visit your workplace, assess what processes you have in place already and help you to plan towards the standard.

The Investors in People framework involves:

- **Plan** – developing strategies to improve the performance of the organisation
- **Do** – taking action to improve the performance of the organisation
- **Review** – evaluating the impact on the performance of the organisation.

The framework is shown as follows:

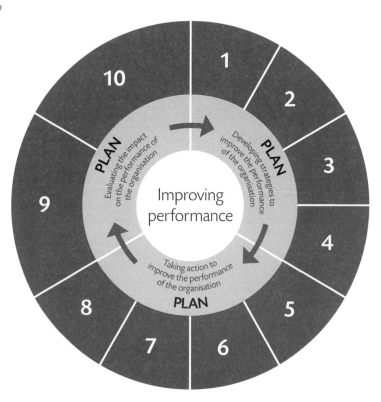

1 Business strategy
2 Learning and development strategy
3 People management strategy
4 Leadership and management strategy
5 Management effectiveness
6 Recognition and reward
7 Involvement and empowerment
8 Learning and development
9 Performance measurement
10 Continuous improvement

Checklist

To achieve the IiP Standard, you must:

- show a thorough understanding of the Standard and its principles
- review your business practices against the Standard
- commit to meeting the Standard and take any action this requires
- provide evidence so that your business can be assessed against the Standard.

For more information, you can go to the Investors in People website at www.investorsinpeople.co.uk or call their helpline on 020 7467 1946.

Regardless of whether your organisation has the IiP Standard, you can access the IiP website, called Your People Manager. This website is aimed at helping managers of small businesses deal with everyday questions, issues and problems associated with managing staff. The site offers best practice advice, in-depth business articles and an opportunity to ask industry experts questions on people management issues. You can access the site through www.yourpeoplemanager.com.

	Produce a learning and development policy and an annual learning and development plan
	Evaluate any learning and development that has been completed, so that you can make changes in the future if needed
	Undertake regular supervision meetings with your staff. They should be frequent enough that the employee is clear about their progress and work priorities
	Undertake an annual appraisal with all your staff
	Be aware of possible personal bias in assessing your staff. Question yourself to avoid unfair judgements
	Deal with performance problems as they arise – don't wait for the annual appraisal
	Follow your disciplinary procedure, or your capability procedure if you have one, in cases of persistent poor performance
	Don't forget your own learning needs – have a personal learning and development plan
	Consider whether your organisation should work towards the Investors in People Standard

Further information

The following organisations offer advice and resources about the subjects covered in this chapter to new and existing employers, often free of charge:

Acas
The following publications can be downloaded from the Acas website:
Advisory Booklet – Employee Appraisal
www.acas.org.uk

Business Link
The Business Link website contains lots of information about training. It covers:

- Training evaluation
- Fitting training to your needs
- Turning underperformance into high performance
- Developing your management team
- Setting up in-house training
- How to find a training provider/ course
- Learning through networking with others
- Skills and training for directors and owners

www.businesslink.gov.uk

Charity Skills
Training courses
www.charityskills.org

Council for Voluntary Service
Your local Council for Voluntary Service may run training sessions for voluntary and community organisations in the area.

Directory of Social Change
Training courses
www.dsc.org.uk

Investors in People UK
Their website is aimed at helping managers of small businesses deal with everyday questions, issues and problems associated with managing staff.
www.investorsinpeople.co.uk

Management Standards Centre
The Management Standards Centre (MSC) is the Government recognised standards setting body for the management and leadership areas. Over the past two years, the MSC has been engaged in a publicly funded project to develop a new set of National Occupational Standards (NOS) for management and leadership.
www.management-standards.org

National Council for Voluntary Organisations (NCVO)
www.ncvo-vol.org.uk

Third Sector Leadership Centre
The Third Sector Leadership Centre aims to be a catalyst to raise the profile of leadership and leadership development across the third sector.
www.thirdsectorleadership.org.uk

UK Workforce Hub
The UK Workforce Hub helps voluntary and community organisations make the best of their paid staff, volunteers and trustees through workforce development.
www.ukworkforcehub.org.uk

A listing of all the useful organisations referred to in this Good Guide can be found at the back of this book with full contact details.

Eight
Parental rights and flexible working practices

This chapter tells you about the following areas:

- Maternity leave
- Adoption leave
- Paternity leave
- Unpaid parental leave
- Emergency leave to deal with a dependant
- Flexible working request

The above rights are all legal rights and are part of the government's agenda to make the work place more 'family friendly'.

We also consider how you can provide a flexible and supportive work environment for all your employees. There may be reasons other than care responsibilities why employees may want flexibility at work, such as to pursue a specific interest or sport.

- Other flexible working practices

Including:

– Flexitime
– Working from home
– Job-sharing
– Career breaks
– Voluntary reduced
– Term-time working
– Supporting employees with caring responsibilities

The charity Working Families estimates that currently one in six working women look after children under 16.

It estimates that one in six of all workers care for elderly relatives and that this proportion is likely to increase as the population as a whole ages.

In addition, with more and more women going out to work, many households do not have anyone at home who can be a full-time carer. It makes sense to ensure that as an employer, you provide flexibility in working arrangements, when carers need it.

'The employee continues to accrue contractual pension rights during any paid maternity leave.'

Maternity leave

Paid time off for antenatal care

Pregnant women are entitled to paid time off to keep appointments for antenatal care made on the advice of a registered medical practitioner, registered midwife or registered health visitor.

Except in the case of her first appointment, a pregnant woman must show you:

- a certificate from a registered medical practitioner, registered midwife or registered health visitor, confirming she is pregnant and
- an appointment card or some other document showing that an appointment has been made.

Duration of maternity leave

Pregnant women are entitled to take up to one year's (52 weeks) maternity leave, regardless of their length of service with you.

Types of maternity leave

Maternity leave is a single continuous period and is made up of two elements:

Ordinary Maternity Leave (OML)
OML lasts for 26 weeks during which the contract of employment continues, and during which the employee continues to receive all her contractual benefits except salary. Contractual benefits might include: contractual annual leave accrual, car or car allowance, mobile phone and reimbursement of professional subscriptions.

Additional Maternity Leave (AML)
AML lasts for a further 26 weeks, during which the contract of employment continues, but only certain terms of the employee's contract apply. Annual leave will continue to accrue, but at the statutory minimum rate of 24 days per year inclusive of bank and public holidays (28 days from April 2009), rather than at the employee's contractual rate, which may be higher. It is of course an option open to you to give the employee accrued annual leave at their higher contractual rate during AML.

During both OML and AML, some terms of the contract continue to apply, such as: the ongoing mutual obligation of trust, confidence and good faith; and terms relating to confidential information and acceptance of gifts.

One important term which continues to apply during OML and AML is the requirement to give you notice of termination of employment, if the employee does not intend to return to work. The notice she must give is that stated in her contract of employment.

Pensions during maternity leave

The employee continues to accrue contractual pension rights during any paid maternity leave. The statutory maternity pay period is 39 weeks (see below), but you may also pay contractual maternity payments for a longer period.

Even though the employee continues in pension scheme membership, she only needs to make pension contributions based on her maternity pay, not on her normal full salary. Employers are only obliged to make pension contributions into the employee's pension scheme for the period of statutory maternity pay ie 39 weeks.

Starting maternity leave

The earliest date a woman can start her maternity leave is the beginning of the eleventh week before the baby is expected. She must provide you with details of the week the baby is expected and the start date of her maternity leave. She should do this by the end of the 15th week before the expected week of childbirth. You must respond to this notification within 28 days and state the date on which you expect your employee to have returned to work after she finishes her full maternity leave entitlement. This will usually be the end of her AML unless she chooses to return at an earlier date.

Compulsory maternity leave

Your employee is not permitted to work during the two weeks immediately after the birth of her baby.

Statutory Maternity pay

Employers should be aware of the following information regarding statutory maternity pay:

- Statutory Maternity Pay (SMP) is payable for a total of 39 weeks to eligible employees. Employees will be eligible if they:
- have 26 weeks service at the 15th week before the week in which their baby is due and
- earn at least the lower earnings limit (£90 per week as at 2008) for national insurance purposes
- If your employee is eligible, SMP is paid at the rate of 90% of average weekly earnings, for the first six weeks of her maternity leave (you can calculate average weekly earnings with reference to the period of eight weeks immediately preceding the 14th week before the Expected Week of Childbirth)
- The remaining weeks will be paid at a rate determined annually by the government, or 90% of the employee's average weekly earnings, whichever is the lower amount. As at April 2008, the rate determined by the government is £117.18

- Statutory Maternity Pay (SMP) is subject to tax and National Insurance deductions and should be paid at the same time as the employee would normally receive her monthly salary
- SMP can start on any day of the week
- SMP should be paid to eligible employees, regardless of whether or not they intend to return to work
- If an employee is not eligible for SMP (for example, because her earnings are too low), she may qualify, based on her recent employment and earnings, for up to 39 weeks' Maternity Allowance, paid direct by Jobcentre Plus.

'Your employee is not permitted to work during the two weeks immediately after the birth of her baby.'

Keeping in touch days

Employees on statutory leave may undertake up to 10 Keeping In Touch (KIT) days. These are days when they can undertake work for you without bringing their entitlement to statutory leave and (where applicable) statutory pay to an end. They cannot do the KIT days during the two-week period of compulsory maternity leave.

There is no obligation for the employee to undertake KIT days and there is no obligation on you as the employer to offer them. However, KIT days can be a really useful way of keeping in contact, so you might wish to agree some KIT days with your employee. You should not subject the employee to any detriment because she does not wish to undertake a KIT day.

The employee's maternity leave is not extended by the number of KIT days she takes.

The Regulations do not state the amount that an employee should be paid for a KIT day, but it is advised that you should pay the employee's normal salary for any day that she works for you. You could reduce the daily pay by the amount of SMP that she would otherwise receive on that day.

Example:
Jane is on maternity leave and is in receipt of £117.18 per week Statutory Maternity Pay (SMP).

Jane's normal daily rate of pay is £80 and she normally works five days per week.

For her KIT day, Jane receives one fifth of her weekly SMP payment, £23.44, plus £56.56 pay, making a total payment of £80.

You are free to make arrangements that are different from the above example, but make sure that both you and the employee are clear in advance on what the employee will receive for her KIT day. Note, also, that any arrangement you make must still comply with the National Minimum Wage Regulations.

Reasonable contact during maternity leave

As an employer, you have a right to make reasonable contact with your employees during maternity leave, to keep her informed of workplace developments.
It is best to agree with the employee, before her maternity leave, what contact will be made and when and how it will be made, so that the contact is seen as supportive rather than intrusive.

In any event, employees on maternity leave should be notified of any vacancies that arise within during their department/organisation during their absence from work and given the opportunity to apply for these vacancies. A failure to do so may result in the employee bringing a claim in the employment tribunal for sex discrimination and constructive unfair dismissal.

Adoption leave

The law provides for 26 weeks ordinary adoption leave and a further 26 weeks additional adoption leave when an employee is newly matched with a child for adoption from an approved adoption agency.

To be eligible for adoption leave, the employee must:

- have been matched with a child to be placed with them by an adoption agency
- have notified the agency that they agree that the child should be placed with them and agree the date of placement
- have been continuously employed by the same employer for at least 26 weeks ending with the week in which they are notified of having been matched with the child.

Adoption leave is available to one member of the couple only; the couple can choose who takes the leave. The other member of the couple may be entitled to two weeks paid paternity leave if they meet the eligibility requirements for paternity leave (see below).

Duration of adoption leave

Adoption leave is a single continuous period and is made up of two elements:

Returning to work after Maternity Leave

A woman on Ordinary Maternity Leave continues to have the right to return to the same job on the same terms and conditions as if she had not been absent, unless a redundancy situation has arisen.

A woman on Additional Maternity Leave continues to have the right to return to the same job on the same terms and conditions. However, if there is some reason (other than redundancy) why it is not reasonably practicable for her to return to the same job (for example, a reorganisation) the employee is entitled to return to another job which is both suitable for her and appropriate in the circumstances, and on terms and conditions that are no less favourable than her previous job.

Returning to work – notice requirements

There is no requirement for your employee to give notice if she intends to return to work at the end of her maternity leave period – she can simply return.

If, however, your employee wishes to change the date of her return to work following statutory leave, she will be required to give you 8 weeks' notice of the intended change (although it is of course open to you to agree to shorter notice).

Health and safety

When a woman is pregnant and during the six months after childbirth, you must take steps to protect her health and safety. You must carry out a risk assessment to identify any risks to your employee's health or that of her child. If you cannot adequately protect her health and safety or that of her unborn child and cannot redeploy her to an alternative post on equivalent terms and conditions, you may need to suspend her on full pay.

Sickness trigger

The employee's maternity leave starts automatically if she is absent from work for a pregnancy related illness during the four weeks before the week her baby is due.

Further information

The information above is a summary of the statutory maternity provisions. The law surrounding maternity leave and pay is relatively complex. For sources of more detailed information, see the end of this chapter.

Future changes

The government has said that it intends to increase maternity pay from 9 to 12 months. This is likely to take effect in 2009.

'When a woman is pregnant and during the six months after childbirth, you must take steps to protect her health and safety.'

Ordinary Adoption Leave (OAL)
OAL lasts for 26 weeks during which the contract of employment continues, and during which the employee continues to receive all their contractual benefits (such as annual leave accrual, car or car allowance, or reimbursement of professional subscriptions) except salary.

Additional Adoption Leave (AAL)
AAL lasts a further 26 weeks, during which the contract of employment continues, but only certain terms of the employee's contract apply. Annual leave will continue to accrue, but at the statutory minimum rate of 24 days per year inclusive of bank and public holidays (28 days from April 2009), rather than at the employee's contractual rate, which may be higher. You could, if you felt appropriate, give employees on adoption leave accrued annual leave at their higher contractual rate during AAL.

During both OAL and AAL, some terms of the contract continue to apply, such as: the ongoing mutual obligation of trust, confidence and good faith; and terms relating to confidential information and acceptance of gifts.

One important term which continues to apply during OAL and AAL is the requirement to give you notice of termination of employment, if the employee does not intend to return to work. The notice they must give is the notice stated in their contract of employment.

Pensions during adoption leave
The employee continues to accrue contractual pension rights during any paid adoption leave. The statutory adoption pay period is 39 weeks (see below), but you may also pay contractual adoption payments for a longer period. Even though the employee continues in pension scheme membership, they only need to make pension contributions based on their adoption pay, not on their normal full salary.

When adoption leave can start
The following guidelines should be followed in the case of Adoption leave:
- Where the child is being adopted in the UK, the employee can choose to start adoption leave:
  - from the date of the child's placement (whether this is earlier or later than expected), or
  - from a fixed date which can be up to 14 days before the expected date of placement, but no later than the expected date of placement

- Where the child is being adopted from overseas, the employee can choose to start the adoption leave:
  - from the date the child enters Great Britain, or
  - from a fixed date (as notified to their employer)no later than 28 days after the child enters Great Britain
- Leave can start on any day of the week
- Only one period of leave will be available, irrespective of whether more then one child is placed for adoption as part of the same arrangement
- If the child's placement ends during the adoption leave period, the employee can continue adoption leave for up to eight weeks after the end of the placement
- Your employee can change their mind about when to start the leave as long as they give you at least 28 days' notice before the original date or the new date the employee wants the leave to start, whichever is later
- Once the employee has provided notice of their intended start date of adoption leave, you must within 28 days, notify the employee of the date on which the adoption leave will end. This will be 52 weeks after the start of adoption leave.

'If you qualify for Small Employers Relief (SER), you can get back 100% of the Statutory Maternity, Paternity or Adoption Pay'

Notice of intention to take adoption leave and pay

The employee should inform you in writing of their intention to take adoption leave no later than 7 days after the day they are notified of having been matched with a child, or as soon as is reasonably practicable. You should ask the employee to:

- state when they expect the child to be placed with them
- state when they want their adoption leave and pay to start
- provide a matching certificate from the adoption agency, as evidence of the planned adoption. You can get a copy of the matching certificate from www.berr.gov.uk
- if adopting from overseas, instead of the matching certificate, provide an 'official notification'*
- make a declaration that the employee has chosen to receive Statutory Adoption Pay rather than Statutory Paternity Pay.

*The law defines official notification as a written notification, issued by or on behalf of the relevant domestic authority, that the authority is prepared to issue a certificate to the overseas authority concerned with the adoption of the child, or has issued a certificate and sent it to that authority, confirming, in either case, that the adopter is eligible to adopt and has been assessed and approved as being a suitable adoptive parent.

Adoption pay

Statutory Adoption Pay (SAP) is payable for 39 weeks (nine months).

Payment is at a rate set annually by the government – currently £117.18 per week from April 2008. The employee should be entitled provided that they have earnings above the Lower Earnings Limit for National Insurance Contributions (£90 as at April 2008).

Keeping in touch days

The employee may undertake Keeping in Touch (KIT) days during adoption leave (see maternity leave section).

Reasonable contact

You have the right to make reasonable contact with your employee during adoption leave (see maternity leave section).

Returning to work after adoption leave

If your employee returns to work during or at the end of the first 26 weeks (ordinary adoption leave), they are entitled to return to the same job on terms and conditions as if they hadn't been away unless a redundancy situation has arisen.

If they take more than 26 weeks (additional adoption leave), they are entitled to return to the same job on the same terms and conditions unless a redundancy situation has arisen.

However, if there is a reason other than redundancy which means that it is not reasonably practicable for the employer to take the employee back to the same job, the employee is entitled to be offered suitable alternative work on terms and conditions that are no less favourable.

Returning to work – notice requirements

There is no requirement for your employee to give notice if they intend to return to work at the end of the adoption leave period – the employee can simply return.

If, however, your employee wishes to change the date of return to work following statutory leave, they are required to give you 8 weeks' notice of the intended change (although it is of course open to you to agree to shorter notice).

Further information

The information above is a summary of the statutory adoption provisions. For sources of more detailed information, see the end of this chapter.

Future changes

The government has said that it intends to increase adoption pay from 9 to 12 months. This is likely to take effect in 2009.

Paternity leave

Two weeks paid paternity leave is available to the person who has or expects to have responsibility for the upbringing of a child. This person could be:

- the child's biological father
- the mother's partner (male or female)
- a person who is adopting, where their partner is taking adoption leave.

To qualify for paternity leave and pay, the employee must have at least 26 weeks continuous service with their employer by the 15th week before the week in which the baby is expected. The employee can take one week or two consecutive weeks, but cannot take two separate weeks.

Paternity leave can start on any day of the week as long as appropriate notice has been given. The leave must be taken:

- within 56 days of the actual birth of the child
- if the child is born earlier than expected, between the date of birth and 56 days from the first day of the expected week of birth
- if the child is adopted, within 56 days of the child's placement.

Paternity pay is at a rate set by yearly the government (currently £117.18 per week from April 2008). An employee will qualify provided that they have earnings which are at or above the lower earnings limit for National Insurance Contributions (£90 per week, as at April 2008).

An employee should complete and sign a model self-certificate SC3 in order to be entitled to Statutory Paternity Pay (SPP). This is available from www.hmrc.gov.uk/forms.

Future change to paternity leave (information as at July 2007)

The Department for Business, Enterprise and Regulatory Reform (DBERR) has issued a consultation paper on the implementation of additional statutory paternity leave and pay (ALP). It appears likely that the scheme will be implemented in 2009. The scheme would enable mothers to pass some of their statutory maternity leave and pay to the father or their partner, if they wish to return to work. This would be in addition to the existing right to two weeks' paternity leave. It would not be possible to start additional paternity leave until 20 weeks after the birth of the baby. For further information see www.berr.gov.uk/consultations.

Recovery of statutory maternity, paternity or adoption payments

If you qualify for Small Employers Relief (SER), you can get back 100% of the Statutory Maternity, Paternity or Adoption Pay you've paid plus 4.5%. Whether or not you qualify for SER depends on the amount of Class 1 National Insurance Contributions (NICs) you were liable to pay to your HM Revenue and Customs Accounts Office in the qualifying tax year.

If you don't qualify for SER, you can get back 92% of the Statutory Maternity, Paternity or Adoption Pay you've paid.

You take the Statutory Maternity, Paternity or Adoption Pay out of your NICs and tax due to be paid in that tax month or quarter. If that's not enough you can take it from next month until the end of the tax year. If you can't wait for the money or if you need it in advance you can write to your HM Revenue and Customs Accounts Office.

For further information on recovery of maternity, paternity or adoption pay, contact your local tax office or see HM Revenue and Customs website www.hmrc.gov.uk.

Offering more generous terms for maternity, paternity and adoption leave

Whilst you must provide the minimum terms required by law, you can provide more generous terms if you wish.

Examples of enhancements that voluntary organisations could make are as follows:

Pay enhancements
- paying a higher rate of maternity and adoption pay, such as the first 2 months at full pay
- providing the 2 weeks' paternity leave at full pay rather than at statutory paternity pay levels.

Leave enhancements
- giving the right to a year's adoption leave to staff from day one, rather than after 26 week's service
- allowing employees taking paternity leave to have additional unpaid leave of up to one year after the 2 weeks paid leave. This may be of interest to individuals who intend to be the principal carer, after the mother has returned to work.

Whilst not all voluntary organisations will be able to offer additional pay, do consider whether you can provide additional unpaid leave to your employees. This is at no or minimal cost to your organisation, yet could be a very valuable benefit to the employee.

'If your organisation is able to do so, you may wish to provide a few days paid parental leave each year'.

Unpaid parental leave

As well as maternity, paternity and adoption leave, parents (mothers, fathers and adoptive parents) have a legal entitlement to unpaid parental leave, if they have a year's service.

The maximum leave which can be taken in total is 13 weeks per child. The leave must be taken by the child's 5th birthday, or if the child is disabled, by their 18th birthday.

Leave can be taken in blocks of 1 week up to a maximum of 4 weeks leave in a year (for each child). If the child is disabled, there is more flexibility: the 4 weeks leave each year does not have to be taken in blocks of 1 week, but can be taken in shorter periods.

The employee must give 21 days notice, prior to taking leave. You can postpone the leave for up to six months, if your business cannot cope with the employee's absence at that time. However, try to agree the leave at the time requested, if at all possible.

Certain terms and conditions of the employment contract will continue to apply during parental leave. These are the same provisions as those that apply to an employee who takes additional maternity leave (see above).

The employee has the right to return to their old job at the end of parental leave of 4 weeks or less. In other words, the employee enjoys the same right as someone returning from ordinary maternity leave in this context.

For employees who have taken a period of parental leave of more than four weeks, employees will have the right to return to the same job in which they were employed prior to the parental leave unless that is not reasonably practicable for the employer. In such a case, the employee will have the right to return to another job which is both suitable and appropriate for the employee to do in the circumstances. In other words, the employee enjoys the same right as someone returning from additional maternity leave in this context.

Enhancements to parental leave

Here are some possible enhancements to parental leave you may wish to consider:

- if your organisation is able to do so, you may wish to provide a few days paid parental leave each year. Many parents may not otherwise be able to afford to take the leave
- you could implement more flexibility, so that employees would be able to take their parental leave in blocks of less than one week, or to take more than four weeks each year
- you could make parental leave available from the first day of employment, rather than after a year's service
- you could widen the coverage of the leave, so that rather than just being parental leave, the leave would be available to all carers.

Emergency time off for dependants

All employees, regardless of their length of service, have a legal right to take a reasonable period of time off work to deal with an unexpected or sudden emergency involving a dependants and to make longer-term arrangements. Employees have a right not to be dismissed or victimised for exercising their right to time off. There is no legal right to payment for the time off.

The law does not say what is a reasonable amount of time, but in most cases, a short period of a few days should be sufficient to make arrangements.

A dependant might be:

- a husband, wife or partner
- a child or parent
- someone living with the employee as part of their family who is dependant on them.

An emergency is when someone who depends on the employee:

- is ill and needs their help
- is involved in an accident or assaulted
- needs them to arrange their longer term care
- needs them to deal with an unexpected disruption or breakdown in care, such as a childminder or nurse failing to turn up
- goes into labour
- dies and there is a need to make funeral arrangements or attend the funeral.

Employees must tell their employer the reason for their absence and how long they expect to be away from work, as soon as practicable. This need not be in writing.

Enhancements to the right to time off for dependants

Many employers offer compassionate leave, whereby an employee is given a short amount of paid time off to deal with a personal situation. The personal situation could include the emergencies outlined above, as well as domestic emergencies such as a flood or electrical failure at home.

Paid compassionate leave of perhaps up to 3 or 5 days per year, could be given, with any additional requirement for leave being unpaid.

'Many employers offer compassionate leave, whereby an employee is given a short amount of paid time off to deal with a personal situation'.

Case study – compassionate leave

Below is the Westwich Association's Compassionate Leave policy:

Paid compassionate leave may be granted for matters such as bereavement or serious illness of a close family member. It will normally be for a maximum of three days for each circumstance that arises, at the discretion of the General Manager.

You should request compassionate leave from the General Manager, or in the case of the General Manager, from the Chair of the Board.

Additional paid days may be granted if needed but must be matched by your taking annual leave days. So, for example, if you need five days leave in total for a particular situation, the first three days may be paid, followed by one day of your own annual leave and a further one paid day.

Paid compassionate leave is given pro-rata for part time employees.

Flexible working requests

The following individuals have the right to apply to their employer for a flexible working arrangement:

- employees who are parents of children under the age of 6
- employees who are parents of disabled children under the age of 18
- employees who are carers of an adult.

The request must be for the purposes of caring for the child or adult. It can cover hours of work, times of work and place of work and could include:

- term-time only working
- decreasing weekly hours of work
- compressed working week
- job-sharing
- later start or finishing time
- working from home
- request for flexi-time.

It might simply be a request to start and finish the working day 10 minutes later, in order to be able to drop a child off at school in the morning.

In the case of an application for the purposes of caring for a child, the employee must:

- be the child's mother, father, adopter, guardian or foster parent, or be married to or be the partner of the child's mother, father, adopter, guardian or foster parent
- have worked with their employer continuously for at least 26 weeks at the date the application is made
- make the application no later than the day before the child's 6th birthday or 18th birthday in the case of a disabled child
- not have made another application to work flexibly under this right during the past twelve months.

In the case of an application for the purposes of caring for an adult, the employee must:

- be caring for or expect to be caring for a person who is in need of care and who is either married to or the partner or civil partner of the employee, a near relative of the employee, or living at the same address as the employee
- have worked with their employer continuously for at least 26 weeks at the date the application is made
- not have made another application to work flexibly under this right during the past twelve months.

Under the legislation there is no definition of care nor any particular level of care required in order to show the person is in need of care.

Carers of adults who request flexible working are likely to be involved with giving help with personal care, mobility, nursing tasks, household tasks and supervision.

The legal right is to request to work flexibly. It does not provide an automatic right to work flexibly as there will always be circumstances when you are unable to accommodate the employee's desired work pattern.

Dealing with a request

It may be that the employee's request is fairly straightforward and you can accommodate it easily and quickly. If this is the case, you may meet the request with no need for a more formal approach.

Alternatively, you may wish to give the request more consideration, in which case you should ask the employee to put the request in writing, and follow the formal statutory procedure below.

The employee's request should provide all relevant details as to why such a change is being proposed and the details of how such an arrangement could operate.

'It does not provide an automatic right to work flexibly as there will always be circumstances when you are unable to accommodate the employee's desired work pattern.'

The process is as follows:

1 Within 28 days of receiving the request, you must arrange to meet with the employee, so that you can both explore the proposed work pattern in depth, and discuss how best it might be accommodated. It also provides an opportunity to consider other working patterns should there be problems in accommodating the work pattern outlined in the employee's application. The employee can, if they want, bring a colleague from your organisation with them to the meeting, as a companion.

2 Within 14 days after the date of the meeting, you must write to the employee to either agree to a new work pattern and a start date; or to provide clear business grounds as to why the application cannot be accepted and set out the appeal procedure. The law specifies eight specific grounds for refusing a request:
- the burden of additional costs
- detrimental effect on ability to meet customer demand
- inability to re-organise work among existing staff; inability to recruit additional staff
- detrimental impact on quality
- detrimental impact on performance
- insufficiency of work during the periods the employee proposes to work
- planned structural changes.

If you do not accept the application, you must state which of the eight ground(s) you rely on and you must provide an explanation as to why that ground applies in the situation.

3 If the employee wishes to appeal against the decision, they must do this within 14 days of being notified of it.

4 Accepted applications will mean a permanent change to the employee's terms and conditions of employment unless otherwise agreed between both parties. If you agree only a temporary or short-term variation, make sure that this is written into the agreement to avoid any misunderstandings. You and the employee might also agree a trial period before a permanent change to the employee's contract is implemented.

If an employee has already made an application for flexible working they cannot make a further application to the same employer within 12 months beginning on the date the previous application was made. This is regardless of whether a previous application has been made in respect of a different caring responsibility ie an employee wishing to make a request to care for an adult would still have to wait a year even if their previous request had been to enable them to care for a child.

Forms to assist at each stage of the process are available at www.berr.gov.uk – go to the section entitled flexible working.

Enhancements to the right to request flexible working
Rather than limit the right to request flexible working to parents only, you could give all employees this right. You might also consider offering flexible working when recruiting people, or for existing staff who have less than 26 weeks service. If a prospective employee must wait the statutory 26 weeks before being able to request flexible working, they may decide not to join you in the first place.

Other flexible working practices

The following practices and support are not legal requirements, but you could offer them to employees as enhancements. It may help you to recruit and retain staff, because flexibility is often highly valued by employees.

Flexitime

A flexitime policy allows employees to choose their own working hours within certain limits. There is a core time during each day when all full time employees must be working, normally the busiest part of the day from 10.00am until around 4.00pm. Outside of the core time, employees can decide at what time they wish to start or finish, as long as they work the required number of hours per week. A small excess of time worked may be carried forward and taken as time off in lieu (TOIL) at a later date. Flexitime can help employees to manage arrangements such as taking children to school or nursery or to follow interests or hobbies. Flexitime gives all employees more control over their working lives and as such can have a positive effect on morale.

Working from home ('teleworking')

More and more employees spend a proportion of their working week working from home. It is now much easier to work from home, with mobile phones, e-mail links and teleconferencing.

Working from home avoids time spent travelling. It may mean that staff can deliver their children to school when they would otherwise not be able to do so. It may mean that you can recruit or retain a disabled worker who finds travelling difficult.

'It may help you to recruit and retain staff, because flexibility is often highly valued by employees.'

Case study – teleworking

Automobile Association

A teleworking initiative was launched in December 1997, initially consisting of 10 call-centre staff moving from an office-based environment to working from home. The pilot expanded in August 1998 to 25 staff, with further expansion planned.

The productivity of teleworkers was found to be 30% higher than office-based staff. Sickness absence was very low and quality of performance very high. Apart from the benefits to the business of reduced absenteeism, increased employee productivity and commitment, the AA has benefited from greater flexibility to deal with unexpected peaks in customer demand.

Teleworkers have cited a variety of benefits: better quality time with family, a more relaxed working environment, reduced expenses and less time wasted in commuting and the associated stress of travelling to work. Several people who could only work part-time previously because of family commitments were able to extend their hours and to benefit from increased salaries.

This new way of working has led to new management practices. Teleworkers have regular one-to-ones with their managers, and monthly team meetings stop any risk of isolation creeping in. Morale amongst the team is high. As well as the direct business benefits of the teleworking project, the AA believes it will assist people who had previously wanted to work, but had been unable to travel, or who had disabilities, family or caring commitments.

Job-sharing

This is a contractual arrangement whereby two employees voluntarily share one full-time job between them. They also share the pay, the holidays and the benefits according to the number of hours each works. Job sharers can share the job in a number of ways, for example:

- 1 week on, 1 week off
- mornings and afternoons
- one works Monday, Tuesday and Wednesday morning; the other workers Wednesday afternoon, Thursday and Friday.

The hours worked by each job sharer do not necessarily need to be the same. For example, one job sharer might be contracted for two days and the other for three days.

Similarly, it may not be necessary to divide the job duties totally in all cases. Both job sharers might be responsible for day-to-day work (and for keeping each other informed at handover times), but they might also have specific projects they work on individually, to suit their specific skills.

Each of the job-sharers should be employed on a permanent part-time contract. See chapter 4 for further information about employment contracts.

If one job-sharer leaves, the other job-sharer retains the right to employment in his or her own right. You could recruit a new job-sharer, or change the job into a part time job.

Job-sharers should co-ordinate the whole job between them, with support from the manager. It is the job-sharers' responsibility to ensure that continuity is maintained throughout the week.

Jobs can be shared at all levels, including at senior levels. Whilst there are additional costs involved in recruiting and training two workers for one job, there are several benefits:

- two individuals typically bring a greater breadth of experience than one
- a person working part-time may be more productive than they would if they were working a full week
- it can be easier to cover periods of annual leave.

Career breaks

Under a career break scheme, an employee can negotiate long periods of time away from work. This may be for 6 months up to perhaps 2 years. The employee and employer keep in touch throughout the period and the employee's job is held for them until the date of return.

The advantage for employers is that the arrangement enables them to retain the skills of the experienced employee who would otherwise have had to forfeit their position.

Career breaks can be taken after maternity or other parental leave, or could be granted to allow an employee to take a qualification, or to travel the world.

'Jobs can be shared at all levels, including at senior levels. Whilst there are additional costs involved in recruiting and training two workers for one job, there are several benefits...'

Voluntary reduced time

Voluntary reduced time, or V-time, schemes allow employees to reduce their hours of work by an agreed percentage over a given period of time. V time might be useful to help employees deal with a short to medium term domestic problem.

There is a right to return to full-time employment at the end of the period. Pay and benefits are reduced proportionately to the reduction in working hours.

This reduction can be achieved by either shortening the working day, the working week or taking block periods off during the year.

Term-time working

This is an arrangement that allows employees with children of school age to be given unpaid leave during school holidays. Such employees remain on permanent full or part-time contracts and typically the salary is spread evenly throughout the year. Further information on term time only contracts is given in chapter 4.

Other support for carers

Employees with childcare problems or problems caring for an older person can cost an employer money. For example:

- the employee may need to take time off to find suitable childcare or nursing care
- the employee may be less productive, due to the stress of the care problems
- the employee may leave, causing additional costs of recruiting and training a new employee.

There are some things that employers can do relatively cheaply to assist employees with their caring responsibilities.

You could provide information. For example, Working Families provides a book called Balancing home and work, which you can order from the Working Families website www.workingfamilies.org.uk or call Working Families on 020 7253 7243.

You can obtain information on local childminders and nurseries from your local authority Under Eights Adviser.

You could provide childcare vouchers. Childcare vouchers have tax and National Insurance (NI) advantages for the employee and NI advantages for the employer. It is possible to provide childcare vouchers at no or minimal cost, because of the tax and NI savings. For further information, see chapter 6.

Case study – people friendly working

The following case study explains what one small charity has done to implement people friendly working practices.

BIBIC (British Institute of Brain Injured Children)

BIBIC is a small national children's charity, which exists purely on voluntary financial contributions.

Previously the charity could have been described as having a long hours culture. Now, it regards itself as people friendly, and recently incorporated 'quality of life at home and at work' into its stated values. Consultation with staff on policies has helped to sustain culture change. Hours worked and leave taken are monitored and BIBIC issues formal written reminders on leave to take.

BIBIC has introduced a range of employee options that were not previously available, or where they were, they were not formalised or functioning well.

Extended unpaid leave and generous paid compassionate leave are in place, which often becomes paid emergency dependency leave depending on circumstances. There is paid leave for medical and related appointments so that staff do not have to lie or take time off in lieu, and leave to attend training/study days if staff are contributing to the community outside their jobs (eg by being a school governor).

Mechanisms have been put in place to allow staff to work at home when necessary, eg loan of laptops.

Job sharing, self-employment, casual work and bank working options have provided additional resources for the charity in covering staff absences/training, whilst allowing staff to achieve personal objectives.

Three key post holders: Finance Manager, Fundraising Manager and Trust Fundraiser have joined BIBIC particularly because they could work from home part of the week. Flexitime has meant that the telephone is answered for an extra hour a day.

All options are in theory open to all levels of staff from day one.

A new willingness to respect and welcome all needs within the staff team has resulted in the successful appointment of several disabled adult volunteers, giving staff a new perspective on social exclusion, and adult needs as well as children's, giving the volunteers a work opportunity, and giving BIBIC additional resources. Staff turnover is reported to have dropped significantly, leading to savings in recruitment costs.

This is an abbreviated case study from the Working Families website.

Checklist

	Know the basic legal rights of employees to all types of parental leave, emergency leave and flexible working
	Consider how you can go beyond the requirements of the law to become a best-practice employer
	If you offer more generous terms, make sure you offer them to all employees equally, to avoid possible discrimination
	Make sure employees know what is available to them
	Build a culture of trust, so that employees have confidence in raising any problems they may have with caring responsibilities
	Conduct informal discussions to find out about the problems an employee may be dealing with, and to help resolve them
	Develop systems at work that ensure employees are not disadvantaged by taking maternity/paternity/adoption leave. Implement effective systems to re-integrate them into the workplace
	Train managers and supervisors to understand the organisation's provisions, the main legal obligations and their own responsibilities in implementing your policies

Further information

The following organisations offer advice and resources about the subjects covered in this chapter to new and existing employers, often free of charge:

Acas
Their website has information on parental rights.
www.acas.org.uk

Business Link
Their website has a tool for managing maternity, paternity and adoption leave.
www.businesslink.gov.uk

Chartered Institute of Personnel and Development (CIPD)
The CIPD has produced a very clear fact sheet on maternity, paternity and adoption.
www.cipd.co.uk

Department for Business, Enterprise and Regulatory Reform (DBERR)
Their website includes standard forms for employers, which you may find to be helpful.
www.berr.gov.ukv

Health and Safety Executive
A Guide for New and Expectant Mothers is available from the HSE website.
www.hse.gov.uk

HM Revenue and Customs
For information on the recovery of maternity, paternity or adoption pay.
www.hmrc.gov.uk

National Council for Voluntary Organisations (NCVO)
www.ncvo-vol.org.uk

Working Families
Their website has information on: maternity, paternity, adoption, flexible working and childcare.
www.workingfamilies.org.uk

A listing of all the useful organisations referred to in this Good Guide can be found at the back of this book with full contact details.

Nine
Handling disputes (discipline/grievance) and dealing with conflict

This chapter helps you deal more easily with what may seem to be the most difficult aspects of employing people: when matters of discipline, grievance or conflict arise. It covers the following areas:

- The legal position
- Statutory procedures and employment tribunals
- Drafting a grievance procedure
- Handling grievances
- Mediation
- Drafting a disciplinary procedure
- Rules
- Handling disciplinary matters – informal action
- Following the formal disciplinary procedure
- Conflict resolution skills

In general, if you are not sure what to do, take advice, because grievance and disciplinary matters can be difficult to deal with. In particular, if the employee raises a grievance at the same time as you are undertaking disciplinary action, you should take advice on how to proceed.

The legal position

There are certain statutory procedures that need to be followed, when dealing with disputes at work.

All employers and employees must follow a simple minimum three-step procedure when dealing with: most dismissals; disciplinary actions such as warnings, demotion or suspension without pay; and grievances. If they do not follow the minimum procedures, any dismissal will be automatically unfair and in addition there may be financial penalties, should the matter go to an employment tribunal.

The three step procedure, for both grievance and discipline cases, involves a written statement (step 1), a meeting (step 2) and an appeal if requested (step 3).

Step 1
In the case of a disciplinary matter, the employer must set out in writing to the employee the employee's alleged misconduct and the reasons why they are contemplating dismissal or considering disciplinary action.

In the case of a grievance, the employee must set out in writing to the employer the grounds of their grievance.

Step 2
The employer and employee must meet.

After the meeting, the employer must inform the employee of their decision and offer the employee the right of appeal.

Step 3
An appeal meeting must occur if the employee requests it.

The employee must be informed of the outcome of the appeal.

Other requirements
The law also states other requirements in connection with the statutory process for grievances and discipline. It states that:

- each step must be followed through without unreasonable delay
- both employee and employer must take reasonable steps to attend each meeting under the procedure and must have the opportunity to state their case
- the meetings must be at a reasonable time and location
- both parties should have all the relevant information and have a chance to consider it prior to each meeting. Prior to the disciplinary hearing the employee should be provided with copies of all correspondence and
- documentation eg witness statements obtained during the investigation, which may be relied on at the hearing

- the employee has the right to be accompanied by a colleague or trade union representative at the meetings
- the appeal meeting should, where possible, be chaired by a manager more senior than the manager who took the decision at step 2
- if the employee or their companion is disabled, the employer must make reasonable adjustments to enable them to participate fully.

Check your procedures
You must make sure that your grievance and disciplinary procedures meet the minimum statutory requirements. If they do not, you must amend them. If you have no disciplinary or grievance procedures in place, you must install at least the minimum procedures.

At any point when you change your disciplinary or grievance procedures, you must inform your employees of their rights and of the procedures they must follow if involved in a grievance or disciplinary matter.

You must tell employees in their written statement of terms and conditions where they can find information about your organisation's grievance and disciplinary procedures.

Statutory procedures and employment tribunals

Grievances

Employees who have a grievance must submit it in writing (under step 1 of the procedure above) and wait for 28 days, before they can make a claim to an employment tribunal. The 28 days is to allow you to respond, but you should aim to respond more quickly than that if you can.

If the employee fails to raise a grievance prior to making a claim to the Employment Tribunal, the Tribunal may not accept the claim. The employee will be advised by the Employment Tribunal to raise a grievance with their employer and wait 28 days for a written response before bringing the claim again. The Employment Tribunal may extend the deadline for the employee to bring a claim whilst this procedure is followed.

If the employee fails to follow the statutory minimum procedure before making a claim concerning a grievance to an employment tribunal and the tribunal makes an award, that award may be reduced by between 10% and 50%. If you as employer fail to follow the statutory minimum procedure, any award may be increased by between 10% and 50%.

Dismissal cases

If the employer fails to follow the statutory minimum procedure in a dismissal case, any dismissal will be automatically unfair. The dismissed employee will in these circumstances receive a minimum basic award of at least 4 weeks' pay (subject to the statutory cap which as of 1 February 2008 is £330 per week). Any additional compensation for the employee will be increased by between 10% and 50%.

If the procedure is not completed because the employee did not follow the statutory minimum procedure, any ensuing award will be reduced by between 10% and 50%.

Note that an employee cannot normally take a case of unfair dismissal against you until the have been employed by you for a year or more. There are some important exceptions to this rule. Notably, any unfair dismissal claim made under the 6 discrimination strands needs no qualifying service. Similarly, there is no qualifying service requirement if an employee brings an unfair dismissal claim on the grounds that they have asserted a statutory right (eg the statutory right to 4.8 weeks annual leave or the statutory right to a written statement of employment particulars) or if they have been dismissed on the grounds of pregnancy or for making a protected disclosure (whistleblowing).

Modified two-step procedure

For the vast majority of cases, you will need to follow the three-step procedure.

There is however a modified two-step procedure which may be used in certain cases.

Modified grievance procedure
This procedure may apply in the case of a grievance if the employee is no longer working for you and:

- both parties agree in writing that it should apply or
- it is not reasonably practicable for one or other party to carry out the standard procedure. This might be the case if, for example, one party has left the country or is seriously ill.

Step 1
The ex-employee sends a written statement of grievance to you.

Step 2
You write back to the ex-employee giving your response to the points raised.

Under the modified grievance procedure the employee does not have any right of appeal.

'Any unfair dismissal claim made under the 6 discrimination strands needs no qualifying service'

Modified disciplinary procedure
This procedure should only be used in a very small number of circumstances, such as a witnessed fight or theft, which might lead to a gross misconduct dismissal. The procedure may be used if you have dismissed someone on the spot. You would then follow up with the two steps outlined below. In general, you are advised not to use the two-step procedure. This is because there is a greater risk that you will be found in an employment tribunal to not have considered the matter properly, and to have dismissed your employee unfairly. You are advised to follow the normal procedure outlined in your organisation's disciplinary procedure.

The modified disciplinary procedure is as follows:

Step 1
You must put in writing the alleged misconduct that led you to dismiss the employee. You should include details of the evidence you relied on and inform the employee of their right of appeal.

Step 2
If the employee wishes to appeal, you must arrange a meeting. You should give the employee your final decision after the meeting.

Circumstances where you do not need to follow the statutory procedures

You need only use the statutory procedures in discipline cases where you are considering taking serious disciplinary action that may result in dismissal (or demotion or suspension without full pay, if your contracts of employment allow for this). In the early stages of disciplinary action, eg verbal warning, you do not need to use the statutory procedures, although you should still follow your organisation's disciplinary procedure.

There are a few circumstances where the statutory procedures do not need to be followed at all. This might be the case if one party is abusive or violent, or where there are factors beyond the control of either party which make it impossible to proceed with the grievance or disciplinary matter (eg in the case of serious illness).

These circumstances would need to be very exceptional and you are advised to seek advice, for example from Acas or an HR specialist, before deciding not to use the procedures at all.

If the employee fails to attend a meeting under the procedure, then the employer, taking account of employee's right to be accompanied and any suggested dates, must rearrange the meeting once.

If the second meeting falls through neither party is under any further obligation to complete procedures. However, it is advisable to try to rearrange the meeting for a further time, where possible. Alternatively, it is also possible to hold a meeting in the employee's absence, if they do not turn up to the meeting and gives no prior notice of this.

Fairness and the statutory procedures

You should note that simply following the three-step statutory procedures will not necessarily mean that an employment tribunal will find in your favour. Your actions must still be reasonable.

You are strongly advised to have grievance and disciplinary procedures that are fuller than the statutory minimum, so that everyone in the organisation is clear about how disciplinary and grievance matters will be handled.

Review of the statutory procedures

The government has announced that it intends to repeal the statutory procedures in their entirety. Any change is unlikely to take effect until April 2009.

Drafting a grievance procedure

An example of a grievance procedure that meets the requirements of the statutory three-step grievance procedure is reproduced below. You could adapt this for your organisation.

When drafting your procedure, make sure you consult with staff and managers before finalising it.

Example
Model grievance procedure

1. Introduction
It is (organisation's) policy to ensure that employees with a grievance relating to their employment can use a procedure that can help to resolve grievances as quickly and as fairly as possible.

2. Principles
- Each step must be followed through without unreasonable delay.
- Both employee and employer must take reasonable steps to attend each meeting under the procedure and will have the opportunity to state their case.
- Meetings will be at a reasonable time and location.
- All relevant information will be provided to both employer and employee in advance of any meeting under the procedure.

- The employee has the right to be accompanied by a colleague or trade union representative at the meetings at step 2 and step 3.
- The appeal meeting at step 3 will, where possible, be chaired by a manager more senior than the manager who took the decision at step 2, or by a Trustee.
- If the employee or their companion is disabled, reasonable adjustments will be made to enable them to participate fully.
- Confidentiality will be maintained. Only those who need to know about the grievance will be informed.
- After the grievance and regardless of the outcome both parties will endeavour to work together in a positive manner.

3. Informal discussions
If you have a grievance about your employment you should discuss it informally with your manager. It is hoped that the majority of concerns will be resolved at this stage.

4. Steps in the grievance procedure
Step 1 – written statement
If you feel that the matter has not been resolved through informal discussions, you should put your grievance in writing to your manager.

Step 2 – meeting
Your manager will arrange to meet with you and will aim to give you a written response within 5 working days. If this is not possible, they will inform you of the reason for the delay and when you can expect a response.

Step 3 – appeal
If you are not satisfied with the response, you may put your grievance in writing to your manager's manager, or to a Trustee, if there is no more senior manager. That individual will arrange to meet with you and will give you a response within 5 working days. If this is not possible, they will inform you of the reason for the delay and when you can expect a response.

Step 3 is the final stage of the procedure and there is no further right of appeal.

'If employees feel that they can raise matters of concern and that they will be listened to, they are likely to raise the concerns at an early stage, when it may be easier to find a resolution.'

Handling grievances

Dealing with matters as they arise
Try to have an open and approachable manner with employees. If they feel that they can raise matters of concern and that they will be listened to, they are likely to raise the concerns at an early stage, when it may be easier to find a resolution. If an employee raises a matter, try and deal with it informally and quickly.

If the employee remains concerned, they may wish to raise a formal grievance. The employee will need to set the grievance out in writing and give a copy to you as their manager.

The grievance meeting
The meeting should be at a reasonable time and location and the employee should make all reasonable attempts to attend. The employee has a legal right to be accompanied by a colleague or trade union representative. If you wish, you can, as an alternative, allow the employee to be accompanied by a friend or family member. Note that the companion has the right to address the meeting, but cannot answer questions on the employee's behalf.

If the employee's companion cannot attend on the day stated, the provisions of section 10 of the Employment Relations Act 1999 apply. This provides that the employee must propose an alternative date within 5 days.

If acceptable, you must then invite all parties to attend at this new time. You are obliged to rearrange the meeting once.

It is advisable for you to have another manager or a human resources specialist present, to assist you in decision making. One of you should take notes of the meeting, or you could arrange for a separate note-taker to attend. Accurate notes of the meeting should be retained.

If appropriate, undertake some investigation into the matter in advance (see below).

You can conduct the grievance meeting as follows:

- introduce the parties and explain the purpose of the meeting
- ask the employee to state their grievance. You should also ask the employee to state what outcome they would like. This can help employees to think about possible solutions, rather than just the problem
- ask the person against whom the grievance has been raised to respond (if relevant)
- ask questions about the issue, to gain a full understanding
- bring in any witnesses, if needed (the witnesses should only attend to answer questions and should then leave the meeting)

- check that everyone involved feels they have had the opportunity to state their case fully
- adjourn the meeting so that you can think about what has been said. Discuss the matter with the person who attended to support you. Take further advice if needed
- bring the employee back to tell them of your decision, how you have come to that decision and that you will confirm it in writing. If you feel you cannot come to a decision that day, tell the employee when they can expect to receive your response in writing
- tell the employee that he or she has the right of appeal if dissatisfied with your decision and confirm this when you write.

Investigation
Sometimes, you may receive a grievance and feel that the matter needs to be investigated before you can hear the grievance.

Alternatively, you may hear a grievance and may feel you are not able to come to a decision, because you find that the matter needs to be investigated further. If this is the case, inform the employee of this at the end of the hearing and after your adjournment. Tell the employee how long you think the investigation will take and when they can expect your decision in writing.

Continued overleaf...

You might undertake the investigation yourself, or you might decide to ask someone independent to investigate. This could be someone from your organisation or, if your organisation is very small, you could ask someone external to the organisation to undertake the investigation.

The independent investigator will normally need to:

- interview the person making the grievance
- interview the person against whom the grievance has been made (if the grievance is against another person)
- interview anyone else who may have been involved (with due regard to confidentiality)
- take formal, signed statements when interviewing
- review any documents relevant to the matter
- produce a brief and factual report on the findings of the investigation. The investigator should avoid including their own opinions in the report, but simply whether the information that has been gathered supports or does not support the employee's version of events.

Investigation

Confidential investigation report – grievance
Date investigation started:
Date finished:
Name of investigator:
Name of employee raising the grievance:
Details of the grievance raised
Details of the investigation conducted (people interviewed, documents reviewed)
Key findings of fact
Signature of investigator
Date

'...the employee does not have the right to know, or have a say in, any action against the other party. This is confidential to management and the party concerned.'

Appeal

If the employee appeals against the decision, you should arrange a further meeting for the appeal to be heard. Where possible, a manager more senior than you should chair the appeal. If you are the most senior manager, a trustee could chair the appeal. If this is not possible, you should hear the appeal as impartially as possible.

The following format can be used for the appeal meeting:

- introduce everyone and explain the purpose of the meeting
- explain what you understand to be the grievance and ask the employee to confirm this or to explain further
- ask the employee what they are still aggrieved about and why
- ask the employee what outcome they are looking for
- ask the manager who made the decision at stage 1 of the grievance procedure for information on why they made the decision they did
- ask if anyone has anything more they want to say
- adjourn the meeting to consider what has been said

- reconvene the meeting to inform the employee of your decision, how you have come to that decision and that you will confirm it in writing. If you need more time, inform the employee in writing on the following day of your decision
- the employee should be clear that the decision is the final stage of the grievance procedure.

You should note that you should not overturn the decision at stage one simply because you would have taken a different decision. The important issue is whether or not you feel that the decision was a reasonable one for a manager to take, regardless of whether you personally would have taken this decision.

If you feel that the decision was indeed reasonable, you could still overturn it, if the employee brings additional information to the appeal meeting that was not available at the stage 1 meeting and if this information changes your perception of the matter.

Difficult situations in grievance matters

Situation 1

If an employee raises a grievance which has been upheld, the employee may ask what action will be taken in respect of the person against whom the grievance was raised.

You should resist telling the employee such information. The employee has the right to know that their grievance has been upheld, and that the organisation will take steps to ensure that the behaviour complained of will not recur. However, the employee does not have the right to know, or have a say in, any action against the other party. This is confidential to management and the party concerned.

Situation 2

Sometimes, in order to protect confidentiality of all concerned, it may not be appropriate for the person raising the grievance to see all the witness statements. There may be damaging and confidential information in the statements. Sometimes, especially in cases of alleged bullying, witnesses are unwilling to come forward unless they know that their statements will not be released apart from to the hearing manager.

Continued overleaf...

If this happens when you are the hearing manager, you should tell the parties the situation. Make sure that you release as much information as possible about the decision and the basis of it, so that the employee raising the grievance can understand as much as possible about why your decision was taken.

Case study – grievance

One of the youth workers at the Westwich Association is aggrieved. He is unhappy that his youth worker colleague, who has just come back from maternity leave, has been given the right to base herself from home.

He has asked to base his work from home also, but has been refused.

He has raised a formal grievance, saying he has been discriminated against on the grounds of his gender.

From the General Manager's point of view, she allowed the youth worker colleague to be based from home, after she received a request to do this. The request was made under the legal right to request flexible working (see chapter 8 for more information) and the General Manager felt it was reasonable to agree in this case. The aggrieved youth worker has no right to request flexible working, because he does not have children under 6 years of age, he does not have a disabled child under 18 and he is not a carer of an adult.

Anyway, the General Manager would not agree to such a request. Whilst she can manage with one part-time youth worker being based at home, there would be insufficient office cover for both youth workers to be out of the office. As far as she is concerned, this is not sex discrimination, she is simply following legal requirements, because her decision to refuse his request is not based on his sex but the requirements of his role.

The General Manager and the employee follow the WA's grievance procedure. The employee is still not happy and goes to appeal, which is heard by a trustee.

Having listened to the points of view of all concerned, including the reasons why the employee is seeking to be based from home, the trustee's decision is that the employee be given some flexibility in working hours. The General Manager is asked to consider the matter again and as a result comes up with a compromise proposal. The employee feels that he has been listened to and is prepared to work with the proposed arrangements.

'Effective mediation can repair work relationships and avoid costly employment tribunals.'

Mediation

Mediation is a voluntary, confidential process, where a neutral third party helps individuals in dispute to work out where are the areas of difference, how they can find common ground and how they can reach a settlement.

Effective mediation can repair work relationships and avoid costly employment tribunals.

Mediation can be used as an alternative to following the grievance procedure, if both parties agree. You could consider including a clause such as the following in your grievance procedure.

Mediation can also be used for all situations of conflict. There is further information about this at the end of this chapter.

Example
Mediation

As an alternative to raising a complaint through the formal grievance procedure or at any stage of the procedure, an employee or the manager may request that the matter is dealt with through mediation. Mediation is voluntary and will only take place if both parties agree.

If mediation is agreed when the formal grievance procedure has already been started, the grievance procedure will be adjourned whilst the mediation takes place. If no mutually acceptable solution is reached through mediation, the procedure will be reconvened at the point of adjournment.

Mediation will take the form of a relatively informal meeting, or series of meetings, involving the employee or employees concerned and the line manager. Meetings may initially be held with the parties separately, if appropriate to the nature of the grievance. The mediation will be conducted by a trained internal or external mediator.

The role of the mediator will be to help the parties in dispute to come to an agreement. The mediator will be independent and neutral to the dispute. The mediator's role is not to decide the matter, but to help the parties towards a mutually acceptable agreement.

If the grievance is resolved through mediation, the mediator will help the parties to draft a written agreement that will be signed by both parties as acceptance of its terms.

Drafting a disciplinary procedure

As well as a grievance procedure, your organisation will also need a disciplinary procedure.

Following is a model disciplinary procedure for small organisations, adapted from the Acas advisory handbook Discipline and grievances at work, available for download from www.acas.org.uk. You can use this model procedure as a basis for your own procedure.

Make sure you consult with staff and managers before finalising your disciplinary procedure.

Acas model disciplinary procedure (small organisations)

1. Purpose and scope
The organisation's aim is to encourage improvement in individual conduct or performance. This procedure sets out the action which will be taken when disciplinary rules are breached or where standards of performance are not reached.

2. Principles
a) The procedure is designed to establish the facts quickly and to deal consistently with disciplinary issues. No disciplinary action will be taken until the matter has been fully investigated.

b) At every stage employees will have the opportunity to state their case and be represented or accompanied, if they wish, at the hearings by a trade union representative or a work colleague.

c) An employee has the right to appeal against any disciplinary penalty.

3. The Procedure

Stage 1 – first warning/performance improvement note

If conduct or performance is unsatisfactory, the employee will be given a written warning or performance improvement note. Such warnings will be recorded, but disregarded after 6 months of satisfactory service. The employee will also be informed that a final written warning may be considered if there is no sustained satisfactory improvement or change. (Where the first offence is sufficiently serious, for example because it is having, or is likely to have, a serious harmful effect on the organisation, it may be justifiable to move directly to a final written warning.)

Stage 2 – final written warning

If the offence is serious, or there is no improvement in standards, or if a further offence of a similar kind occurs, a final written warning will be given which will include the reason for the warning and a note that if no improvement results within 12 months, action at Stage 3 will be taken.

Stage 3 – dismissal or action short of dismissal

If the conduct or performance has failed to improve, the employee may suffer demotion, disciplinary transfer, loss or seniority (as allowed in the contract) or dismissal.

Statutory discipline and dismissal procedure.

If an employee faces dismissal – or action short of dismissal such as loss of pay or demotion – the minimum statutory procedure will be followed. This involves:

Step one – a written note to the employee setting out the allegation and the basis for it

Step two – a meeting to consider and discuss the allegation

Step three – a right of appeal including an appeal meeting

The employee will be reminded of their right to be accompanied.

Gross misconduct
If, after investigation, it is confirmed that an employee has committed an offence of the following nature (the list is not exhaustive), the normal consequence will be dismissal without notice or payment in lieu of notice:

– theft, damage to property, fraud, incapacity for work due to being under the influence of alcohol or illegal drugs, physical violence, bullying and gross insubordination.

While the alleged gross misconduct is being investigated, the employee may be suspended, during which time he or she will be paid their normal pay rate. Any decision to dismiss will be taken by the employer only after full investigation.

Appeals
An employee who wishes to appeal against any disciplinary decision must do so (state name or job title of a senior manager) within five working days. The employer will hear the appeal and decide the case as impartially as possible.

Once the procedure has been written, you need to be sure that all employees are familiar with it and have access to a copy. You also need to be certain that all managers and supervisors are fully trained in its operation.

Disciplinary Rules

Acas advises that organisations should have disciplinary rules and that these should be clear and in writing. Consulting with employees when you develop the rules will help with acceptance and understanding.

Make sure that your managers understand the rules and that they enforce them consistently.

All employees should know about the rules and have access to a copy of them. If you have a staff handbook, you could include your rules in that document. Alternatively, in a small organisation, you might simply display your rules on the staff notice board.

You may need to make special effort to ensure that employees with little experience of working life, and employees for whom English is a second language, understand what is expected of them.

Following are some example subject areas for rules, drawn from the ACAS advisory booklet on discipline and grievances at work, available from www.acas.org.uk:

Example
Subject areas for rules

Timekeeping
- arrival times
- lateness.

Absence
- authorising absence
- approval of holidays
- notification of absence
i) who the employee tells
ii) when they tell them
iii) the reasons for absence
iv) likely time of arrival/return
- rules on self-certification and doctor's certificates.

Health and safety
- personal appearance – any special requirements regarding, for example, protective clothing, hygiene or the wearing of jewellery (employers should be aware that any such requirement must be solely on the basis of health or safety, and should not discriminate between sexes or on the basis of race, disability, sexual orientation or religion or belief)
- smoking policy
- special hazards/machinery/chemicals
- policies on alcohol, drug or other substance abuse.

Use of organisation facilities
- private telephone calls
- computers, email and the internet
- company premises outside working hours
- equipment.

Discrimination, bullying and harassment
- equal opportunities
- rules/stance on harassment relating to race, sex, disability, sexual orientation, religion or belief.

Gross misconduct
The types of conduct that might be considered as 'gross misconduct' (this is misconduct that is so serious that it may justify dismissal without notice).

Handling disciplinary matters – informal action

Informal action is when a manager raises a concern with an employee about their conduct or performance. It is prior to the formal disciplinary procedure. The aim is to improve conduct or performance so that the formal disciplinary procedure does not need to be invoked.

When someone is not performing well or their conduct is of concern, deal with it at the time. A quiet word in private may be all that is needed to set the employee back on track. Explain exactly the problem as you see it. Ask the employee for an explanation and check the explanation if possible.

If the reason is lack of the required skill, give the employee training and support to achieve the required performance level within a reasonable period.

Consider finding the employee suitable alternative work, with their agreement.

Explore all options with the employee, but you should still make sure that the employee understands that their performance or conduct is not acceptable.

Keep following up any concerns in regular supervision and appraisal meetings (see chapter 7 for further information).

In some circumstances, the problem may be temporary and can be resolved without a need for further action. Here is an example from the Acas advisory booklet on discipline and grievances at work.

Example
Informal action

A valued and generally reliable employee is late for work on a number of occasions causing difficulty for other staff who have to provide cover. You talk to the employee on his own and he reveals that he has recently split up with his wife and he now has to take the children to school on the way to work. You agree an adjustment to his start and finish times and make arrangements for cover which solves the problem.

Following the formal disciplinary procedure

If the individual's conduct does not improve within a reasonable timescale, or if there is a recurrence of the misconduct, you will need to invoke the disciplinary procedure.

Investigation into allegations

A situation where an employee is consistently late for work is not likely to require a major amount of investigation. However, in some circumstances, such as alleged fraud or abuse, you may need to suspend the employee on full pay and organise a thorough investigation, before convening a disciplinary hearing. You should explain to the employee that suspension is a neutral act to allow investigation – it does not imply guilt.

It may be appropriate for a separate manager or someone external to the organisation to undertake such an investigation.

Make sure that the investigation is undertaken quickly. It is very stressful to be on suspension awaiting a disciplinary hearing.

The principles of investigating a disciplinary matter are the same as those outlined earlier in this chapter for grievance hearings. The investigator will normally need to:

- interview the person who made the allegation
- interview the person against whom the allegation has been made
- interview anyone else who may have been involved (with due regard to confidentiality)
- take formal, signed statements when interviewing
- review any documents relevant to the matter
- produce a brief and factual report on the findings of the investigation. The investigator should not include their own opinions in the report.

The findings of the investigator, plus notes of interviews/witness statements should be made available to the following people:

- the manager who will hear the disciplinary matter. This should not be the same person that conducted the investigation. The disciplinary hearing should be conducted by someone independent ie another manager
- the employee against whom the allegations have been made.

The documentation should be received sufficiently in advance of the disciplinary meeting for those affected to be able to consider it.

If you are contemplating dismissal, it is particularly important to give this information to the employee in advance. You also need to specify in advance exactly what the employee has done, or failed to do that may result in disciplinary action or dismissal. The law does not allow you to present this information only at the hearing.

Opposite is an example format for the report:

Example confidential investigation report-disciplinary matter

Date investigation started:
Date finished:
Name of investigator:
Name of employee against whom the allegation has been raised:
Details of the allegation:
Details of the investigation conducted (people interviewed, documents reviewed)
Key findings of fact
Signature of investigator
Date

The disciplinary meeting

The meeting should be at a reasonable time and location and the employee should make all reasonable attempts to attend. The employee has a legal right to be accompanied by a colleague or trade union representative. Tell the employee in advance of this right. If you wish, you can, as an alternative, allow the employee to be accompanied by a friend or family member. Note that the companion has the right to address the meeting, but cannot answer questions on the employee's behalf.

If the employee's companion cannot attend on the day stated, the provisions of section 10 of the Employment Relations Act 1999 apply. This provides that it is advisable for you to have another manager or a human resources specialist present, to assist you in decision making and to take notes of the meeting. Accurate notes of the meeting should be retained.

You can conduct the disciplinary meeting as follows:

- start by introducing those present and by explaining the format of the meeting
- explain your understanding of the allegation
- unless the matter is very straightforward, such as poor timekeeping, in which case you can gather the facts yourself, a separate manager should normally have conducted an investigation into the matter. You should ask that manager to present their findings to the hearing
- ask the employee to comment on what is said. You should give the employee full opportunity to present their side of the story and to say anything they wish to
- if needed, bring in witnesses and allow all parties to question them on their evidence
- ask the investigating manager to sum up
- ask the employee to sum up
- summarise your understanding of the facts (but do not give your views about the facts at this stage)
- adjourn the meeting to consider the matter in private. Discuss it with the person who attended the meeting to support you. Take advice from a Human Resources practitioner if needed

- reconvene the meeting to give your decision and confirm this in writing. If you need more time, reconvene the meeting to tell the employee that you will give your decision in writing on the following day or as soon afterwards as you can. Inform the employee of their right to appeal
- throughout the hearing, make sure you demonstrate an open mind and keep your approach formal and polite.

Coming to a decision

In coming to a decision, you should take all matters into account, including the thoroughness of the investigation and on the balance of probabilities, is the case against the employee proven? If you feel that the case against the employee is not proven, no disciplinary penalty should be imposed. If you feel that the case is proven, then you should consider:

- what is a reasonable penalty in this circumstance? In considering this, review your disciplinary procedure and the rules of your organisation. Consider any similar cases in the organisation in the past and what action was taken
- are there any mitigating circumstances which might make it appropriate to lessen the penalty?
- does the employee already have current disciplinary warnings?

'When an individual's performance is poor, this will require particularly sensitive handling'.

If you are considering dismissal, what is the reason? The reason must be one allowed by the law, that is:

- capability or qualifications of the employee
- conduct of the employee
- redundancy
- contravention of a duty or restriction
- some other substantial reason

In normal circumstances, you should not dismiss an employee unless you have previously given one or more warnings. The exception to this is in cases of gross misconduct (ie very serious matters such as theft, fighting, assault or neglect of service users), where you may dismiss summarily without prior warnings and without pay in lieu of notice.

The appeal meeting
If the employee wants to appeal against your decision, they should do so in writing. If possible a manager more senior than you or one or more trustees should hold the appeal hearing.

The employee may be accompanied at the meeting by a colleague or trade union representative or, if your procedures allow, a friend or family member.

Here is a format for the appeal meeting:

- the person chairing the appeal should explain the purpose and format of the appeal
- the employee should be given the opportunity to explain the grounds for their appeal
- the person chairing the appeal should ask for clarification if required from the manager who took the original decision
- witnesses may be brought in if necessary, but a full re-hearing of the case should normally be avoided
- once all parties have said what they wish to about the matter, the hearing should be adjourned
- the person chairing the appeal should consider all the matters raised and then reconvene the meeting to inform the employee of their decision. This should be confirmed in writing. If more time is needed, the employee should be told this and a decision should follow in writing as soon as possible afterwards.
- the employee should be informed that there is no further right of appeal.

Coming to a decision – appeals
The person hearing the appeal must consider whether, in all the circumstances, the original decision was a reasonable management decision to take and whether the procedure was followed appropriately.

The person hearing the appeal should set aside whether they would have taken a different decision in the circumstances. The only thing to be assessed is whether the original decision was within the range of reasonable management decisions, based on reasonable evidence and reasonable belief.

The person hearing the appeal should also consider whether any new evidence has been presented that may change the decision. If this is the case, they should consider it carefully, before confirming or overturning the original decision.

Matters of poor performance
When an individual's performance is poor, this will require particularly sensitive handling. Chapter 7 provides additional information about how to deal with performance problems within the disciplinary procedure.

Conflict resolution skills

As well as dealing with formal matters of discipline and grievance, you are likely to come across day-to-day situations of conflict.

The Acas advisory booklet on managing conflict states: "Conflict at work takes many forms. It may be that two workers simply don't get on; or that an individual has a grievance against their manager. Conflict may take the form of rivalry between teams; or it may be apparent by the lack of trust and cooperation between large groups of employees and management."

The information in this section is drawn from that advisory booklet, which is available for download from www.acas.org.uk.

Responding to conflict

There are three common responses to conflict:

Fight
You react in a challenging way. At work this might mean shouting or losing your temper.

Flight
You turn your back on what's going on. This is a common reaction – by ignoring a problem you hope it will go away.

Freeze
You are not sure how to react and become very passive. You might begin to deal with the issue but things drift or become drawn out through indecision.

The above three reactions are almost instinctive. However, there is a fourth way – facing it. This means approaching a problem in a calm and rational way with a planned approach.

Below is a checklist of ways in which Acas suggests that we can manage conflict:

X	train managers (or yourself, if you are the only manager) to handle difficult conversations with employees
X	have clear discipline, grievance and dispute procedures for dealing with conflict
X	consider outside help where necessary
X	encourage open expression of opinions
X	recognise the importance of feelings
X	listen to what people have to say
X	focus on interests not positions and personalities.

'...there is a fourth way – facing it. This means approaching a problem in a calm and rational way with a planned approach.'

Interests rather than positions/personalities

This last point in the above list is important. Often in a conflict situation, we concentrate on our position – 'We need to do things this way and there is no other way'. We can also concentrate on personalities – 'he is so stubborn!' Such approaches tend to entrench positions, rather than resolve the conflict.

As an alternative, try finding out about the other person's interests. Put another way, find out about their concerns and what they want to achieve. Share your concerns too. In this way, you may start to find common ground. So in the above example, you could say 'let's think for a moment about what we both need to achieve and set aside the way we want to do it.'

Upgrade your skills

Here are some skills that Acas suggests are important for resolving conflict:

- listen to what employees say and try and pick up on any underlying causes of unhappiness or stress
- question employees in a measured and calm way, putting them at ease and giving them the chance to speak freely
- reframe what's been said so that problems can be seen in a different light and explored further (eg if someone says: 'he just doesn't understand me!', you could reframe with 'you feel he is not aware of how you feel?')
- build teams by making connections between the interests of the individual and that of the team or company
- lead by example and set the right tone for the way people communicate with each other
- respect diversity and put in place an equality policy (see chapter 2).

Using mediation

Mediation is the most common form of conflict resolution. It involves an independent, impartial person helping two individuals or groups reach a solution that is acceptable to everyone.

Earlier in this chapter, we have outlined how mediation may be used as an alternative to the grievance procedure. It may be useful in other situations of conflict too.

Mediation is not prescriptive. It helps the parties involved to make progress in resolving their differences. It does not make judgments or determine outcomes.

Continued overleaf...

A mediator will:	
X	be seen as impartial and independent
X	come without any emotional or political baggage
X	develop new ideas based on their experience
X	use tried and tested techniques for getting people talking and listening and reaching compromises
X	protect and sustain the ongoing relationships at work.

How mediation works

A mediator will often meet the parties in dispute separately, perhaps several times, and then together. They may use appropriate techniques to help determine the underlying causes of the problem – for example, using diagnostic workshops can help groups to agree on their common concerns.

Finding a mediator

If you want to use an external mediator, you could search the internet to find out about organisations offering mediation. Alternatively, you could review NCVO's list of approved consultants. To find out more, contact NCVO on 0800 2 798 798 or textphone 0800 01 888 111 or e-mail helpdesk@ncvo-vol.org.uk.

Acas also provides mediation services, you can contact them on 08457 47 47 47.

Preventing future conflict

You can learn a great deal from conflict. Chapter 1 of this guide outlined the Acas model workplace. To recap, below are the areas that Acas outlines as the model workplace. Acas suggests that these same points are some of the common matters that many employers need to address during or after periods of individual and group conflict, or to avoid conflict occurring in the first place.

Put systems and procedures in place
- establish formal procedures – for dispute resolution, grievances and disciplinary issues
- explain plans – link individual performance targets to the overall business plans so everyone feels involved
- listen – consultation is the key to involving employees in decision-making
- reward fairly – pay is seldom far from people's minds
- work safely – think about use of computers, smoking, stress and drugs as well as noise, dust and chemicals.

Checklist

Develop relationships

- value employees – how would most employees describe the culture within the organisation?
- treat fairly – check the law on discrimination and the meaning of harassment
- encourage initiative – think about job design and developing individuals
- balance personal and business needs – flexible working patterns could help to improve the work-life balance of employees and the effectiveness of the business
- develop new skills – it is worth thinking about Investors in People (IiP) to promote training and communication.

Work together

- build trust between employee representatives (ie union representatives) and management – relationships add value to the organisation by creating a system of effective working and discussion to respond to change.

	Make sure your grievance and disciplinary procedures comply with the statutory minimum procedures
	Draft disciplinary rules, so that staff know what is expected of them. Make sure all staff have access to a copy of the rules
	Follow principles of fairness and reasonableness in dealing with any grievance or disciplinary matter. Always follow your procedures and always investigate fully
	Consider the use of mediation in grievance cases, and situations of conflict, where appropriate
	Review the Acas advisory booklet on managing conflict at work and then consider if you might deal with confrontation and conflict in new and more effective ways
	Seek human resources or legal advice when in doubt

Further information

The following organisations offer advice and resources about the subjects covered in this chapter to new and existing employers, often free of charge:

Acas

The following publications can be downloaded from the Acas website:

- A self-help tool to producing grievance and disciplinary procedures
- The Acas Advisory Handbook Discipline and grievances at work
- The Acas Code of Practice on disciplinary and grievance procedures
- Advisory Booklet – Managing Conflict.

www.acas.org.uk

Business link
www.businesslink.gov.uk

Department for Business, Enterprise and Regulatory Reform (DBERR)

Their website has several documents about the statutory dispute resolution procedures. There is also a useful publication targeted at smaller employers, called 'Disciplinary, dismissal and grievance procedures, guidance for employers'. This publication includes standard letters that you can use in disciplinary cases. www.berr.gov.uk

National Council for Voluntary Organisations (NCVO)

NCVO has a paid-for publication called You're Not Listening to Me!, which has lots of practical advice on mediation. www.ncvo-vol.org.uk

A listing of all the useful organisations referred to in this Good Guide can be found at the back of this book with full contact details.

Ten

Managing absence and attendance

High levels of absence can be a problem for any organisation. If you are a small employer with little flexibility to re-allocate work, employee absence can be especially difficult to deal with. Quite apart from the operational problems, high levels of employee absence can affect morale. It can also be costly: the Chartered Institute of Personnel and Development 2007 employer survey found that the average cost of absence per employee per year was £659. The survey also reported a significant increase in stress at work with 31% of employers reporting an increase in stress-related absence.

Legal requirements

There are certain legal requirements which affect the management of employee absence.

Disability Discrimination Act 1995 (DDA)

The DDA says that if an employee has a disability, you must make reasonable adjustments so that the employee is not treated less favourably than other employees.

Health and Safety at Work Act (HSWA) 1974

Under the Health and Safety at Work Act, you have a responsibility to protect the health and safety of your employees. If your employee is more vulnerable to physical or psychological risk on return to work because of their illness, injury or disability, you have an extra responsibility to protect them.

Employment Rights Act 1996 and Employment Act 2002 (Dispute Regulations) 2004

If you need to dismiss an employee on the grounds of ill health, you must follow the statutory minimum dismissal procedure. You must also follow a fair procedure.

Data Protection Act 1998

If an absence record contains specific medical information relating to an employee, this is deemed sensitive data and you must gain the employee's consent to process it. You can achieve this via a general clause in the written statement of terms and conditions of employment (see chapter 4).

Maximising staff attendance

Employees who have high motivation and job satisfaction are likely to have better attendance. Acas comments that "although some absence is outside management's control, levels of absence can be reduced when positive policies are introduced to improve working conditions and increase workers' motivation to attend work."

There are certain things that all employers can do to encourage a work environment which maximises staff attendance. Here are some suggestions:

- provide good physical working conditions and high health and safety standards
- try and provide interesting and varied work, where staff are given responsibility to take decisions about their work
- encourage team working
- give new starters, particularly younger employees, thorough induction training
- have effective policies and practices on equality and discrimination
- give as much flexibility as you can, so that employees can fulfil their work as well as their domestic responsibilities
- support staff through difficult periods, to help them to maximise attendance. For example, you could agree with them a temporary reduction in hours (and pay) or you could pay for a course of counselling

Employee well-being initiatives
The CIPD (Chartered Institute of Personnel and Development) 2007 employers' survey found that employers are increasingly managing employee health rather than simply employee absence. Employers are developing a number of measures to promote employee well-being – 42% of surveyed employers had implemented at least one measure, compared with 25% in 2006.

Here are some examples of the well-being initiatives reported in the CIPD survey:

- employee assistance programmes
- stop smoking support
- health screening, healthy canteen options and subsidised or discounted gym membership
- the development of stress management policies and practices. This might mean introducing stress audits to help measures the levels and causes of stress in your organisation, as well as potential initiatives to address these. For further information on stress, see chapter 11
- improvements to working conditions and environment.

You may not be able to afford all the above areas, but you could do the following:

- offer counselling via an employee assistance programme – many schemes are now set up at a reasonable cost (see chapter 6)
- direct staff to the free NHS stop smoking services – see www.gosmokefree.co.uk
- contact your local gym and see if you can negotiate a group or charity discount for your employees.

Case study – employee well-being

The CIPD's report What's happening with well-being at work? cites one small organisation, Scotia, with 17 employees, that has promoted employee well-being at work. Below is an extract from the CIPD report:

The Scotia approach has involved a package of initiatives that are complementary and mutually supportive. This added up to an overall package with a big impact on employee well-being.

*Well-being information is displayed widely in the offices, including in the toilets!

*Regular one-to-one and group meetings are held where employee well-being is the sole topic of discussion.

*Employees have the time to attend external well-being courses free of charge.

*Employees have free access to all the organisation's services, for example the health services they provide to clients.

*Personal alarms are provided for female employees concerned about leaving the office in the dark.

*No smoking and healthy eating is strongly encouraged.

*A fresh water fountain, a juicer and full kitchen facilities are available for staff, and they are encouraged to use them as an alternative to snacking.

*Regular reminders and discussions occur on 'hot' topics, such as drugs, exercise, healthy eating, and stress.

Scotia have stated: 'Profits are up, we have no retention problems, and we do not have to advertise to recruit new staff. We are well known and well respected in the area."

Sickness notification and certification requirements

You should make clear to your employees how they need to notify you if they are not well enough to come into work. On their return, you should ask them to produce a self-certificate for absences of 7 days or less; and a doctor's certificate for absences of more than 7 days. You should make clear that failure to adhere to your organisation's certification and notification requirements, or unauthorised absence, will be treated as a disciplinary offence and may result in them not receiving statutory sick pay (SSP) or occupational sick pay (if offered by your organisation). See chapter 6.

Example
Statement on certification and notification requirements

Westwich Association: sickness absence certification and notification requirements

If you are unable to attend work due to sickness, you must call to speak with your immediate manager, no later than the time that you would be due to start work. If your immediate manager is not available, you should ask to speak with the General Manager.

You should keep in contact with your manager on a daily basis, or less than this if agreed with your manager.

If your absence is for 7 days or less, you must, on your return to work, fill in a self-certification form and pass it to your manager. A form is available on the shared drive on the computer network, or from the Administrator.

If you are absent for more than 7 days, you must complete a self-certification form and provide a doctor's certificate. If your absence is for more than 14 days, you must send in medical certificates regularly during your absence.

If you fail to adhere to the above requirements, or if your absence is unauthorised, the matter may be treated as a potential disciplinary offence.

Example self-certification form

The Westwich Association Self-certificate
Note – this form must be completed for ALL periods of sickness. For a period of sickness lasting more than 7 calendar days in a row, a medical certificate is also required.

Name:

Date illness began (including non-working days):
Date you were better (including non-working days):
First date of absence from work:
Date of return to work:

Reason for absence:	**Did you attend hospital** Yes/No
	Clinic Yes/No
Please briefly describe symptoms:	**Doctor** Yes/No
	Did you receive medication from your doctor Yes/No
	Did you purchase medication from a chemist Yes/No
Give details of any accident:	

I understand that if I provide inaccurate or false information about my absence it may, depending on the circumstances, be treated as gross misconduct and result in my summary dismissal from the organisation.

Signature .... **Date** ....

I confirm that the employee was absent from work on the above dates.

Date of return to work interview........................

Signature .... **Date** ....

Sickness notification and certification requirements

If your employees tend to have only occasional days off sick, and you pay them full pay for such days, you may get into a habit of not recording these absences. However, problems can arise if:

- the 'odd day off sick' becomes a regular thing or
- a short-term sickness becomes a longer-term situation.

If you do not keep records from the beginning, it will be more difficult to check the details of an employee's sickness absence. Further, you are legally required to keep records on levels and dates of absence and sickness, for SSP (statutory sick pay) purposes. You will not be able to do this unless you keep accurate records.

You can adopt a simple record system for each of your employees. The following recording forms are adapted from the Acas advisory booklet on Personnel Data and Record Keeping, available for download on the Acas website at www.acas.org.uk.

Example individual absence record

Individual record of absence								
Employee name:								
Week no	Absent					Sick pay due in week/ month	Sick pay running total	Comments
	M	T	W	TH	F			
1								
2								
3								
4								
5								
6								
7								
8								
9								
10								
11								
12								
Etc								

'...you are legally required to keep records on levels and dates of absence and sickness, for SSP (statutory sick pay) purposes.'

Example organisational absence record

Monthly summary of absence																
Employee name	Date in month															
	1	2	3	4	5	6	7	etc	22	23	24	25	26	27	28	29	30	31

A= authorised absence
U = unauthorised absence
S = certified sickness
US = uncertified sickness
L = lateness

'The Chartered Institute of Personnel and Development employer survey 2007 states that return to work interviews are judged to be one of the most effective management actions in increasing employee attendance.'

Time lost to sickness

You can assess the percentage of time lost due to sickness each year in your organisation. This can be helpful in assessing year on year trends and checking whether or not you have a problem.

You could use the following formula to work out the percentage of time lost:

$$\frac{\text{Total absence days}}{\text{Total available days}} \times 100$$
$$\text{in the period}$$

So, for example, if the total days lost to absence over the year was 82 and the total working days available to your organisation was 2,600 (ie working days excluding weekends/rest days and holidays), then the formula would be:

$$\frac{82}{2,600} \times 100$$

This would give the percentage of time lost to absence as 3%.

You might then check your percentage absence rate against other organisations, to see how serious the problem is and to decide whether action is needed. You may be able to get figures for other organisations through local employers' groups or your local Council for Voluntary Services (CVS).

As a guide to national figures on absence, the Chartered Institute of Personnel and Development 2007 employer survey found the following:

- the average level of sickness absence was 3.7%
- the most commonly quoted target for absence was around 3%.

You can analyse your absence in different ways, to find out whether most of your absence is due to long-term sickness, short-term absence or unauthorised absence and lateness. You should discount any periods of pregnancy-related illness.

Reasons for absence

You will need to know not only the amount of absence in your organisation, but also the reasons. This will help you to tackle the cause. If the most frequent reason for absence is work related stress, your actions may be different compared with if the most frequent reason is back pain.

As well as the recorded reasons on medical certificates, you could consider holding a meeting with a group of employees to have an open discussion about reasons for absence, and how absences could be minimised.

The CIPD absence management tool suggests the main factors influencing absence as:

- role and organisational factors (job satisfaction, working conditions etc)
- medical factors
- external and social factors (domestic responsibilities, other issues outside of work).

The CIPD's absence management tool gives a checklist of possible absence causes and possible approaches to minimise absence. You can access the tool and the checklist from the CIPD website at www.cipd.co.uk.

For further ways of analysing and measuring absence, see the Acas self-help guide to attendance management, which you can download from www.acas.org.uk.

Return to work interviews

A return to work interview is a meeting that you as a manager hold with your employee when they returns to work after sickness, either after a single day off or, more often, after a longer period. The Chartered Institute of Personnel and Development employer survey 2007 states that return to work interviews are judged to be one of the most effective management actions in increasing employee attendance.

The aims of a return to work interview are:

- to support the employee back into the workplace
- to ensure that the employee is fit to return to work
- to discuss if any reasonable adjustments need to be considered.

A possible format for the meeting is:

- check that the employee is feeling better
- receive the self-certificate or doctor's certificate from them
- tell them that they have been missed
- tell them about any workplace developments
- check what work priorities they have
- help them re-prioritise if needed
- go through their attendance record if there are any areas of concern
- Follow up after the meeting, as outlined in the sections below, as needed.

Trigger points

Some organisations use trigger points in their absence policies. These trigger points are identified times at which certain action will be taken. The trigger points can be useful to make clear to managers what they must do when; and to employees what they can expect to happen and when.

In respect of short term absence, a trigger point would be the stage at which managers should undertake a review of absence over a given period and consider, with the employee, what action needs to be taken to improve their attendance.

A review might automatically be triggered when an employee is absent X number of times in Y months. Some organisations use a combination of duration and frequency as their triggers. For example, a trigger could be seven days or three absences in a 12-month period.

In respect of long-term absence, the trigger points might be the stages at which the organisation will:

- contact the individual by telephone
- institute a home visit
- seek a formal prognosis from its occupational health adviser and/or the individual's GP
- reduce or discontinue occupational sick pay.

The example absence policy towards the end of this chapter includes the use of a trigger point.

Dealing with short term recurring absence

If an employee is repeatedly absent for short periods of one or two days at a time, this can be disruptive for the organisation as well as detrimental to the employee's own work performance.

Earlier in this chapter, the importance of return to work interviews as an effective way of reducing absence has been highlighted.

In addition, there will be a need to investigate the reasons for the frequent short-term absence. Each case will be different.

Absence review meeting

Once the trigger point (see above) has been reached, you should meet with the employee to hold an absence review meeting. This is not a disciplinary meeting, but a joint problem-solving meeting. It is likely to be a longer meeting than the return to work meeting.

Prior to the meeting, you should gather statistical data on the employee's absence and on absence generally in the organisation. You should review the reasons given for the absence. The purpose of gathering this information is not to jump to conclusions, but to help you to identify the issues to explore with the employee.

At the absence review meeting, you should:

- explain to the employee, and try to help them understand, that their absence presents a problem to the organisation
- try and determine the reasons for the absence – specifically whether the absence is medical or non-medical
- discuss possible ways of reducing the absence in the future
- aim to keep the meeting frank and open, not blaming the employee, but explaining the problem to the organisation of their level of absence.

You should note that frequently, the employee themselves may not know the reasons why their absence is high and there may be a number of factors, including lifestyle issues or underlying stress. There may be genuine reasons for absence, but sometimes the impact on attendance is being exaggerated.

If some underlying medical explanation is possible, the case should be dealt with accordingly (that is, with the aim of addressing the medical issue in order to help improve attendance).

Ultimately, if there is no resolution to the sickness problem, any dismissal will be on the grounds of capability (see section on dismissal below). If, on the other hand, no medical explanation can be found, any dismissal may be on the grounds of misconduct arising out of the employee's poor attendance record. If the matter appears to be a misconduct issue, the disciplinary procedure should be followed (see chapter 9).

Medical investigation

Where there may be medical causes for the absence, it will be appropriate to seek the employee's permission to contact the employee's GP for a medical report. In any case, it will generally be appropriate to get a report from the individual's GP before taking any significant action in respect of absence levels, particularly if it could lead to formal disciplinary processes or even dismissal. You could in addition perhaps seek the advice of professional occupational health advisers.

You can find out about the process of undertaking a medical investigation later in this chapter.

'...the employee themselves may not know the reasons why their absence is high and there may be a number of factors, including lifestyle issues or underlying stress'

You will still need to exercise judgement, though – even where there are clearly genuine health factors affecting attendance, you will still have to judge whether these appear to justify the levels of absence and whether any action might be taken to alleviate the problem.

Taking other action

Here are some of the actions that you might consider, depending on the outcome of the absence review meeting:

- amendments to the employees working hours (if feasible)
- discussion on change in work
- provision of medical support to assist the employee
- discussing lifestyle changes.

You should support the employee, but also make clear that it is their responsibility to attend regularly and that you expect attendance levels to improve within a specific timescale. You should set a date for review. You might make clear what will happen if attendance does not improve (eg disciplinary action if relevant or formal warnings that employment is at risk on the grounds of incapability).

If, after warning, the employee's attendance does not improve, you may be looking at possible dismissal.

An important case was International Sports Company Ltd v Thompson (1980) in which the EAT (Employment Appeal Tribunal) explained the procedures that employers should follow in cases of frequent short-term absence. The EAT said that there should be:

- a fair review by the employer of the employee's attendance record and reasons for the absences
- an opportunity for the employee to make representations
- appropriate warnings of dismissal if the situation doesn't improve.

The EAT concluded that if there was no adequate improvement in the attendance record after this procedure, dismissal would be justifiable.

When dismissal is being contemplated, the EAT has suggested that employers should consider the following factors:

- the nature of any illness, if applicable
- the likelihood of any further absences recurring
- the length and frequency of the absences and the periods of attendance between them
- the employer's need for the work to be done by a particular employee

- the impact of the absences on other employees
- the adoption and exercise of fair and consistent absence policies and procedures
- taking account of the employee's personal assessment in the ultimate decision
- the extent to which the difficulty of the situation and the position of the employer have been explained to the employee.

If you are contemplating dismissal of an employee on grounds of short-term absence, please also refer to the section on terminating employment at the end of this chapter.

Dealing with long term absence

Where an employee experiences long-term ill health, it is important to take action early on. If your policy includes trigger points (see above), use these as your guide on when to take action.

Research has indicated that early intervention and support in cases of long-term ill health is effective in getting employees back to work sooner. The longer the period of time off sick, the less likely the employee is to return.

You should:

- monitor the employee's absence record
- consult regularly with the employee about their health and the support you can give them to improve their attendance or return to work
- set time limits on assessing the situation and tell the employee
- let them know if their job is at risk, and why
- obtain medical reports, seeking the employee's consent first
- consider adjustments to the employee's work or work environment
- only consider dismissal as a last resort, after exploring all other avenues with the employee. See the section below on termination of employment.

The process should involve genuine consultation and two-way communication to establish the medical position.

How you deal with the matter will depend on the specific situation. The following are some examples.

'Research has indicated that early intervention and support in cases of long-term ill health is effective in getting employees back to work sooner'.

Example 1
long-term absence with a relatively clear end date

David has broken his leg and it is anticipated that he will be off sick for 2 months. A full recovery is anticipated.

David's manager takes the following actions:

- keeps in contact with David
- pays occupational sick pay (to which David is entitled for 9 weeks at full pay, in any 12 month period)
- towards the end of David's sick leave and in agreement with David, passes him some work which he is able to do from home.

Example 2
long-term ill health with no clear date for improvement

Julie has long-term ill health problems which have led to increasing periods of time off work. It is uncertain as to whether she will be able to return to her previous duties.

Her manager:

- keeps in regular contact
- ensures Julie receives her Occupational Sick Pay entitlement
- seeks Julie's agreement to gaining a medical report from her GP

Once the medical report has been received, her manager arranges a formal meeting with Julie. Julie has the right to be accompanied by a work colleague or trade union representative but in this circumstance and bearing in mind Julie's ill health, her manager agrees that her partner should accompany her.

At the meeting, Julie and her manager review the medical report and discuss all available options, including reducing her hours of work on a permanent basis, phasing her return to work or making adjustments to the work. Redeployment to a different job is also discussed, although Julie's manager makes clear that no alternative job is currently available.

The Doctor's report has indicated that some improvement may be anticipated in around 2 months' time, so Julie and her manager agree that a further report will be sought then and another formal meeting arranged. The manager lets Julie know that all reasonable adjustments will be explored to get her back to work but that ultimately, her job is at risk if she is unable to return within another 3 months. This is because of the operational difficulties caused by her absence.

Julie's manager confirms the outcome of the meeting in writing and keeps in touch with Julie, prior to the next formal meeting. She also suggests that Julie comes in to see colleagues at lunchtimes when she can, in order to keep in touch.

If, after the next formal meeting, there is no improvement, Julie's manager will need to consider whether termination of Julie's employment is reasonable and necessary. If it is, Julie's manager will need to consult with Julie fully and will need to follow the statutory dismissal procedure (outlined later in this chapter).

Continued overleaf...

Medical investigation

Example 3
long-term absence with adjustments made

Chas has suffered from lower back pain, on and off for several years, leading to spells of short term certificated absence. He is currently absent due to his bad back and is awaiting physiotherapy.

His manager has kept in touch with him each week and has encouraged him to call into work for a chat and to keep in touch both with what is happening at work and with his colleagues.

Chas's wait for physiotherapy will be a few weeks and there are problems covering his work. The manager has talked to Chas about this problem and his health and they agree that he should be examined by an independent occupational health practitioner for advice on the best course of action.

After speaking to the occupational practitioner, Chas agrees to return to work for a few hours each day on a temporary basis until he completes the course of physiotherapy.

As he finds it painful to sit or stand for long periods, adjustments are made to accommodate this. Arrangements are made to make the journey to and from work as easy as possible by allowing him to start and finish outside the rush hours and reserving a parking place near his place of work.

The manager and Chas review his work area and job and establish that the chair provided for him does not provide enough support. A more supportive chair is provided. His colleagues agree to help with any lifting required in the job.

During this ongoing process, the organisation also increases awareness of back injuries among its staff, by distributing relevant leaflets, providing training on the manual handling of materials and carrying out risk assessments on each job.

Gaining access to medical records
Where an employee has a health problem preventing them from attending work, you will need medical information on the employee's fitness to work now and in the future. This will help you in determining your duty of care (for example, to make reasonable adjustments if there is a disability). You can obtain a medical report from the employee's GP and if relevant, their consultant.

Please note that if you end up dismissing an employee on the grounds of ill health and you have not first sought medical information, it is likely that the dismissal would be found to be unfair.

Seeking consent
In accordance with the Access to Medical Reports Act 1998, the employee is entitled to withhold consent to your obtaining a medical report on them. If the employee gives consent, they are entitled to see the report before it is sent to you.

If the employee refuses to give access to medical records, then you are entitled to make a decision on employment based on the facts available to you. You should inform the employee of this in writing, including that your decision could result in dismissal.

'If the employee refuses to give access to medical records, then you are entitled to make a decision on employment based on the facts available to you'

In some circumstances, more than one report may be needed, especially if the employee is off sick for an extended period, or the employee disputes the contents of the first report.

Process

You should draft a consent form for the employee to sign, making it clear that they are giving consent to their GP to supply a medical report. Here is an example consent form, from appendix 4 of the Acas self-help guide to attendance management:

Consent to a medical examination

The reasons for a medical examination have been explained to me. I have read an explanation of the Access to Medical Reports Act 1988 supplied to me by my Manager.

I consent/I do not consent to a medical report being prepared following the medical examination and/or assessment by a doctor of my employer's choice.

I will inform my Employer should I require access to any medical report which is prepared following the medical examination/assessment prior to it being sent to the Employer.

Signed:

You should send the consent form to the GP along with a list of questions relating to the illness/absence and details of the role of the employee in your organisation. The more information that is supplied to the GP, the more likely it is they will be able to make an assessment and comment on the suitability of the role and any reasonable adjustments. A model letter to send to the GP is contained in section 3 of the CIPD Absence Management Tool, obtainable from www.cipd.co.uk.

Referral to occupational health professionals

As well as seeking a GP report, you could consider referring the employee to have a medical examination with an occupational health adviser. An employee does not have to agree to undergo a medical examination, unless there is a clause in the contract requiring this. The CIPD's absence management survey 2007 found that referring employees to occupational health professionals was considered to be the most effective approach to managing long term absence. Referrals to occupational health advisers are also important in resolving short-term absence problems.

How to find an occupational health professional

Smaller voluntary organisations are unlikely to be able to employ their own company doctor, but there are several providers of occupational health services (eg Corporate Health). Many GP surgeries also offer occupational health services on a retained basis for smaller employers. The NHS occupational health service, NHS Plus, is another option to consider (see www.NHSplus.nhs.uk). Alternatively, you could contact the Faculty of Occupational Medicine by telephone on 020 7317 5890, or visit www.facoccmed.ac.uk.

'Re-organise or re-design the job to enable the employee to continue to carry out their work. Financial support for any adjustments may be available from the government's Access to Work scheme.'

What the occupational health professional does

An occupational health adviser does not have access to the employee's medical records. However, they are able to advise on matters related to the stated medical condition, such as:

- whether the absence is consistent with the stated medical condition
- what measures you as an employer might be able to take to assist the employee back to work as soon as possible
- what the employee themselves may be able to do to get themselves back to work as soon as possible
- whether any adjustments to work may need to be made
- the timescale over which the employee may be able to return, or a statement that the employee is not likely to be able to return
- whether additional information may be required, and if so, the appropriate sources for this information.

If you employ less than 250 employees, you can access free telephone advice on occupational health from Workplace Health Connect, which is a government-funded service. Go to www.workplacehealthconnect.co.uk, or call 0845 609 6006.

Making decisions based on medical information

Medical information will give you information on which you can base your decisions regarding the future of the employee. There is a considerable amount of judgment involved in using medical information. GP's information may, for example, be relatively non-committal. You need to weigh up the evidence from the GP, from occupational health advisers as well as the views and information from the employee themself.

You might take one of several options, based on the medical information you have available:

- to re-organise or re-design the job to enable the employee to continue to carry out their work. Financial support for any adjustments may be available from the government's Access to Work scheme. You can find out information about Access to Work from the Disability Employment Adviser at your local Jobcentre Plus
- to consider finding alternative work for the employee
- to take no action, either pending a further medical report after a set period of time, or because there is a set return date which is reasonable
- to consider termination of employment, on the grounds of ill health and after consultation with the employee. If you are considering termination, you must follow the procedures outlined in the section later in this chapter on termination of employment.

Absence and employees with disabilities

The Disability Discrimination Act 1995 says that if an employee has a disability, you shouldn't treat them less favourably than employees who do not have a disability.

You are also under an obligation to make reasonable adjustments to enable the employee to undertake their job in circumstances where they would otherwise be at a substantial disadvantage in comparison with persons who are not disabled. The adjustments you agree will depend on the requirements of the individual.

For example, if an employee with Multiple Sclerosis has periods when they are not able to work, a possible adjustment might be to allow the employee to work on the basis of annual hours – so that there is more flexibility on when the work must be undertaken.

Even if the employee does not have a disability, it is still good practice, and will benefit your organisation, if you make adjustments to enable each employee to maximise their attendance.

Some examples suggested by the Health and Safety Executive are:

Adjustments to working arrangements:
- allowing a phased return to work
- changing individual's working hours
- providing help with transport to and from work
- arranging home working
- allowing an employee to be absent from work for rehabilitation treatment.

Adjustments to premises:
- moving tasks to more accessible areas
- making alterations to the premises.

Adjustments to a job:
- providing new or modifying existing equipment and tools
- modifying work furniture
- providing additional training
- modifying instructions or reference manuals
- modifying work patterns and management systems
- arranging telephone conferences to reduce travel
- providing a buddy or mentor
- providing supervision
- reallocating work within the sick employee's team
- providing alternative work.

Consult with the employee to find out what adjustments may assist. You could also seek the advice of the Disability Employment Adviser at your local Jobcentre Plus.

Terminating employment due to ill health

Long-term absence or frequent persistent short-term absence can be very difficult to deal with in a small organisation. You will be trying to keep the employee's job open but on the other hand, you may need to replace the employee to get the job done.

At some point, the time may come when you are not able to hold open employment for any longer, because of the employee's inability to do the job and because adjustments, including transfer to another job, are not practicable.

If this is the case, and even if the employee is disabled, it may be fair for you to dismiss the employee.

Dismissals due to ill health can be complex. You are advised to take advice from an employment lawyer or human resources specialist.

Remember that the employee is unwell and will be more vulnerable than usual. You will need to proceed with great care and sensitivity. It is really important that you consult with the employee. This means you take into account the employee's views on when they would be capable of returning and the type of work they feel they would be able to do. You should balance this against your own assessment, backed up by professional medical opinion.

If termination of the employee's contract is contemplated, or other actions such as a move to a lesser job, you must have given prior notification to the employee that employment is at risk and you must follow the minimum statutory procedure under the Statutory Dispute Regulations from the Employment Act 2002. This involves:

Step 1
A written note to the member of staff, setting out the fact that termination of the employee's contract is contemplated and the basis for it, ie absence from work.

Step 2
A meeting to discuss the matter, after which a decision should be taken.

Step 3
A right of appeal against any decision taken at stage 2. The appeal should normally be heard by a more senior manager, or if there is none, a trustee or trustees not previously involved in the matter.

The member of staff should be given full opportunity to state their point of view at both the step two meeting and any appeal. They should be informed prior to the meetings of their right to be accompanied by a colleague or trade union representative. As an alternative, you may want to give the employee the right to be accompanied by a friend or family member.

You should note that in addition to the minimum statutory procedure, you must also adopt a fair procedure. Your reason for dismissal must be genuine (ie capability) and you must be reasonable in treating this as a reason for dismissal.

Should termination of employment result, the employee should be given paid notice, in accordance with the requirements of their employment contract.

Review of the statutory procedures
The government has announced that it intends to repeal the statutory procedures in their entirety. Any change is unlikely to take effect until April 2009.

'Dismissals due to ill health can be complex. You are advised to take advice from an employment lawyer or human resources specialist.'

Developing a sickness absence policy

It is a good idea to have a sickness absence policy, so that staff know what is expected of them, the support and payments they will have when off sick and what may happen if they do not adhere to the requirements of the policy.

The policy could cover the following areas:

A statement of intent
This could explain that your organisation's policy is to support staff who may be on long term sick leave, to make adjustments to work or premises to accommodate individuals and to hold jobs open wherever possible.

Notification and certification requirements
This would explain what you expect staff to do if they are not able to come to work, and what certificates they must produce. The consequences of not complying with the system should be spelled out.

Return to work interviews
Your policy on return to work interviews.

Sickness payments
Details of any occupational sick pay, over and above Statutory Sick Pay.

Frequent short-term absence
Your procedures in the case of frequent short-term absence.

Long-term absence
Your procedures in the case of long-term absence.

Referral to a medical specialist
Circumstances where you may refer an employee to a medical specialist.

Reference to other areas of support
A reference to other time off to which employees may be entitled (such as for emergencies involving dependents, parental leave) – see chapter 8 for more information.

The Acas self-help guide to attendance management has a model absence policy, with guidance notes to assist you. The guide is available to download in full at www.acas.org.uk. The model policy is reproduced on the following pages.

Introduction	Comments/guidance notes
	Set out here the purpose and principles of the policy, along with any definitions of terms. Use straightforward language and write directly to employees, using 'you' rather than 'the employee'.

1. Principles

The purpose of this policy is to set out what treatment you can expect from the Company if you suffer sickness or injury or if you are absent from work for other reasons.

Your attendance is important to the business and is monitored. This policy identifies points at which the Company will take action if your sickness absence reaches unacceptable levels.

The overriding aim is to ensure a healthy, productive workforce, not to punish you for being unwell. However, the Company cannot ignore the effects on the services and on other employees of lateness or absence from duty, whatever the cause.

Comments/guidance notes:

You should be aware of the health and safety implications in the event of an accident at work. For more information contact the Health and Safety Executive's Infoline on 0845 345 0055.

More information on 'trigger points' is given in Section 6 of this policy.

It is important to outline clearly the aims of the policy and to stress the effects on the business of high levels of absence.

2. Statutory Sick Pay

You are entitled to Statutory Sick Pay (SSP) when you are absent from work due to sickness.

The main features of the scheme are:

- The first three days of incapacity are unpaid (called 'waiting days')
- Further sickness is paid at the rate of £75.40 a week (revised annually in April) for up to 28 weeks.
- Once SSP is exhausted, an employee normally transfers onto benefits, paid directly by the Department of Work and Pensions (DWP).
- If two periods of sickness are separated by less than eight weeks (56 days) then they are linked and the employee need not serve the waiting days again.

Comments/guidance notes:

An employer must operate the Statutory Sick Pay (SSP) scheme as a minimum. In order to qualify for SSP an employee must have done some work for the employer and be earning at least £90 a week (2007). More information on qualifying for SSP is available from Her Majesty's Revenue and Customs www.hmrc.gov.uk or phone the employer's helpline on 08457 143 143.

3. Sickness whilst on holiday
If you are sick whilst on holiday the Company will consider any requests to change arrangements. However, the Company reserves the right to insist that you still take your previously-booked annual leave and to pay holiday pay accordingly. Sick pay will not be paid for periods where you are receiving holiday pay.

If you wish to cancel any booked leave and use the entitlement at another time then you should inform your line manager as soon as possible. The Company will then decide whether to allow the change and will inform you as soon as possible.

If an employee is sick during a period of annual leave (or if a period of annual leave falls whilst an employee is off sick) they cannot receive both sick pay and holiday pay for the same period of time. It is prudent to outline a policy to ensure both employer and employee are aware of how such a situation will be handled. The Company could allow employees to cancel their leave and take it at another time.

4. Company sick pay scheme

Many employers pay sickness benefit over and above the SSP entitlement in order to attract and retain good staff.

A company sick pay scheme that is funded through an insurance policy may require that medical information is sought in certain cases. If the Company chooses to exercise its discretion then it may have to fund sick pay directly if the insurance policy will not pay. It may be appropriate to refer to the insurance policy terms and conditions within this policy, attaching a copy of the relevant terms.

5. Short-term absence
Your manager will formally review your absence record if in any three month period there are three separate periods of absence (whether these are certificated or not), or if there is an unacceptable pattern of absence, for example, regular time off on Mondays or Fridays.

Frequent spells of short term absence are troublesome and costly to employers because of their unpredictability. Tighter monitoring procedures which help to control such absences can also improve overall efficiency.

The organisation has to decide at what stage absence levels become 'unacceptable'. Some organisations have set up systems where managers are alerted to an individual's absences through the use of 'trigger points'. Remember the trigger is for investigation not for automatic sanctions such as a warning.

Continued overleaf...

6. Long-term absence.

'Long-term absence' is a period of sickness which lasts longer than two calendar weeks.

The Company takes a sympathetic view about genuine ill-health problems and will provide a supportive approach to all employees in such circumstances.

Your line manager will monitor your absence and will counsel you through a period of sickness absence. If, after discussion, it appears that you are likely to be away from work for more than four weeks, your manager will telephone you every fortnight and visit, with your consent, your home every month. These arrangements may be varied by agreement.

(Home visits should always be made by the manager and another Company representative. Where the employee is female one of the Company representatives should also be female.)

The Company will make contact to find out the reason for your sickness (including requesting medical information where appropriate), the likely duration of your sickness and if there are any steps that the Company or you can take to speed your return to work.

Ultimately, if absence does reach problematic levels then the Company may have no choice but to dismiss you. The point at which this action may be taken will depend on the nature of your work and the difficulty caused to the company by your continued absence. Dismissal will be regarded as a last resort and the company will try to ensure that the following criteria are fulfilled:

- Relevant medical information is sought and considered.
- Alternative duties or working arrangements are examined.
- Your views will be taken into account.

Before any dismissal the company will comply with any applicable statutory dismissal procedure.

There is no universally accepted definition of 'long-term absence' but it is good practice for each organisation to have its own definition.

If an employee is off sick for an extended period then action should be taken to ensure that the lines of communication remain open and that adequate steps are being taken to ensure the employee's prompt return to work. The example policy sets out actions that could be taken in such a situation, the definitions of long-term absence and of the actions to be taken.

Possible options could include:

- Lighter duties
- Altered hours
- Purchase of specialised equipment
- Alternative work
- Flexible working.

A dismissal in these circumstances should not come 'out of the blue', it should be the final step in a consultation process.

'Frequent spells of short term absence are troublesome and costly to employers because of their unpredictability. Tighter monitoring procedures can improve overall efficiency.'

7. Return to work interviews

When you return to work from any absence (excluding holidays) your line manager will interview you on the first day you return or as soon as reasonably practicable after that. They will check that you are fit to return, update you on any important matters you have missed and may discuss your absence record if appropriate.

Return to work interviews help to ensure that employees are aware that their absence has been noticed and their attendance is valued. It also allows managers to discover any underlying problems that are causing the absence and try and solve them before absence reaches problematic levels.

8. Medical information

If your absences reach excessive levels, the Company may require medical information about your condition from your GP and/or a specialist practitioner of the Company's choosing.

If the Company requires information from a specialist practitioner, the Company will pay for the examination and for any expenses that you incur.

If the Company needs a report from your GP, the Company will comply with the Access to Medical Reports Act 1988, which requires that:

– The Company obtains your written consent before we contact your GP.
– You are given prior access to the report and can refuse the Company access to it if you wish.
– You can ask your GP to alter the contents of the report if you feel it is inaccurate. If your GP does not wish changes to be made, you can ask your GP to attach a statement of your views to the report.

However, you should be aware that if you refuse to supply relevant medical information the Company may have no choice but to make decisions about your likely return to work based on the information that is available.

Therefore, it is in your best interests to disclose medical information.

Decisions about whether the employee is likely to return to work are far easier to make and will be more easily seen to be fair if they are made in the light of appropriate medical information. A doctor is the most qualified person to make judgments on medical issues and employers should refrain from making such judgments themselves wherever possible. An example of a letter to a GP requesting medical information about an employee is shown in Appendix 3.

It is possible to get access to medical information with the appropriate consent from the individual employee.

It is often useful for an organisation to have a doctor (or occupational health specialist) who is familiar with the workplace and who can give an informed second opinion in any particular case. It may be a condition of medical insurance that such advice is sought regularly from company doctors.

If advice is sought both from a doctor acting for the company and one acting for the employee then it is more likely that any accusations of bias can be avoided.

Continued overleaf...

9. Promoting a healthy workforce
The Company will give you the opportunity to attend regular health screenings. This can help pinpoint medical conditions early on and encourage you to lead a healthy life style.

The Company has also arranged for discounts for employees at local health clubs.

Health programmes can pay for themselves through, reduced sickness absence and higher morale.

An alternative policy is available in the absence management toolkit, which you can access from the CIPD website at www.cipd.co.uk.

Checklist

	Maximise staff attendance with good management practice and employee well-being initiatives
	Establish clear notification and certification procedures for cases of employee absence and make sure employees adhere to them
	Keep records of absence. Analyse your records periodically to check for problems or trends
	Implement a system of return to work interviews
	Use trigger points to identify when further action should be taken
	If an employee is suffering from long-term ill health or regular short-term illnesses, take the following steps: • consult with the employee about their absence, their return and any reasonable adjustments • set time limits for assessing the situation • let the employee know if their job is at risk and why • obtain medical reports • consider adjustments
	Follow the minimum statutory dismissal procedures if you are contemplating dismissing an employee on the grounds of ill health
	Develop a policy on managing sickness absence

Further information

The following organisations offer advice and resources about the subjects covered in this chapter to new and existing employers, often free of charge:

Acas
The following publication can be downloaded from the Acas website:
- Self-help guide to attendance management (includes a model absence policy)
- Advisory Booklet on Absence and Labour Turnover
- Personnel Data and Record Keeping
www.acas.org.uk

Business link
The Business Link website has some information on managing absence.
www.businesslink.gov.uk

Chartered Institute of Personnel and Development (CIPD)
Their website has an excellent and comprehensive toolkit on managing sickness absence, produced in collaboration with the Health and Safety Executive, the CIPD and Acas.
www.cipd.co.uk

Faculty of Occupational Medicine
www.facoccmed.ac.uk

Health and Safety Executive (HSE)
The HSE has a section on managing absence on its website.
www.hse.gov.uk

National Council for Voluntary Organisations (NCVO)
www.ncvo-vol.org.uk

NHS Plus
A network of NHS occupational health (OH) departments across England, supplying quality services to non-NHS employers.
www.NHSplus.nhs.uk

Workplace Health Connect
A free government service for employers with under 250 staff.
www.workplacehealthconnect.co.uk

A listing of all the useful organisations referred to in this Good Guide can be found at the back of this book with full contact details.

Eleven
Health and safety

This chapter gives an overview of what employers will need to know and do about health and safety.

Your health and safety obligations

Your main health and safety obligations are outlined below.

General duties of employers

The Health & Safety at Work Act 1974 places a general duty on you as employer to ensure the health, safety and welfare of employees and others who may be affected the actions of the Company, so far as is reasonably practical. The phrase "so far as is reasonably practicable" appears throughout much of H&S legislation and in simple terms means that the amount of cost, time, trouble and effort involved must be proportionate to the level of risk.

The general duties extend to:

- providing safe equipment and safe systems of work
- ensuring that articles and substances are used, handled, stored and transported safely
- providing information, instruction, training and supervision necessary to ensure the health and safety of employees
- providing safe workplaces with safe means of entering and leaving the workplace
- providing a healthy work environment with adequate welfare facilities.

You can download guides to each of the following regulations at www.hse.org.uk, or order them from HSE Books.

Produce a health and safety policy

Under the Health and Safety at Work Act 1974, you must have a written, up to date health and safety policy if you employ 5 or more people. The policy must be brought to the attention of all employees and be easily accessible. Failure to have a policy in place is an offence and could lead to a fine.

See later in this chapter for information about writing a health and safety policy.

Carry out risk assessments

The Management of Health and Safety at Work Regulations 1999 say that employers must undertake a suitable and sufficient assessment of risks to both employees and others who may be affected by their work activities. A risk assessment is a vigilant examination of what could cause harm to people so that you can assess if you need to take further precautions. If you employ five or more people, you should record the significant findings of your risk assessments.

It is also a legal requirement for you to undertake special risk assessments on young persons (anyone under 18) and any woman who is pregnant or breastfeeding.

You can download information about risk assessments from the Health and Safety Executive (HSE) website at www.hse.gov.uk, then search for risk assessments. A particularly useful document is 5 Steps to Risk Assessment. If you want information in hard copy, you can contact HSE Books on 01787 881165.

Register with the local enforcing authority for health and safety

Under the Offices, Shops and Railway Premises Act 1963, any employer who intends to employ someone to work in an office or shop must notify the appropriate enforcing authority beforehand. This is done by completing form OSR1 and sending two copies to the appropriate authority as shown on the form. You can get a copy of OSR1 from www.hse.gov.uk.

Display a current certificate of Employers' Liability Insurance

You can find out more information from the leaflet Employers' Liability (Compulsory Insurance) Act 1969: a guide for employers. You can download this leaflet at www.hse.gov.uk or contact HSE Books for a hard copy.

Display the Health and Safety Law poster

The law says that if you employ anyone, a Health and Safety Law poster must be displayed at all times giving information to employees about health, safety and welfare. Names and locations of safety representatives and health and safety responsibilities need to be inserted onto the pro forma poster, which you can get from HSE Books by calling 01787 881165 or going to their website at www.hsebooks.com.

Report certain injuries, diseases and dangerous occurrences

Under the Reporting of Injuries, Diseases and Dangerous Occurrences Regulations 1995 (RIDDOR), you must report certain work-related health and safety incidents. The reportable instances are:

- deaths, including the death of an employee within one year of being injured as the result of a notifiable accident
- major injuries
- where an employee or self-employed person has an accident resulting in them being off work for more than three days
- any gas incident
- injuries to members of the public that require them to go to hospital
- work-related diseases

- specified dangerous occurrences that could potentially have resulted in death, injury or ill health.

You can find out further information about reporting arrangements from the HSE publication about RIDDOR, downloadable at www.hse.gov.uk, or you can order it from HSE Books.

Keep an accident book

In addition to the reporting requirements above, which apply to all employers, you must also provide an accident book, if you employ ten or more people or if your premises is a factory. The book is for employees, or people acting on their behalf, to enter details of accidents leading to injury. Accident records have to comply with the Data Protection Act 1998 and you must therefore not allow personal details and information to be seen by anyone reading or making an entry in an accident book. A way of doing this is to have tear-out pages. The Health and Safety Executive have published an Accident Book with pages which can be retained separately. It is available from HSE Books.

Provide first aid facilities

The Health and Safety (First Aid) Regulations 1981 require you to make adequate and appropriate provision for first aid. For further information, see the Health and Safety Executive booklet about first aid, at www.hse. gov.uk, or obtain it from HSE Books.

Consult with your employees about health and safety matters

If you have a recognised trade union, then you must consult with the safety representatives appointed by the union. If the trade union requests it, you must set up a safety committee.

You must also consult with employees not covered by trade union safety representatives. If there is no recognised trade union, you can consult with employees either individually or via representatives.

All representatives must be given reasonable training, time off with pay, facilities and help to enable to them to undertake their role.

For further information, see the leaflet Consulting Employees on Health and Safety, available for download at www.hse.gov.uk or from HSE books.

Provide a safe and healthy work place

Under the Workplace (Health, Safety and Welfare) Regulations 1992, there are a number of requirements covering matters such as the provision of adequate space for employees, maintenance of the workplace, conditions of floors, safe access routes, and control of temperature, lighting, ventilation and cleanliness. This is the regulation that states that there must be adequate welfare facilities in place, drinking water available, places for hanging clothing etc.

Ensure minimum standards for the use of machines and equipment

Under the Provision and Use of Work Equipment Regulations 1998, you must ensure minimum standards for the use of machines and equipment with regard to suitability, maintenance and inspection.

Further, you must ensure that employees have received sufficient information, instruction and training before using any equipment and that only authorised people are allowed to use the equipment.

You must ensure that guards or covers intended to protect against contact with dangerous parts are fitted at all times.

Manual handling

The Manual Handling Operations Regulations 1992 state that, wherever possible, you should aim to avoid the need for employees to undertake manual handling (lifting).

If manual handling cannot be avoided, then the operations must be assessed and risks of injury eliminated or reduced by using mechanical means wherever practicable. Failing this, the risk assessment should identify other options such as redesign of task/layout, limiting size of loads, team lifting or training in safe lifting techniques.

The HSE recommend a maximum lifting weight of 25kg for a man and 16kg for a woman, but these limits vary depending upon matters such as the size and strength of the person and the shape of the load. The important thing is that employees should not be required to lift anything that they feel is beyond their capability.

Provide protective clothing /equipment

The Personal Protective Equipment at Work Regulations 1992 state that you must provide protective clothing or equipment to control those health and safety risks that cannot be adequately controlled by other means or as a backup to other control measures. Personal Protective Equipment (PPE) must always be considered a last resort.
You must assess and select suitable equipment taking into account the individual, compatibility with other PPE, comfort and any other additional risks the PPE may introduce.

You must provide PPE free of charge and provide information, instruction and training in the use, maintenance and storage of PPE.

Ensure safe use of VDUs

The Health and Safety (Display Screen Equipment) Regulations 1992 introduced measures to prevent repetitive strain injury, musculo-skeletal disorders, fatigue and eye problems when using VDUs (visual display units).

You must make a suitable and sufficient assessment of each workstation and surrounding work environment, together with any specific needs of the individual, to identify any risks. The assessment will highlight any areas where change may be needed.

You must also give free eyesight tests on request, ensure that VDU operators have sufficient breaks from using the equipment and provide health and safety information about the hazards and safe use of the equipment to each VDU operator.

'If you have more than 5 employees, you must have a health and safety policy. This should show who will do what, when and how they will do it.'

Use of hazardous substances

You are required to carry out risk assessments in respect of the handling, storage and use of hazardous substances as required by the Control of Substances Hazardous to Health Regulations 2005.

In the first instance you must establish whether a substance is hazardous by looking at the label or obtaining the safety data sheet for the substance.

The COSHH assessment will establish: who might be affected by the substance and how; the level of risk; and the required control measures necessary to eliminate or reduce the level of risk.

The safety data sheet must be retained and be accessible in an emergency.

A guide to the regulations can be downloaded from www.coshh-essentials.org.uk. There is also information on the HSE website.

Assess risks relating to electricity

The Electricity at Work Regulations 1989 place a duty on employers to control risks associated with the use of electricity in their premises. This includes fixed installations and portable appliances such as heaters, kettles and microwaves.

You must ensure that electrical equipment is suitable for the task, regularly inspected and properly maintained. Steps should be taken to avoid electrical overloading that can leads to fires.

All electrical work in the premises must only be undertaken by a competent person.

Assess fire risks

The Regulatory Reform (Fire Safety) Order 2005, which came into effect in October 2006, replaces the need to have fire certificates.
Instead, the onus is on the employer or person in control of the premises to undertake a fire risk assessment.

A responsible person with limited formal training or experience, should be able to carry out a fire risk assessment.

They should understand the relevant risks people may be exposed to and be able to identify the general fire precautions that need to be taken.

You can do an online risk assessment, which takes you through each stage, at the Fire Protection Association website at www.fpa-fireriskassessment.com.

Discrimination on health and safety grounds

Under the provisions in the Employment Rights Act 1996, employees are protected from dismissal or victimisation by an employer for a health and safety related reason, for example bringing to the employer's attention matters which potentially breach health and safety regulations.

Employees who act as health and safety representatives must not be dismissed or subjected to a detriment for carrying out or proposing to carry out duties in connection with preventing or reducing risks to health and safety at work.

If a dismissal occurs for any of the above reasons, the dismissal will be automatically unfair.

Drafting a health and safety policy

If you have more than 5 employees, you must have a health and safety policy. This should show who will do what, when and how they will do it.

You also need to carry out risk assessments to identify any risks and record the outcome of the assessments.

You can combine the policy and risk assessment into an annual (or more frequent if required) health and safety plan.

When you draw up or review your plan, you should discuss it with your employees or their health and safety representatives.

You can get advice on your health and safety policy/plan from Workplace Health Connect. This is a government-funded organisation, which provides free health and safety advice to employers of 250 staff or less. You can find their details at www.workplacehealthconnect.co.uk, or by calling 0845 609 6006.

The Royal Society for the Prevention of Accidents (RoSPA) suggests you take the following practical steps to draw up your plan.

How to draw up a health and safety plan

Start with a single sheet of A4 paper.

Write it in your own words and make it fit your company's needs.

Divide it up into sections:

On one side, in simple terms, write down your overall health and safety objectives (see below).

Next outline responsibilities (from director level down to the newest recruit).

Then outline the arrangements you have in place for achieving a safe and healthy working environment (for example, carrying out risk assessments; providing necessary training and information; monitoring health and safety performance; accident/incident reporting; first aid; general fire safety; obtaining professional advice; and so on).

Now turn the sheet over and on the other side write down the results of your risk assessments, detailing hazards, what could happen and any rules or control measures that need to be in place and appendices giving other useful information.

Don't make the plan any longer than it needs to be. Keep it as simple as possible.

Remember, if it is to be of any value at all, it has to be a working document which your employees will actually refer to and read.

When you have drafted your plan, ensure that it is signed and dated by the Director or Chief Executive as the person with overall responsibility for formulating, implementing and developing the policy.

You need to set aside time to explain your plan to staff, explaining the contribution of managers and every member of the team to its successful development and the formulation and implementation of procedures.

Example health and safety plan

The example health and safety plan/policy below is from the Royal Society for the Prevention of Accidents (RoSPA), at their website at www.rospa.com/occupationalsafety

The Go-ahead Manufacturing Company: Health and Safety Action Plan

Part A. What we're trying to do.

We aim to:

- avoid accidents and damage to people's health and cutting corners on health and safety to try and save time and money
- ensure that we pay as much attention to health and safety as any other key business objective
- always follow safe systems of work
- avoid buying in unsafe products
- work to legal requirements as a minimum standard to be achieved
- always insist on high standards of health and safety when dealing with others
- strive for continuous improvement in health and safety performance.

How we're going to do it.
We will always:

- make sure we consider health and safety whenever we plan anything (however small)
- identify hazards, assess risks to see whether our control measures are adequate or need to be improved and (see below)
- set ourselves measurable health and safety standards and targets with dates for implementation
- monitor how well we are achieving them (for example, through inspection) and record results

- report and record all accidents and incidents and investigate them to see why we have not been able to prevent them
- consult everyone to get their views about possible health and safety problems and solutions;
- communicate all necessary health and safety information
- provide necessary training for everyone so they can meet their health and safety responsibilities
- get advice from outside competent specialists whenever we need it
- meet basic workplace welfare requirements, have appropriate first aid and fire precautions and employers liability insurance
- make time every three months to see how we're doing, record our findings, and, where necessary, set new targets for improvement.

Who is responsible for what?

- Josephine Soap, as overall managing director, has overall responsibility for health and safety in the company
- Joe Soap and Tom Thumb, as supervisors must make sure safe systems of work are always followed and carry out regular monitoring
- Every member of staff must co-operate in following safe procedures, report problems and make suggestions for improvements
- Our contractors and suppliers must provide us with all necessary safe information and co-operate with our health and safety requirements.

Signed

Josephine Soap, *Managing Director.* 1/11/2004

Directors' responsibilities

The Health and Safety Commission has published guidance on the health and safety responsibilities of board directors of all types of organisation.

The guidance may be relied upon in court as an example of good practice, and health and safety inspectors may use it as a point of reference when carrying out inspections.

The guidance lists five main action points:

- the board should accept formally and publicly a collective role in providing health and safety leadership in their organisation
- each member of the board should accept their individual role in providing health and safety leadership for the organisation
- the board should ensure that all board decisions reflect health and safety intentions as articulated in an organisational health and safety policy statement
- the board should recognise its role in the act of engaging the active participation of workers and improving health and safety
- the board should ensure it is kept informed of and alert to the relevant health and safety risk management issues; the HSE recommends that a member of the board should be designated health and safety director for this purpose.

For further information, see the publication Directors' responsibilities for health and safety, available for download from the HSE website at www.hse.gov.uk, or from HSE Books.

Part B. The Go-ahead Manufacturing Company Record of Risk Assessments (example format)

Hazards

What could cause harm?
Machinery?
Chemicals?
Manual handling?
Electricity etc?

Risks

What could happen?
How bad could it be?
How likely is it?
Who could be affected?

What is the risk level, high medium or low?

Control Measures

What do we need to do to prevent harm?
Is it adequate?

Do we need to do more? If so, by when?

The Working Time Regulations

The Working Time Regulations 1998 (as amended) place certain restrictions on the working time of employees and make certain requirements of employers in terms of rest breaks and paid annual leave. The Regulations implement the provisions of the European Working Time Directive. The Health and Safety Executive (HSE) is responsible for enforcement of the Regulations. It is a criminal offence for an employer to fail to comply with the provisions of the Working Time Regulations.

The Regulations apply not only to employees but also to the wider category of workers. See chapter 4 for further information about the differences between a worker and an employee.

Working time

Under the Regulations, working time means any period during which the individual is working, is at the employer's disposal and is carrying out their activities or duties. Working time includes:

- any period during which the employee is receiving training in connection with the job
- travel time during the working day (eg the journey between two work places or clients)
- time spent waiting at the place of work for work to be allocated

- time spent working away from home
- time on call at the workplace (see below)

Working Time does not include:

- the journey to or from the workplace and home
- time resting at the end of the working day, even if the worker is required to stay away from home overnight
- time spent on call when away from the workplace and not carrying out duties.

The 48-hour week

The Working Time Regulations state that employees must not work, on average over a 17-week period more than 48-hours per week. The averaging period extends to 26 weeks in some circumstances, eg care homes where 24-hour cover is required. The working hours include any overtime.

If you require an employee to work more than the average 48 hours, the employee must first sign an opt out, formally agreeing to this.

Employees must not be pressured to sign an opt-out agreement. If they have opted out, they may opt in again, subject to a maximum of 3 months notice.

Time spent on call at the workplace

In October 2000 the European Court of Justice gave judgement in a case concerning the status of on-call time (1). The judgement related to doctors employed in primary health care teams although a similar approach has been taken by the courts in other areas. It indicated that on-call time would be working time when a worker is required to be at their place of work. When a worker is permitted to be away from the workplace when on-call and accordingly free to pursue leisure activities, on-call time is not working time.

(1) Sindicato de Médicos de Asistencia Publics (SIMAP) - v - Conselleria de Sanidad y Consumo, confirmed in subsequent cases.

This case has direct effect in the UK, although the European Commission has not yet passed primary legislation to finally clarify this point. As the law currently stands, though, this may have an impact on your organisation if you run residential care homes. This is because the whole period of time members of staff spend on a sleep in will be considered to be working time.

'It is a criminal offence for an employer to fail to comply with the provisions of the Working Time Regulations.'

This means that these staff may be working in excess of the maximum 48 hours average. If you have not agreed opt outs from the 48-hour week with these staff, you are advised to do the following:

- check their average weekly working hours, including the sleep in period
- if average weekly working hours are in excess of 48, take legal or HR advice on the latest situation and whether you may need to agree opt outs with your staff and/or discuss with them changing hours of work.

Please note that sleep ins may also be considered as working time for the purposes of the minimum wage. This is following a case decision in January 2006 in the UK Employment Appeal Tribunal (Mrs E MacCartney v Oversley House Management), where a live-in care centre manager who was required to be on call and within three minutes of the workplace was held by the employment appeal tribunal to be working for the purposes of both minimum wage and working time rights.

The practical effect of this is not that you need to pay the minimum wage for each hour spent on a sleep in. However, you do need to ensure that the average pay of your employees, over a reference period such as a month and taking into account all hours worked including sleep in hours, does not fall below the minimum wage.

For more information about the minimum wage, please see chapter 6.

Keeping records

You are not required to keep a record of employees' working hours, but you must keep a record of the names of those who have opted out of the 48 hour average working week.

The right to rest breaks

Workers have a legal right to the following rest breaks:
An uninterrupted rest break of 20 minutes, if the worker's daily working time is more than 6 hours. The rest break may be unpaid:
- a daily rest period of 11 consecutive hours
- an uninterrupted weekly rest period of not less than 24 hours, although this can be aggregated to one uninterrupted rest period of 48 hours over a 14 day period.

Night work

A night worker is someone who works at least three hours at night-time as a normal course. Night-time is defined between 11pm and 6am, although workers and employers may agree to vary this.
Night workers should not work more than eight hours daily on average, including overtime where it is part of a night worker's normal hours of work.

Nightly working time is calculated over 17 weeks, but can be longer in some situations.

A night worker cannot opt-out of the night work limit.

Exempt workers

Managing executives whose working time is unmeasured are exempt from the Working Time Regulations. There are certain other exemptions. For example, shift workers are exempted from the right to daily and weekly rest periods, but must be afforded adequate compensatory rest within a reasonable time. Compensatory rest should be sufficient to make up for the rest period that the worker has missed.

Annual leave

The Regulations say that you must give your workers and employees a minimum of 24 days paid leave annually (pro-rated for those working part time). The 24-day requirement includes the 8 UK public and bank holidays. The 24 days will increase to 28 in April 2009.
For further information about paid annual leave, please see chapter 6.

Stress at work

Young workers

There are different provisions that regulate the working time of young workers (ie those over school leaving age but under 18). In summary, these provisions are as follows:

- a limit on the hours of work to 8 per day
- a maximum working week of 40 hours
- an uninterrupted rest break of 30 minutes where the normal working day is more than 4.5 hours
- a rest period of not less than 48 hours in a 7 day period. This cannot be aggregated over a 14 day period
- no provision for averaging weekly working time over a reference period
- no opt-out
- restrictions on night work – young workers should not ordinarily work at night, although there are certain exceptions.

Collective agreements and workforce agreements

The Working Time Regulations allow for collective agreements or workforce agreements, which may modify or exclude certain provision of the Working Time Regulations. A collective agreement is an agreement between an employer and a trade union; a workforce agreement is an agreement between an employer and employee representatives, or if the employer has less than 20 workers, between the employer and the majority of workers.

Employers and workers can agree that night work limits and rights to rest breaks may be varied, with the workers receiving compensatory rest. They may also agree to extend the averaging period for the 48-hour week from 17 weeks up to 52 weeks.

For further information on the Working Time Regulations, see the Department for Business, Enterprise and Regulatory Reform website at www.berr.gov.uk/employment.

According to the Health and Safety Executive (HSE), each case of stress-related ill health leads to an average of 30.9 working days lost. Almost 13 million working days were lost to stress, depression and anxiety in 2004–2005.

One of your responsibilities as an employer is to ensure that work is not overly stressful. A certain amount of pressure helps people to achieve their best, but too much stress can be damaging to health and can lead to lower productivity and higher sickness absence.

'Help people to prioritise work, cutting out unnecessary tasks and providing time-management training if necessary.'

Stress audit

To find out whether stress is a problem in your organisation, you could undertake a stress audit. Basically, this involves talking to staff about their jobs and gaining an understanding from them as to: what they find stressful and why; and what they do not find stressful and why. You could use the HSE Management Standards for stress to assist you in the audit. You can find the standards at www.hse.gov.uk/stress/standards. Once you have completed the audit, you can determine a plan of action if needed.

Tackling the causes of workplace stress

If you have identified particular stress problems in your organisation, the next step is to tackle the causes.

The following is advice taken from the Business Link website. You can find this by going to www.businesslink.gov.uk and searching under stress.

Dealing with workplace stress

If overwork is a problem, consider how you might reduce people's workload. Ensure targets are challenging but realistic. Help people to prioritise work, cutting out unnecessary tasks and providing time-management training if necessary. Encourage delegation of work where possible, and try to delegate work yourself.

Make sure staff take their holiday entitlement – and take your own.

Check individuals are well-matched to the jobs you give them. Make sure your recruitment and selection procedures help you to achieve this.

Make sure every employee has a well-defined role – and that they know what this is.

Review people's performance so they know how they're doing. Reviews also allow you to get feedback from employees about potential problems and identify any training they may need.

Where possible give employees more autonomy, allowing them to plan their work schedule and decide how to tackle problems.

Adopt a management style that encourages employees to discuss problems with you. Provide them with opportunities to express ideas about their work.

Keep staff informed about your business' direction and make sure you tell them about significant changes to the business.

Ensure you have effective discipline and grievance procedures to tackle bullying and harassment.

Encourage employees to achieve a better work-life balance.

Take a sympathetic approach to any personal problems employees may have – a relationship break-up or family illness. Discuss with the individual what support may help them. This might be a period of time off, or a period of more flexible working.

'The employer is usually entitled to assume that an employee can withstand normal job pressures'

Good management practice

Lots of the good management practice described elsewhere in this guide will help to ensure that your employees are motivated rather than stressed by their work. If there is stress, the information in this guide will help to ensure that employee stress levels do not go undetected. For example: see the guidelines on diversity and non-discrimination at chapter 2; induction and probation in chapter 5; staff supervision in chapter 7; and flexible working in chapter 8.

Case law and stress

There have been some employment tribunal cases in recent years concerning employee stress. In some cases, employees have been awarded significant sums in compensation where an employer has failed to take steps to protect the employee's psychological health and safety. Case law indicates the following:

- unless the employer knows of a particular problem or vulnerability, it is usually entitled to assume that an employee can withstand normal job pressures
- no occupation should be regarded as intrinsically dangerous to health
- to trigger an employer's duty to take steps, the indications of likely harm to the employee's health must be obvious enough for the reasonable employer to realise that something should be done

- where an employer offers a confidential counselling service, it is less likely to be in breach of its duty
- however, merely offering the confidential counselling service is not enough – there is also a need to review and monitor the situation, once the employee's condition has been brought to the employer's attention.

Personal stress

Make sure you also deal with your own stress if you need to. The Business Link website at has some practical suggestions about dealing with your own stress. See www.businesslink.gov.uk and search under stress.

Guides on managing stress

The Health and Safety Executive has a guide to workplace stress, which you can download from the section of the HSE website about stress, at www.hse.gov.uk/stress. Alternatively, you can order it from HSE Books. Acas also has a guide about stress, which you can download from www.acas.org.uk, by searching for 'advisory booklet stress'. Alternatively, you can order it from Acas Publications, telephone 08702 42 90 90.

The CIPD (Chartered Institute of Personnel and Development) has recently published three resources about managing stress. These are:

Managing stress at work: A competency framework for line managers

Line management behaviour and stress at work: Guidance for line mangers

Line manager behaviour and stress at work: Advice for HR.

These and CIPD's other resources on stress management can be found at www.cipd.co.uk/subjects/health/stress.

Case study – tackling stress at a care home

The following case study is taken from the
Health and Safety Executive website.

Background
Care giving in old people's homes involves providing
assistance with activities of daily living (walking, bathing,
feeding, etc) and emotional support (companionship)
for residents who often have reduced physical or
mental capacity.

Problem
Physical and mental demands on staff are high.
The home in question was originally designed for
residents who were relatively independent, however
as residents have aged, their dependency levels have
naturally increased and some now require much greater
support. As a result, staff have reported considerable
physical and mental strain and there has been a marked
increase in the rate of sickness absence from stress-
related illnesses, such as depression and anxiety.

Assessing the risks and finding solutions
Workers, managers, safety representatives and
specialist staff discussed the issue through the home's
health and safety committee. It was found that there
were predictable patterns in demands on caregivers,
which allowed the following measures to be brought in:

Work schedules were adjusted to increase staff
numbers during hours of peak demand.

The roles of auxiliary nursing staff were clarified to
ensure that both they and specialist staff knew their
responsibilities and needs regarding support.

Greater power to make decisions was given to certain
groups of workers.

Results
Care staff reported a more manageable workload, an
increase in perceived support from management and
other care givers, and greater ownership of their work.
Although some had greater responsibilities, this was
welcomed as a positive development.

The success of these interventions has also contributed
to a substantial reduction in stress-related sickness
absence.

Problems of work overload and constrained resources
have been reduced by targeting resources at
particularly busy areas or times.

Consulting with and involving staff and their
representatives 'on the ground' was a simple way of
ensuring that this was done effectively and fairly.

Smoking

With effect from 1 July 2007, the Health Act 2006 made smoking in workplaces and public places unlawful. This follows similar bans in Wales, Northern Ireland and Scotland.

Given that an estimated 25% of the UK population are smokers, the implications of this landmark change cannot be underestimated.

Premises must be smoke free if they are enclosed or substantially enclosed and are:

- open to the public
- used as a place of work by more than one person
- a place where members of the public might attend for the purpose of receiving goods or services from persons working there.

Work in this context includes voluntary work.

The effect is that all indoor workplaces must be smoke free, including any existing designated smoking rooms. The ban also covers premises which have a roof or ceiling, and which are at least 50% surrounded by walls. This could apply to a variety of structures including covered smoking shelters located on the exterior of buildings.

In addition to premises, the smoking ban applies to work vehicles that are used by more than one person.

Your staff are still allowed to smoke in places which are not enclosed or substantially enclosed, although you are free to decide to outlaw smoking in such areas too, if you consider appropriate.

Exemptions

There are exemptions in the legislation for: prison cells; rooms in residential care homes; and certain rooms in mental health units. The exemptions, however, only apply to the person occupying the room and their guests. Care workers, for example, will not be able to smoke at work, although residents will be permitted to smoke in their rooms or in a dedicated smoking room if provided by the care home.

No smoking signs

As an employer, you are also obliged to ensure that no-smoking signs are displayed in a prominent position at each entrance to your premises. These signs should be: no smaller than an A5 piece of paper; display the no-smoking symbol; and display the words 'No smoking. It is against the law to smoke in these premises.'

No-smoking signs must be displayed in all smoke-free vehicles. There are no restrictions on the size of the sign, nor any compulsory wording. However, a sign must be displayed in a prominent position in each compartment of the vehicle.

Your legal liability

Whilst your employees must not smoke in a smoke-free place, please note that you also commit an offence if you fail to prevent smoking in a smoke-free place.

There are, however, three possible defences. These are:

- that you took reasonable steps to cause the person in question to stop smoking
- that you did not know, or could not reasonably be expected to know, that the person in question was smoking
- that on other grounds it was reasonable for you not to comply with the duty.

It is advisable that you have a clear policy statement on smoking, so that staff are clear about where they cannot smoke. You can find an example smoking policy at www.smokefreeengland.co.uk.

'You could alert smokers to the NHS website www.gosmokefree.nhs.uk, or to the availability of free NHS support to quit smoking.'

Matters to consider

If you allow smokers to continue to smoke outside, then one thing that is often divisive between smokers and non-smokers is the question of cigarette breaks. Since smoking rooms have become a thing of the past, cigarette breaks will have to be taken outside, which may serve to make them longer. If you do not currently have provisions or policies relating to when and how frequently employees may take cigarette breaks, you may wish to consider introducing one.

The most prudent course of action might be to settle on an approach to smoking breaks that does not give smokers an advantage over non-smokers. An example might be to allow smoking breaks, but require smokers to make the time up at the end of the day or by having a shorter lunch break. Whatever approach you choose, enforcing the policy will be much easier if it is contained in a clear policy document which is distributed to all staff in advance of its coming into force.

If an employee is caught smoking in the workplace, this will be a disciplinary offence and you should follow your normal disciplinary procedure.

Supporting staff to give up

As a matter of good practice, you might consider what support you could give to encourage and support smokers to give up. For example, you could alert smokers to the NHS website www.gosmokefree.nhs.uk, or to the availability of free NHS support to quit smoking.

Here is the smoking policy introduced by the Westwich Association:

Case study – smoking policy

It is the policy of the Westwich Association not to permit smoking in any part of its premises. This is to comply with current law and to ensure the health and safety of all staff. This policy has been introduced after consultation with all employees and volunteers.

If you wish to smoke, you may do so only outside the main building. Please consider the impression you are giving as an employee or volunteer of Westwich Association and ensure that you dispose of cigarette stubs appropriately.

The Westwich Association encourages employees and volunteers to give up smoking and advises them to review the NHS website www.gosmokefree.co.uk, to see what resources are available to assist them.

However, the Association fully recognises the right of individuals to smoke if they wish.

Volunteers are asked to agree smoking breaks with their supervisor.

Those staff who wish to take a smoking break during the working day may do so once during the morning and once during the afternoon. In order to be fair to smokers and non-smokers, it is the Association's policy that the time spent by staff on a smoking break should be taken from the lunch break, or added on to the end of the working day.

Any employee or volunteer found to be in breach of these rules may be subject to disciplinary action.

Checklist

☐	Make sure you have an up to date health and safety policy
☐	Notify your staff of the policy and make sure they know where to find it
☐	Consult with your staff or staff representatives on health and safety matters
☐	Ensure all staff have health and safety training during their induction
☐	Staff must be given training on specific risks they might face such as manual handling and violence
☐	Carry out risk assessments on every aspect of your operations. Make sure they include manual handling, chemical, fire and stress risks; keep them up to date; and act on the results
☐	Carry out a stress audit
☐	Make sure you have safety data sheets for all potentially dangerous materials you use – including cleaning fluids, and ensure all chemicals are clearly marked
☐	Make sure all VDU users have an ergonomic assessment and are offered free eye tests
☐	All electrical equipment and gas appliances should be tested regularly
☐	Make sure you have first-aiders amongst your staff and sufficient first aid boxes

☐	Make sure: work spaces are kept tidy and clean; floors and stairs free from obstruction and non-slip; there is sufficient space for staff; temperature and ventilation is kept at a comfortable level all year; there are sufficient toilets and other facilities
☐	Make sure you have a smoking policy
☐	Ensure that there clear and sufficient fire signs and instructions; you have regular fire drills; fire alarms and smoke detectors are checked regularly
☐	Make sure all reportable accidents and occurrences recorded and reported and that you have an accident book
☐	Get employers Liability Insurance
☐	Make sure all managers and management committee members receive health and safety training
☐	Ensure you comply with the requirements of the Working Time Regulations
☐	Ensure you comply with the no smoking regulations

Further information

The following organisations offer advice and resources about the subjects covered in this chapter to new and existing employers, often free of charge:

Acas
The following publications can be downloaded from the Acas website:

• Advisory Booklet – Stress at Work.
• Advisory Booklet – Health and Employment.
www.acas.org.uk

Business link
The Business Link website has a section on its website about health and safety. The information on the Business Link website has been developed in conjunction with the Health and Safety Executive, specifically for small/medium sized employers
www.businesslink.gov.uk

Chartered Institute of Personnel and Development (CIPD)
Their website has the following resources about managing stress:

• Managing stress at work: A competency framework for line managers
• Line management behaviour and stress at work: Guidance for line managers
• Line manager behaviour and stress at work: Advice for HR.
www.cipd.co.uk

Department for Business, Enterprise and Regulatory Reform (DBERR)
Their website has a guide to the Working Time Regulations
www.berr.gov.uk

Fire Protection Association (FPA)
Their website has information on fire precautions and a very useful online fire risk assessment.
www.thefpa.co.uk

Go Smoke Free
This is the NHS website designed to help smokers give up.
www.gosmokefree.nhs.uk

Health and Safety Executive (HSE)
Their website has a wealth of information on all aspects of health and safety at work.

The following publications are available from HSE:

• An Introduction to Health and Safety for Small Businesses

• Charity and Voluntary Workers: A guide to health and safety at work. This is not available on the website, but you can obtain it from HSE Books

• Health and Safety Starter Pack, which contains most of the basic health and safety advice you need to help your organisation comply with the law and protect its employees. The pack includes copies of the HSE Accident Book, the Health and Safety Law Poster, and the publication 'Essentials of Health and Safety at Work'.
www.hse.gov.uk

Royal Society for the Prevention of Accidents (Rospa)
www.rospa.com/occupationalsafety

Smoke free England
Their website has information on the no-smoking legislation.
www.smokefreeengland.co.uk

Unison
Their website has a 'health and safety zone', containing lots of useful and accessible information.
www.unison.org.uk

Workplace Health Connect
Their website provides free health and safety advice to employers of up to 250 workers.
www.workplacehealthconnect.co.uk

A listing of all the useful organisations referred to in this Good Guide can be found at the back of this book with full contact details.

Twelve
Employee relations

The subject of employee relations covers the relationships between an employer and its employees. It is about individual relationships as well as group (collective) relationships. It may involve communication, consultation or collective bargaining.

Communicating and consulting with your employees

Communication, consultation or collective bargaining are defined by Acas (in its guide to the Information and Consultation Regulations)

Communication is concerned with the interchange of information and ideas.

Consultation goes beyond this and involves managers actively seeking and then taking account of the views of employees before making a decision.

Collective bargaining is the process by which employers and recognised trade unions seek to reach agreement through negotiation on issues such as pay and terms and conditions of employment. It is quite different from consultation where the responsibility for decision-making remains with management.

Employees who feel that little notice is taken of them at work, that they are not appreciated or that their views and comments are not heard, are likely to feel less positive about their work and be less productive.

Conversely, effective communication and consultation and acknowledgment of good performance are likely to have the following benefits:

- avoidance of misunderstandings, because staff will understand the organisation, its performance and constraints
- better individual performance, because employees will understand what they need to achieve, how and why
- greater support for management decisions, because employees will have been more involved in decision taking
- better management decisions, because of employee involvement
- fewer staff grievances.

Below are some practical steps you could take to ensure that you are communicating and consulting appropriately with your employees.

Hold face-to-face meetings
Have regular team meetings and one to one meetings.

Chapter 7 gives more information about one to one staff supervision meetings.

Communicate in writing
Written communication may be via a notice board, e-mail, memo, a staff newsletter, your intranet (if you have one) or a staff handbook. If staff in your organisation are based at more than one work location, written communication will be especially important, so that messages do not become confused.

Undertake group communication and consultation
Unless your organisation is very small (eg under 50 employees), it is helpful to communicate and consult not only with individuals but also with staff representatives or trade union representatives. Collective consultation and communication can help with joint learning and problem solving. In addition, collective consultation allows you to make workforce agreements on workplace policies, procedures and the application of some aspects of the law, notably the Working Time Regulations (see chapter 11).

Continued overleaf...

In some circumstances, you may be under a legal obligation to inform and consult your employees (see section on Information and Consultation Regulations below).

Good practice in communication and consultation
Follow the gidelines below in order to show good practice:

- try and act in an open manner, with an open door policy and frequent informal discussions with staff
- encourage staff to give their views and suggestions
- hear what they have to say with an open mind. If your decision is to do nothing, say why. If you have taken up a suggestion, make sure that you tell staff that you have done this and thank the person who suggested it
- make sure that your communications reach all staff, including part-time staff, staff who work from home and other staff who may be overlooked
- as a general principle, be generous in your communication. You cannot over-communicate.

Legal requirements
As an employer, you are required to:

- consult employee representatives over planned collective redundancies and transfers of undertakings (Trade Union and Labour Relations (Consolidation) Act 1992, Transfer of Undertakings (Protection of Employment) (Amendment) Regulations 1987 and Transfer of Undertakings (Protection of Employment) Regulations 2006). See chapters 13 and 14 for further information
- consult safety representatives of recognised trade unions (Safety Representatives and Safety Committees Regulations (SRSCR) 1977)
- consult on health and safety any employees not in groups covered by trade union representatives. You can choose to consult them directly or through elected representatives (Health and Safety (Consultation with Employees) Regulations (HSCER) 1996)
- include in your annual report action that has been taken to inform, consult and involve employees (Companies Act 1985), if you have more than 250 employees
- provide information and consult in certain circumstances (Information and Consultation Regulations 2004). Further information about these Regulations is given later in this chapter.

Staff surveys

One method of finding out about what your employees think is to undertake a staff attitude survey. Staff surveys may be administered by an external organisation, so that your staff feel able to give their opinions in an open and confidential manner. The external organisation will also be able to benchmark the results of your staff survey with similar organisations.

If yours is a very small organisation, you probably won't need to undertake a formal survey, but you may find it useful to hold a meeting, perhaps facilitated by an external person, in which staff are asked to give their views about your organisation.

The areas covered in a staff survey might include:

- the organisation as a place to work
- equality and fairness
- communication
- consultation
- job satisfaction
- appraisal and supervision
- opportunities for development
- pay and benefits
- other areas staff wish to highlight.

Give staff feedback about the outcome of the survey and tell them what you intend to do as a result. Make sure you do what you say you will do, or the whole process is likely to lose credibility.

On the next page is an example survey that you could use as a basis for your own staff survey.

Example staff survey

[Organisation] is keen to be a good employer, with good employment procedures and practices. We want to make sure that we are treating everyone in a fair, honest and open manner.

Please could you answer the following questions, to help us assess how well we are doing. Please tick the relevant box, to indicate how you rate [organisation's] practice in each of the areas listed.

	Very fair	Mostly fair	Often unfair	Very unfair	Don't know
Recruitment and selection					
Training and development					
Induction and probation					
Internal career progression					
Pay and benefits					
Performance review					
Communication and consultation					
Accessibility of buildings					
Opportunities to work flexibly					
Other adjustments made to accommodate individuals					
Handling of disciplinary matters					
Handling of grievance and harassment matters					
Day to day decisions managers make					

Please now provide comments in the box below to support the above answers. Could you give:

• examples of what we have done well
• examples of what we have done less well
• your suggestions on how we could improve.

Thank you for your time. Please now return this survey to............... in the envelope provided. You do not need to put your name on the survey and your responses will be treated in confidence.

'Typically, recognition covers negotiation on pay, conditions of employment, training and health and safety.'

Trade unions and collective bargaining

A trade union is an organisation which exists to support its members at work.

Recognition

A trade union may be recognised in a workplace, which means that the employer agrees to negotiate about certain items. What is negotiated depends on the contents of a recognition agreement. Typically, recognition covers negotiation on pay, conditions of employment, training and health and safety. Recognition agreements may be informal, but a formal, written agreement helps avoid misunderstandings.

The negotiations between union and employer are called collective bargaining and the employees who are covered by collective bargaining are called a bargaining unit.

Whether or not a trade union is recognised in an organisation, individual employees have the following rights:

- to choose to be a member or not to be a member of a trade union. A dismissal which is found to be on the grounds of trade union membership or non-membership is automatically unfair, regardless of an individual's length of service
- to have the right to be accompanied by a trade union representative in formal grievance or disciplinary meetings.

Unions normally also provide benefits to members in addition to their collective bargaining and representational role. They may provide discounted services and products as well as financial and legal advice.

Trade union recognition – voluntary basis

Union recognition can occur on a voluntary basis. This means that the employer and union agree to recognition without using any legal procedures.

Organisations and unions wanting to set up a recognition agreement can gain support from Acas (see contact details at the end of this chapter).

If you are considering voluntary recognition of a trade union, consult carefully with your employees to see what they want. There may be a large number of your workforce who are already members of a particular union, so it may make sense to meet with an official from this union. If there are a smaller number of union members, you could ask officials from different unions who represent members in your area of work to meet with you and your employees. The main unions representing members in the voluntary sector can be found on the TUC's Worksmart website at www.worksmart.org.uk.

Trade union recognition – statutory basis

A trade union can make an application for statutory recognition provided that you, together with any associated employers, employ 21 workers or more.

The union must first submit a written request to you for recognition and you have 10 days from receipt to start negotiations or to refuse the request.

If you refuse the request or no agreement is reached, the union can apply to the Central Arbitration Committee (CAC). The union must be able to show that 10% of workers in your organisation (or in a particular part of it – a bargaining unit) belong to the union and that the majority are likely to favour recognition. If it cannot show this, its application will not be accepted.

The CAC will issue a declaration that the union is recognised for the bargaining unit in question, if:

- the employer accepts that the union enjoys the support of a majority of the workforce or
- the CAC is satisfied that more than 50% of the bargaining unit are members of the union seeking recognition.

If the CAC cannot issue a declaration, it will arrange for a secret ballot of the bargaining unit to be conducted. The union must have support of a majority of those voting in the ballot and at least 40 per cent of those entitled to vote to achieve recognition.

The union must wait three years before making a new application if it fails.

Rights of recognised trade unions

A number of statutory rights arise when a trade union is recognised, including:

- the right to receive certain information from you for collective bargaining purposes
- the right to receive information on health and safety and occupational pension schemes
- the right to paid time off for officials for trade union duties, training and activities
- the right to reasonable time off (which need not be paid) for trade union members during working hours to take part in the activities of the union

- the right to be consulted if your organisation proposes to dismiss as redundant 20 or more employees over a period of 90 days or less
- the right to be consulted and informed about any transfer of the business and, in certain circumstances, the right to be recognised by the new employer
- the right to appoint a safety representative
- rights for Union Learning Representatives to reasonable paid time off to carry out their duties and to undergo training.

In addition, if a union has been recognised by the statutory recognition route (as opposed to voluntary recognition), then there is a legal right to:

- collective bargaining about pay, hours, and holidays as a minimum
- consultation on training
- not to be derecognised for at least three years.

Content of recognition agreements

The recognition agreement should set out procedural arrangements for bargaining.

While collective bargaining agreements are not normally legal documents, the outcome of collective bargaining (such as a pay increase) may be incorporated into employees' contracts of employment and in this way it becomes legally enforceable.

On the next page is an example collective bargaining agreement:

Example collective bargaining agreement

Recognition and procedural agreement between _____

_____Nursing Home_____

_____and UNISON, 1 Mabledon

Place, London WC1H 9AJ

1. DEFINITION OF TERMS

In this Agreement:

The Nursing Home – refers to Nursing Home and Subsidiaries

The Union refers to UNISON

Staff refers to all employees of the Nursing Home

2. COMMENCEMENT DATE

This Agreement commences on

3. OBJECTIVES

3.1 In drawing up this Agreement, the Nursing Home and the Union recognise that the Nursing Home exists to serve its patients. The purpose of this Agreement is to ensure that employment practices in the Nursing Home are conducted to the highest possible standards within the resources available, and that equal opportunities are offered to employees or prospective employees and that the treatment of staff will be fair and equitable in all matters of dispute.

4. GENERAL PRINCIPLES

4.1 The Nursing Home and the Union accept that the terms of this Agreement are binding in honour upon them but do not constitute a legally enforceable agreement.

4.2 The Union recognises the Nursing Home's responsibility to plan, organise and manage the work of the Nursing Home in order to achieve the best possible results in pursuing its overall aims and objectives.

4.3 The Nursing Homes recognises the Union's responsibility to represent the interests of its members and to work for improved conditions of employment for them.

4.4 The Nursing Home and the Union recognise their common interest and joint purpose in furthering the aims and objectives of the Nursing Home and in achieving reasonable solutions to all matters which concern them. Both parties declare their common objective to maintain good employment relations.

5. UNION REPRESENTATION

5.1 The Nursing Home recognises UNISON as the Trade Union with which it will consult and negotiate on all matters set out in Clause 8.2. of this Agreement.

5.2 The Nursing Home will inform all new employees of this Agreement and will encourage them to join the union and provide facilities for them to talk to a representative as part of their induction procedure.

5.3 The Nursing Home accepts that the Union's Members will elect mutually agreeable representatives in accordance with their Union Rules to act as their spokespersons in representing their interests.

5.4 The Union agrees to inform the Nursing Home of the names of all elected representatives in writing within five working days of their election and to inform the Nursing Home in writing of any subsequent changes, each time within five working days of the change having taken place. Persons whose names have been notified to the Nursing Home shall be the sole representatives of the UNISON membership.

5.5 The Nursing Home recognises that Union representatives fulfil an important role and that the discharge of their duties as Union representatives will in no way prejudice their career prospects or employment with the Nursing Home.

6. UNION MEETINGS AND OTHER FACILITIES

6.1 Meetings of Union Members may be held on the Nursing Home premises outside working hours and there shall be no restriction on the frequency or duration of such meetings.

6.2 Union meetings may be held on the Nursing Home premises inside working hours provided that prior consent for such meetings shall be obtained from the Nursing Home by the Union. Such consent shall not be unreasonably withheld. The Union shall provide the Nursing Home with a timetable of regular Union meetings or give at least three working days notice of the intention to hold a meeting as appropriate.

6.3 The Nursing Home agrees to provide reasonable and defined facilities to the Union representatives to enable them to discharge their duties including the provision of a notice board and reasonable use of telephones, photocopiers and computers.

6.4 Subject to at least seven days notice and the agreement of the Nursing Home, Union representatives will be granted special leave without loss of pay to attend training courses run by the Union or other appropriate bodies which are relevant to the discharge of their Union duties.

6.5 Union representatives will be permitted to take reasonable paid time off during working hours to enable them to carry out their duties under this Agreement as provided for under the Trade Union and Labour Relations (Consolidation) Act 1992.

6.6 Subject to reasonable prior notice and the consent of the Nursing Home which shall not unreasonably be withheld, Union representatives will be permitted reasonable time off during working hours for the purpose of taking part in Trade Union activity as defined under the Trade Union and Labour Relations (Consolidation) Act 1992.

6.7 Subject to reasonable prior notice, employees who are Union Learning Representatives may take reasonable time off during working hours to fulfil their role.

6.8 In all other respects, elected Union representatives shall conform to the same working conditions as all other employees.

7. CHECK-OFF SYSTEM

7.1 It is agreed that a check-off system will operate whereby the Nursing Home will deduct Union dues from the salaries of Union Members and pay them to the Union each month with a schedule of payments.

7.2 The Union will co-operate with management in devising and implementing a system to secure the completion of authorisation forms for deduction of subscriptions from salaries. The Union will also afford full co-operation to management in advising members of any increase in subscriptions.

8. JOINT NEGOTIATING COMMITTEE

8.1 The Nursing Home and the Union agree to set up a joint Negotiating Committee consisting of representatives of both sides.

8.2 The joint Negotiating Committee shall be governed by a written constitution which should cover such areas as:

Hours of Work
Holiday and Sickness Arrangements
Pensions
Overall Salary Structure
Pay Awards
Health and Safety
Equal Opportunities Policies
New Technology
Training and Recruitment
Staff Amenities
Redundancy and Redeployment
Disciplinary and Grievance Procedures
Any other item which both sides agree to refer.

9. GRIEVANCE AND DISCIPLINE

9.1 The Nursing Home recognises the Union's right to represent the interests of all or any of its members at any stages during grievance and disciplinary procedures and to call in Union representatives who are not employees of the Nursing Home wherever this is considered appropriate.

9.2 The Nursing Home undertakes to inform the Union representatives immediately of the name of any UNISON staff member faced with disciplinary action to enable the Union to make appropriate arrangements for representation. This information will be limited to the name of the member only.

9.3 Union representatives will be permitted to spend reasonable paid time inside working hours to discuss grievance or disciplinary matters with affected employees.

10. VARIATIONS

10.1 This Agreement may be amended at any time with the consent of both parties.

11. TERMINATION

11.1 The Agreement shall not terminate except by mutual consent.

for UNISON

SIGNED:

DATE:

for Nursing Home

SIGNED:

DATE:

'While management may consult a staff committee, they are under no obligation to act on the feedback they receive.'

Statutory de-recognition

In certain circumstances, an employer may wish to derecognise a union.

There are two main grounds for de-recognition:

- the employer no longer has a workforce of 21 or more workers
- the union no longer has enough support from workers in the bargaining unit – the group of workers the union represents.

There are certain procedures which must be followed in cases of statutory de-recognition. For further information, see www.berr.gov.uk/employment

Dealing with collective disputes

Where a union is recognised, there will normally be a written procedure on how disputes will be dealt with. The example procedure below is from the ACAS advisory handbook for small firms at www.acas.org.uk/media.

Example

Dispute procedures

General principles

The purpose of this agreement is to introduce a procedure to establish a sound and effective relationship between the organisation and the trade union. The union accepts that it is the organisation's responsibility to operate as efficiently as possible and the employer accepts that it is the union's responsibility to protect and further the interests of its members. The organisation and the trade union will make every effort to resolve all differences through negotiation and will refrain from all forms of industrial action until this procedure has been completed.

The negotiating procedure will have three stages

Stage 1

A shop steward may raise an issue with (designated manager). (Designated manager) will meet the shop steward to discuss the matter. Stage 2 will be entered if there has been no agreement within two weeks of the shop steward first raising the issue.

Stage 2

The Chief Executive will meet with the shop steward and full time union officer to discuss the issue. If there is no agreement within six weeks of the shop steward first raising the issue, then the third stage may be entered.

Stage 3 – Third party assistance

The organisation, the trade union or both parties jointly may ask Acas to assist with the resolution of the issue by conciliation. If Acas is unable to help the parties to a conciliated solution, then at the request of both parties jointly, Acas may be asked to appoint an arbitrator. Management and trade union agree to be bound by the arbitrator's decision.

Signed for the organisation:

Signed for the trade union

Other forms of collective employee relations

Organisations which do not recognise trade unions may have either a staff committee or a joint committee.

Staff committee

This is made up of staff representatives elected from amongst the workforce. Depending on the make-up and size of the organisation, there may be more than one committee in an organisation. A staff committee may meet as frequently as needed, such as monthly, quarterly or biannually.

While management may consult a staff committee, they are under no obligation to act on the feedback they receive. This is different from the negotiation that will take place with a recognised trade union.

A staff committee will not normally have independent resources of its own, or access to external expertise. This means it will probably rely on you as an employer to provide employee relations and employment law advice as well as staff training for the representatives.

Joint committee

A joint committee is a consultation committee that includes union and non-union representatives. A joint committee may be set up when management do not wish to enter into a recognition agreement with a union. This may be because there is not enough employee support for full recognition, or where the majority of employees are not union members.

The Information and Consultation Regulations

The Information and Consultation of Employees Regulations 2004 came into effect on 6 April 2007, for organisations with at least 100 employees. From April 2008, the Regulations will also apply to organisations with at least 50 employees.

The Regulations require employers to inform and consult employees in certain circumstances, although the requirement to inform and consult does not operate automatically. It is triggered either by a valid request from employees for an Information and Consultation (I&C) agreement, or by employers choosing to start the process themselves. A valid request from employees consists of a request (or a series of cumulative requests made over a 6 month period) by at least 10% of the employees in the organisation (subject to a minimum of 15 and a maximum of 2,500 employees).

'Whistleblowers who make wider disclosures (eg to the press) may still be protected, but there are certain criteria that must be met.'

If a valid request is received, an employer must enter into negotiations with the workforce on how and on what the employer will inform and consult its workforce in the future. If within 6 months, an agreement has not been reached, a statutory default agreement will come into play. This will have to include the standard information and consultation provisions set out in the Regulations. The standard provisions are that employers will need to inform and consult with employee representatives about:

- the organisation's economic situation
- employment prospects
- decisions likely to lead to substantial changes in work organisation or contractual relations, including redundancies and transfers.

Pre-existing agreements

If there is already a pre-existing agreement approved by employees on information and consultation with the workforce and if a valid employee request is received for a new agreement, the employer may ballot the workforce to ascertain whether it endorses the request by employees. If the employer chooses not to ballot the workforce, they will come under the obligation to negotiate a new agreement.

Where a ballot is held, and 40% of the workforce and a majority of those who vote, endorses the employee request, the employer would come under the obligation to negotiate a new agreement. Where less than 40% of the workforce or a minority of those voting endorses the employee request, the employer does not come under an obligation to negotiate a new agreement, and a three-year moratorium on further employee requests would begin.

To be valid a pre-existing agreement must:

- be in writing
- cover all the employees in the undertaking
- set out how the employer will inform and consult the employees or their representatives. The legislation does not impose any requirements or set any restrictions, on the method, frequency, timing or subject matter of the information and consultation arrangements set up under pre-existing agreements
- be approved by the employees. This would include support indicated by a simple majority among those voting in a ballot of the workforce; a majority of the workforce expressing support through signatures; or the agreement of representatives of employees (including trade union and other appropriate representatives) who represent a majority of the workforce.

Protection for information and consultation representatives

An employee who is an information and consultation representative will be able to:

- claim automatic unfair dismissal if dismissed for carrying out their duties (or in connection with being a candidate for the post)
- complain to an employment tribunal if they suffer a detriment related to their duties.

The Department for Business, Enterprise and Regulatory Reform (DBERR) has produced guidance on the legislation which is available at www.berr.gov.uk/files.

Acas has also produced some good practice advice which is intended to help organisations develop and maintain effective information and consultation arrangements. It is available at www.acas.org.uk.

Public interest disclosure (whistleblowing)

The Public Interest Disclosure Act 1998 gives legal protection from detriment, to workers who disclose information about wrongdoing in their organisations. The term workers includes not only employees but also contractors providing services, most agency workers, home workers and trainees on vocational and work experience schemes.

Detriment may take a number of forms, such as denial of promotion, facilities or training opportunities which the employer would otherwise have offered. Whistleblowers may make a claim to an employment tribunal if they feel that they have suffered such a detriment.

Whistleblowers who are employees are also protected against unfair dismissal. If the dismissal is found by an employment tribunal to be due to making a protected disclosure, it is automatically unfair. Compensation is unlimited and there is no qualifying length of service to make a claim.

The legislation does not give protection to whistleblowers in all circumstances. Protection is only available if the disclosure is a qualifying disclosure and a protected disclosure. The whistleblower must also have made the disclosure in good faith.

Qualifying disclosure

To be a qualifying disclosure, the disclosure has to fall within one of the following areas:

- a criminal offence
- failure to comply with a legal obligation, including a contractual obligation
- miscarriage of justice
- health and safety
- environmental matters
- deliberate concealment of any of the above.

The subject matter of the disclosure can concern matters outside the UK.

A qualifying disclosure needs only to be the reasonable belief of the worker making it. It is not necessary for it to be factually correct.

In respect of failure to comply with a legal obligation, the disclosure will be a qualifying disclosure even if the legal obligation does not exist, provided that the whistleblower was of the belief that the legal obligation existed.

Protected Disclosure

The disclosure must be a protected disclosure. This concerns to whom the qualifying disclosure is made.

The Public Interest Disclosure Act 1998 (PIDA) protects a whistleblower if they raise a concern about wrongdoing internally and in most cases, with an external regulator.

An external regulator might be an organisation such as the Health and Safety Executive or the Commission for Social Care Inspection.

External disclosure:

- must first be raised with the employer or a prescribed person, or
- has not been raised internally because the worker believes evidence would be destroyed or they would be penalised.

The whistleblower must:

- have a genuine belief in the information being disclosed
- not make the disclosure for personal gain
- show it is reasonable to make the disclosure.

Whistleblowers who make wider disclosures (eg to the press) may still be protected, but there are certain criteria that must be met. There must be a belief in the substantial truth of the information; a valid reason for the wider disclosure; the disclosure must be a reasonable step to take; and the disclosure should not be for reasons of personal gain.

Internal procedures

A clear procedure for raising concerns about the organisation can allay fears from both managers and employees that the raising of a serious concern may be mishandled. The employee may be concerned about repercussions on their employment and the employer may be concerned about adverse publicity that could result.

The Chartered Institute of Personnel and Development gives the following advice about a whistleblowing procedure:

What should a whistleblowing procedure contain?

Employers should make clear to employees what to do if they come across malpractice in the workplace. This should encourage employees to inform someone with the ability to do something about the problem. Guidance will need to reflect the circumstances of individual employers, but should make clear that:

*the kinds of actions targeted by the legislation are unacceptable and the employer attaches importance to identifying and remedying malpractice (specific examples of unacceptable behaviour might usefully be included).

*employees should inform their line manager immediately if they become aware that any of the specified actions is happening (or has happened, or is likely to happen).

*in more serious cases (eg if the allegation is about the actions of their line manager), the employee should feel able to raise the issue with a more senior manager, bypassing lower levels of management.

*whistleblowers can ask for their concerns to be treated in confidence and such wishes will be respected.

*employees will not be penalised for informing management about any of the specified actions.

It is preferable to deal with whistle blowing separately, rather than as an extension to or part of an existing grievance procedure, whilst cross-referencing procedures on discipline and grievances.

Source – CIPD Fact sheet on Whistle blowing, February 2007

'The employee may be concerned about repercussions on their employment and the employer may be concerned about adverse publicity that could result.'

Checklist

For further information, go to the website of the Chartered Institute of Personnel and Development (CIPD). There is some useful introductory guidance on whistle blowing and the Public Interest Disclosure Act 1998. It is at www.cipd.co.uk.

There is also a lot of useful information on whistle blowing at the Public Concern at Work website www.pcaw.co.uk.

	Establish regular verbal and written communication and consultation with your employees
	Encourage staff to give their views. Make sure they know their views are valued and taken into account
	Review the Acas advisory booklet on managing conflict at work and then consider if you might deal with confrontation and conflict in new and more effective ways
	Seek feedback from your employees about working in your organisation. Consider undertaking a staff survey
	Recognise a trade union where the majority of your workforce are in favour, ideally following a voluntary, rather than a statutory process
	Establish a clear recognition agreement between your organisation and the trade union
	Give to recognised trade unions the rights afforded to them by law
	As an alternative to trade union recognition (and unless your organisation is very small), consider establishing a staff committee or joint committee
	Adhere to the requirements of the Information and Consultation Regulations. Consider developing with your employees an Information and Consultation agreement, if you do not have one already
	Do not discriminate against individuals on the grounds of trade union membership or non-membership, or on the grounds of being an information and consultation representative
	Make clear to employees, ideally via a brief procedure, how they can raise concerns (whistleblow) if they identify wrong-doing

Further information

The following organisations offer advice and resources about the subjects covered in this chapter to new and existing employers, often free of charge:

Acas
The following publications can be downloaded from the Acas website:

- A leaflet on communicating with your employees
- An advisory booklet about communication and consultation
- An advisory booklet on representation at work
- Information about trade unions and representation

www.acas.org.uk

Business Link
Their website has a section on employee representatives and trade unions.
www.businesslink.gov.uk

Chartered Institute of Personnel and Development (CIPD)
Their website has some useful introductory guidance on whistleblowing and the Public Interest Disclosure Act 1998.
www.cipd.co.uk

Department for Business, Enterprise and Regulatory Reform (DBERR)
Their website has guidance on the Information and Consultation Regulations.
www.berr.gov.uk

National Council for Voluntary Organisations (NCVO)
NCVO has a paid-for publication called You're Not Listening to Me!' which has lots of practical advice on mediation. www.ncvo-vol.org.uk

Public Concern at Work
Their website has information on whistleblowing.
www.pcaw.co.uk

Trades Union Congress
The Trades Union Congress (TUC) is the national organisation which represents trade unions in Britain. It acts as a voice for working people and promotes the rights and welfare of people at work.
www.tuc.org.uk

UK Workforce Hub
The UK Workforce Hub has good practice case studies on employee relations, as well as up to date employment news. Go to www.ukworkforcehub.org.uk.

Worksmart
Their website, run by the TUC, which provides help and information on workplace issues for union and non-union members.
www.worksmart.org.uk

A listing of all the useful organisations referred to in this Good Guide can be found at the back of this book with full contact details.

Thirteen
Redundancy

Whilst this chapter gives an overview of how to handle redundancies, please note that redundancy is one of the most technically complex areas of people management and you may wish to take specialist and/or legal advice.

As far as possible, you will want to ensure job security for your employees. However, sometimes this may not be possible and you may need to make staff redundant.

Legal definition of redundancy

The law says that a redundancy occurs when:

- the employer has ceased, or intends to cease, to carry on the business for the purposes of which the employee was so employed or
- the employer has ceased, or intends to cease, to carry on the business in the place where the employee was so employed or
- the requirements of the business for the employee to carry out work of a particular kind, in the place where they were so employed, has ceased or diminished or are expected to cease or diminish.

Collective consultation

Collective consultation means consulting with employee representatives.

Section 188(1) of the Trade Union Labour Relations (Consolidation) Act states:

'where an employer is proposing to dismiss as redundant 20 or more employees at one establishment within a period of 90 days or less, the employer shall consult about the dismissals all the persons who are appropriate representatives of any of the employees who may be affected by the proposed dismissals or may be affected by measures taken in connection with those dismissals.'

Thus collective consultation is required where you may be making 20 or more employees redundant. You should note that even if you do not end up dismissing 20 employees as redundant, if there is a possibility that this number may end up redundant, you should still undertake collective consultation.

Timing of collective consultation

The law says that the consultation should begin in good time, that is:
- at least 30 days before giving notice of the first dismissal if between 20 and 99 employees are to be dismissed within a 90-day period
- at least 90 days before giving notice of the first dismissal if 100 or more employees are to be dismissed.

Electing representatives

If the affected employees are represented by an independent trade union recognised for collective bargaining purposes (see chapter 12 for further information on trade union representation), you must inform and consult an authorised official of that union. This may be, for example, a shop steward, a district union official or, if appropriate, a national or regional official. You are not required to inform and consult any other employee representatives in such circumstances, but you can do if you wish.

If your organisation does not recognise a trade union, you will need to consult either with existing representatives (for example, a staff or joint committee) or new ones specially elected for the purpose. If you want to consult with existing representatives, their remit and method of election or appointment must give them suitable authority from the employees concerned. Employee representatives elected for the purposes of health and safety, for example, would not give suitable authority.

Continued overleaf...

'There is also a legal onus on you to take all reasonable measures to avoid the need for redundancies.'

There are certain rules on the way the elections must be handled. For further information on these rules, you can refer to document number PL833, Redundancy Consultation and Notification, available from job centres. Alternatively you can download information from the website of the Department for Business, Enterprise and Regulatory Reform (DBERR). Go to www.berr.gov.uk and search for 'redundancy consultation and notification.'

If you give your employees the opportunity to elect representatives and they fail or decide not to do so, then you have fulfilled your obligations and may simply consult with the employees direct.

Fairness

Consultation must be fair, that is, you should meet with the representatives while the redundancy proposals are still at an early stage. They should be given enough information on the proposed redundancies and enough time to digest it before making an informed response. You must genuinely consider their response.

Content of consultation

The following information must be disclosed in writing to employee representatives:

- the reasons for the proposals
- the numbers and descriptions of employees it is proposed to dismiss as redundant
- the total number of employees of any such description employed by the employer at the establishment in question
- the proposed method of selecting the employees who may be dismissed
- the proposed method of carrying out the dismissals, taking account of any agreed procedure, including the period over which the dismissals are to take effect
- the proposed method of calculating any redundancy payments, other than those required by law, that you propose to make.

You could also provide information on:

- arrangements for reasonable time-off with pay to seek alternative work
- assistance with job seeking, such as access to computers, help with writing CVs or completing application forms
- any arrangements to offer voluntary redundancy (see later in this chapter).

The outcome of consultation

You are not obliged to agree with or implement the employee representatives' responses, but the law does require you to consult 'with a view to reaching an agreement'. There is also a legal onus on you to take all reasonable measures to avoid the need for redundancies.

Informing the Department for Business, Enterprise and Regulatory Reform (DBERR)

If you intend to make 20 or more employees redundant, you must also notify the Department for Business, Enterprise and Regulatory Reform (DBERR) in writing. Form HR1 is available from your local Jobcentre Plus for this purpose.

The reason for this advance notification is so that the Department for Business, Enterprise and Regulatory Reform (DBERR) has an opportunity to provide help in finding alternative work or retraining for the employees who may be made redundant.

Notification does not mean the redundancies will necessarily take place, but simply that you foresee a situation where redundancies are likely.

Individual consultation

The minimum time limits for notification are:

- at least 30 days before the first dismissal if between 20 and 99 employees are to be dismissed within a 90-day period
- at least 90 days before the first dismissal if 100 or more employees are to be dismissed within a 90-day period

If you do not notify DBERR in advance of making 20 or more employees redundant, you may incur a fine.

Regardless of whether you have undertaken collective consultation as outlined above, you must always consult individually with affected employees. If you do not, the redundancy dismissal may be found to be unfair if you are taken to an employment tribunal.

The law says that where possible, you should undertake consultation when the proposals are still in their formative stage.

- you should provide adequate information on which affected employees can respond
- you should give a reasonable time (eg at least two weeks) for the consultation process
- you should give conscientious consideration to any points raised

Quite apart from the legal requirements, there are good practice reasons to consult; the Acas guide to Redundancy Handling, available from www.acas.org.uk, states:

'The purpose of consultation is to provide as early an opportunity as practicable for all concerned to share the problem and explore the options. It can stimulate better co-operation between managers and employees, reduce uncertainty and lead to better decision making... representatives or individual employees may be able to suggest acceptable alternative ways of tackling the problem or, if the redundancies are inevitable, ways of minimising hardship'.

Subject of consultation
Individual consultation needs to cover the same areas as collective consultation.

You should put your consultation in writing, as well as meeting with employees to consult with them. A written consultation document can help avoid confusion about what will happen and employees can refer to it after you have met with them.

Continued overleaf...

Who to consult with

You should consult primarily with those whose jobs may be made redundant. However, you should also consult about your proposals with anyone else who may be affected, such as the managers of those who may be made redundant.

Make sure you don't forget people who are absent from work, such as employees on maternity leave or long-term sick leave.

Remember also that redundancy can affect the morale of those who aren't being made redundant. You may want to consider ways you can reassure these employees about their future in your organisation.

Case study – how the Westwich Association undertook consultation concerning a potential redundancy situation

The Westwich Association (the WA) had for some time employed a part time book keeper. The Treasurer, a qualified accountant, had taken responsibility on a voluntary basis for producing management and annual accounts.

As the WA grew, the Treasurer became unable to keep undertaking this work. The WA felt that it would need to pay for accountancy support instead.

Having considered various options, the WA felt that the most appropriate option might be to appoint a part-time financial accountant, who would prepare management and annual accounts as well as undertake all book keeping.

Because their funding was limited, they would not be able to keep on a separate book keeper.

The WA therefore entered into a consultation process with the book keeper about the proposed change and the impact on his job.

First, the General Manager met with the book keeper to explain the situation. She made sure that she met him mid-week, rather than on Friday afternoon, so that he could discuss the situation further with her at work on the following day, if he wished.

She explained:

- That the WA proposed to replace his current post with a more senior post of accountant.

- The reasons for the proposal – that there was a need for accountancy support as the Treasurer was no longer able to undertake this work.

- That should the proposal go ahead, the book keeper could apply for the higher position, but if he were unsuccessful and there were no other suitable alternative employment, his post would be redundant and statutory redundancy pay would be payable.

'Remember also that redundancy can affect the morale of those who aren't being made redundant. You may want to consider ways you can reassure these employees about their future in your organisation.'

- The proposed timescale for change.

At the end of the meeting, she gave the book keeper a letter containing the information she had talked through with him. Here is the letter:

Dear Paul

CONSULTATION ON REDUNDANCY OF YOUR POST

I write to let you know that Westwich Association is proposing a restructuring of the way that financial management and administration is conducted. Up to now, you have undertaken book keeping work, with our Treasurer having responsibility, on a voluntary basis, for producing management and annual accounts. Our Treasurer is no longer able to fulfil this role.

This proposed restructuring will directly affect you, as the proposal is to replace your role with the role of Financial Accountant. This post would prepare management and annual accounts as well as undertake all book keeping. Because our funding is limited, we would not be able to keep on a separate book keeper.

I must stress that at this stage, no firm decisions have been made. This letter is intended to start a formal consultation process with you. You may have thoughts on how we could achieve our objective in different ways and we are genuinely keen to hear these.

Should the proposal go ahead, you will be given the opportunity to apply for the Financial Accountant post and we would discuss with you reasonable training to achieve the requirements of the role.

Should you be unsuccessful in applying for the accountant post, you would be entitled to redundancy pay at statutory levels.

I and the Trustees would like your response within two weeks of today, ie (date). I am happy to discuss the matter with you at any time during the two week consultation period.

At the end of the two weeks, we will take a decision on how to proceed. Should the proposal to replace your job go ahead, we will continue to consult with you throughout the process.

I appreciate that this is an uncertain time and would like to take this opportunity to thank you for all the good work you do. This proposal is in no way connected with the quality of your work.

Yours sincerely

Freda Platt
General Manager

'Some organisations select individuals for redundancy on the basis of last in, first out. You are advised to avoid such criteria, or only use them if they can be objectively justified.'

Measures to avoid or minimise redundancy

You should make every effort to avoid or minimise redundancies. For example, if you know your funding will decrease and you will need to reduce the number of paid staff, you could:

- restrict the recruitment of permanent employees, either to new or to vacant posts
- reduce the use of temporary employees
- fill vacancies, where possible, from amongst existing employees
- reduce (with agreement) the hours of work of existing employees.

Make sure you consult with employees about your plans to minimise redundancies. They may have some useful suggestions.

Selection process

If, having taken steps to avoid or minimise redundancies, the number of employees still exceeds requirements, redundancy may occur.

If there is only one post that you propose to make redundant, for example because the funding for that post is coming to an end, then it will normally be clear that the person in that post should be redundant.

In other circumstances, such as if you have two staff doing the same job and in the future you only need one, you will need to apply selection criteria.

You should have clear and published selection criteria for redundancy. Selection criteria might simply be along the lines of an assessment of the suitability of an individual's skills, experience and potential for the remaining posts. You might also take into account the individual's disciplinary record or attendance record. However, if you take into account attendance, care should be taken to exclude any periods of absence that relate to maternity and you should also make sure that you do not treat disabled people any less favourably than non-disabled people. You will need to score employees against the selection criteria, in order to come to a decision about who to make redundant.

Some organisations select individuals for redundancy on the basis of last in, first out. You are advised to avoid such criteria, or only use them if they can be objectively justified. This is because the practical effect of these criteria may be that younger workers are more likely to be selected for redundancy, This could be found to be age discrimination. In addition, female employees tend to take more breaks in employment than male employees, and therefore tend to have shorter service with an employer. This could give rise to a claim of sex discrimination.

Do not use part-time status as a selection criterion. This would be unlawful discrimination against part-time workers. Given that more women tend to take part-time work than men, it could also amount to sex discrimination.

Do not discriminate against an employee who is pregnant. Apply exactly the same selection criteria as for other employees. If an employee is on maternity leave, make sure that you still include her in the selection process and do not forget to consult with her about the proposed redundancies.

Suitable alternative employment

You should not select someone for redundancy because you consider that it is time for them to retire. This would not be a valid selection criterion and would be discriminatory on the grounds of age. There are separate procedures for retirement – please see chapter 16 for further information.

Where possible, try and redeploy otherwise redundant employees to suitable alternative work in your organisation. If you employ only a few people, there may be few opportunities for alternative employment, but make sure you still consider all available options with each affected employee.

If there is alternative employment, it will be considered to be suitable alternative employment if it is at broadly the same level, with similar duties, hours and terms and conditions.

If you can offer alternative employment, you need to put the offer in writing, showing how the new employment differs from the old. You need to make the offer before the employment under the previous contract ends. In accordance with the law, the new job should start either immediately after the end of the old job or after an interval of not more than four weeks.

Any employee who is under notice of redundancy has a legal right to a trial period of four weeks in the alternative job. The trial period begins when the previous contract has ended.

The effect of the trial period is to give the employee a chance to decide whether the new job is suitable without necessarily losing the right to a redundancy payment. This trial period can be extended for retraining purposes by an agreement which is in writing, specifies the date on which the trial period ends and sets out the employee's terms and conditions after it ends.

As the employer, you should also use the trial period to assess the employee's suitability. Should you or the employee feel that they are unsuitable for the post, the employee will normally preserve the right to the redundancy payment under the old contract.

However, if the employee unreasonably refuses the alternative employment (either before the trial period or at any time during it), they may lose any entitlement to redundancy pay. Unreasonable refusal might be where the difference between the old and new jobs is negligible or where the employee rejects the changes a new job might involve, before investigating whether they are feasible. The burden of showing that an employee was unreasonable in refusing to accept suitable alternative employment generally lies with the employer.

Continued overleaf...

If the only available alternative employment is at a lower salary level, then the employee should still be offered it, if they have the relevant skills and knowledge. The employee may prefer this to redundancy. However, in this circumstance, a refusal to take the lower paid job would be reasonable and the employee would still be entitled to redundancy pay.

Voluntary redundancy

Sometimes in a redundancy situation, an employer may ask for volunteers for redundancy or individuals may come forward to volunteer for redundancy.

You can agree to voluntary redundancy if the remaining workforce have the skills and experience you need for the organisation in the future. However, if the skills of the person volunteering are still required in the organisation, and no one else has these skills, you would be reasonable to refuse the request for voluntary redundancy.

Statutory dismissal procedure

If, after consultation, you feel that certain redundancies are necessary, you must follow the statutory dismissal procedure. (NB however, that you do not have to follow the statutory dismissal procedure in a collective redundancy situation, that is, if you intend to make 20 or more employees redundant).

The statutory dismissal procedure is as follows:

Step one – written statement
You must send or give a letter to the employee, stating that the employee's post has been selected for redundancy, the reasons for this, and inviting the employee to a meeting to discuss the situation. You must give reasonable notice of the date of the meeting.

Your letter must include a full statement of circumstances which led you to contemplate the dismissal on grounds of redundancy. If you have gone through a selection process (see above), you should also include details of the selection pool and the employee's scores awarded against the selection criteria.

Step two – meeting
You should discuss the proposed redundancy with the employee. You should discuss suitable alternative work that the employee may be interested in.

'Meetings should allow both employer and employee to explain their cases.'

You should give the employee the opportunity to state their point of view at the meeting.

You should confirm when the employee's employment will end and how much notice will be worked.

You should explain the appeals process, requirements during the notice period and time off provisions.

You should follow up the meeting with a redundancy notification letter.

Step three – appeal
The employee must inform you if they wish to appeal on the grounds of unfair selection for redundancy. You can set a reasonable time limit for receipt of the appeal eg 5 working days from the date of your letter confirming the outcome of stage 2.

You should then:

- invite the employee to attend a further meeting
- arrange for the appeal meeting to be chaired by another manager (more senior if possible) or a panel of trustees who were not involved in the original decision to dismiss on grounds of redundancy
- give the employee the opportunity to state their view at the meeting
- adjourn the meeting to consider what the employee has said

- communicate the final decision to the employee in writing, after the meeting and not at the end of the meeting. This means you have time to consider all information carefully and there is less pressure and likelihood of a reactive decision.

The law says that in following the above 3-step process:

- each step and action should be taken without unreasonable delay
- the timing and location of meetings should be reasonable
- meetings should allow both employer and employee to explain their cases
- the employee may be accompanied at both the original and the appeal meeting by a colleague or trade union representative. If you wish, you may allow the employee to bring a friend or family member instead of a colleague or trade union representative.

Notice of redundancy

If, having met with the employee in accordance with the statutory procedure and as outlined above, you decide to confirm the employee's redundancy, you will need to issue the employee with written notice of redundancy. You can issue this notice, even if the employee has appealed against the redundancy and the appeal meeting has not yet taken place.

This notice should state the employee's last day of service with your organisation and the redundancy payments that will be made (see next section in this chapter).

The employee is entitled to the statutory notice of one week's notice after 1 month's service up to 2 years, then 2 weeks notice after 2 years, 3 weeks notice after 3 years, and so on up to a maximum of 12 weeks notice after 12 years service. If the employee's contract states a notice entitlement above the statutory amount, then this higher notice must be given.

Continued overleaf...

'Redundancy payments are, according to current legislation, free of tax and National Insurance up to a maximum of £30,000.'

Redundancy payments

Sometimes, it may not be possible to give full notice. This may be because the work will run out before the employee's notice period expires. If it is not possible for notice to be given, pay in lieu of any unexpired period of notice can be added to the final redundancy payment. Pay in lieu of notice is, according to current legislation, free of tax and national insurance, provided that there is no provision for pay in lieu in the contract of employment. If however the employee's contract of employment specifically states that pay in lieu may be given instead of actual notice, then the payment is deemed to be a contractual payment and as such is subject to tax and national insurance.

Statutory redundancy pay is payable to employees who have at least two years' continuous service.

Statutory redundancy pay is not payable to an employee who is offered suitable alternative employment before the date on which redundancy is due to take place but unreasonably refuses that employment.

You must fund the payments from your organisation's funds; the government does not reimburse you for these payments.

Amount of payment

Payment is as follows, for each complete year of service, up to a maximum of 20 years:

- for each year of service at under age 22 – half a week's pay
- for each year of service at age 22 but under 41 – one week's pay
- for each year of service at age 41 or over– one and a half week's pay.

Please note that since the introduction of the Age Discrimination Regulations in 2006, employees of 65 and above and employees aged under 18 are entitled to redundancy pay. This was not previously the case.

A week's pay

The government says that the maximum payable as a week's pay is £330 (as at 1 February 2008). This means that employers do not by law have to pay more than £330, even if the employee's weekly pay is more than this (however, some organisations choose to pay more, see section below on enhanced redundancy provisions).

If an employee's weekly pay is less than £330, then you should pay this lesser amount.

You should calculate a week's pay based on the employee's contractual entitlement at the date on which you give the minimum notice to which the employee is entitled.

You can use a ready reckoner for calculating redundancy payments if you go to the website of the Department for Business, Enterprise and Regulatory Reform (DBERR) website at www.berr.gov.uk and type 'redundancy ready reckoner' in the search box.

Redundancy payments are, according to current legislation, free of tax and National Insurance up to a maximum of £30,000.

Holidays accrued but not yet taken should also be paid on termination of employment. Holiday pay is subject to tax and National Insurance.

Assistance with job seeking

Employees who are under notice of redundancy and have been continuously employed for at least two years have a legal right to reasonable time off to look for work or to arrange for training for new employment.

Leaving before the expiry of notice

The law states that during an individual's period of contractual or statutory notice, they can write to their employer to say that they wish to leave early. The employer needs to write back within 7 days and either agree (in which case redundancy payments would be made) or state that it is not operationally feasible for the employee to leave early. For example, if the individual has 5 years service, they would be entitled under law to 5 weeks' notice. Their contract may say less or more than this (eg 4 weeks or 8 weeks). The higher of these notice periods is the one that needs to be taken into account.

If an individual wishes to leave early during a period of extended redundancy notice (for example, if you are giving more notice of redundancy than their contract or statute requires) then there is no entitlement to receive redundancy pay.

Enhanced redundancy provisions

You could consider enhancing your redundancy provisions beyond legal requirements in the following ways:

- offer employees the opportunity for collective consultation, even where not legally required
- arrange for longer than 4 weeks as a trial period in suitable alternative employment. However, make sure that this extension of the trial period is agreed by both parties
- when going through the statutory dismissal procedures, allow the employee to be accompanied by a friend or family member, as an alternative to the legal right to be accompanied by a colleague or trade union representative
- give as long notice of redundancy as possible – longer than statutory or contractual requirements where you can
- allow all employees, including those with less than 2 years service, to have time off for job seeking
- contact other employers with a view to canvassing for any vacancies which may be suitable for the redundant employees
- contact the local job centre to inform them of the skills and abilities of your redundant employees
- consider providing redundancy guidance/counselling, which might include: guidance on how to find another job; advice on completion of application forms; guidance on attending interviews

- make enhanced redundancy payments if you can. If you wish to make enhanced redundancy payments, you should note that any age brackets you use should be the same as the statutory scheme, in order to avoid falling foul of age discrimination legislation. These age brackets are outlined earlier in this chapter and are: under age 22; age 22 to under age 41; age 41 and over. So, for example, you could use the age brackets of the statutory scheme, but give one week's actual pay per year of service, rather than only paying up to the statutory maximum for a week's pay
- be as flexible as possible in allowing staff to leave, with no loss of redundancy pay, before the expiry of notice.

'You should note that the termination of a fixed-term contract is also considered to be a redundancy situation in law.'

Disabled employees

If a disabled person may be affected by redundancy, you may need to make adjustments to your redundancy and redeployment processes. You will need to consult with the disabled employee and if needed take advice. Here are some examples of what you may need to do.

Make adjustments to the consultation process
If one of your employees is visually impaired, for example, you may need to provide the consultation document in larger text or on a tape.

If one of your employees has a learning disability, you may need to ensure that the language you use is accessible and you may need to provide the consultation document on tape. You may also need to arrange for a supporter to assist the employee during the consultation process.

Make adjustments to the selection process
If you have an employee with chronic fatigue syndrome (ME), you may need to adjust the selection process so that the individual can rest between, for example, an interview and a written test.

Make adjustments to any possible alternative job
You will need to consider a disabled person's suitability for an alternative job after any reasonable adjustments have been applied. It would not be appropriate, for example, to disallow a disabled employee who could not drive, if adjustments could be made to the job or the way the job was carried out, to remove the requirement to drive.

Employees on fixed term contracts

You should note that the termination of a fixed-term contract is also considered to be a redundancy situation in law. You may have fixed-term contracts where, for example, you have limited funding for a particular project.

Consultation on redundancy in this circumstance may be less than in other cases, because the employee will be aware that the term of their post is coming to an end. However, you will still need to consult with the employee about matters such as:

- any ideas they have for keeping the post going
- possible alternative employment
- any ways of minimising hardship to them.

You will also need to follow the statutory dismissal procedure and, if the employee has two years service or more, you must pay redundancy payments.

You can find a case study about the termination of a fixed term contract in chapter 4.

Checklist

	Give early warning of possible redundancy situations. Consult collectively where the law requires. Always consult with individuals
	Select fairly for redundancy based on published criteria. Ensure selection for redundancy does not discriminate directly or indirectly against a particular group of employees based on their gender, maternity status, religion, race colour, ethnic or national origins, disability, age or sexual orientation
	Consider ways to minimise or avoid redundancies, for example by reducing the use of temporary staff, redeployment or reducing (with agreement) hours of work
	Consider whether any suitable alternative employment exists and if so, offer it to otherwise redundant employees
	Provide redundancy guidance/counselling, if possible, for employees selected for redundancy
	Accept voluntary redundancies where possible
	Follow statutory dismissal procedures when making staff redundant
	Give employees selected for redundancy their notice entitlement
	Make redundancy payments where applicable
	Allow employees under notice of redundancy to leave early if possible
	Make suitable and reasonable adjustments throughout the process for disabled employees
	Prepare p45 certificates for all departing employees

Further information

The following organisations offer advice and resources about the subjects covered in this chapter to new and existing employers, often free of charge:

Acas
The following publication can be downloaded from the Acas website:

• Advisory Booklet – Redundancy Handling
www.acas.org.uk

Business link
Their website has information on its website about redundancy.
www.businesslink.gov.uk

Department for Business, Enterprise and Regulatory Reform (DBERR)
Their website has several documents on redundancy.
www.berr.gov.uk

HM Revenue and Customs
Their website has information on the tax treatment of redundancy.
www.hmrc.gov.uk

National Council for Voluntary Organisations (NCVO)
www.ncvo-vol.org.uk

A listing of all the useful organisations referred to in this Good Guide can be found at the back of this book with full contact details.

Fourteen
TUPE Transfers

This chapter gives introductory guidance. However, the TUPE Regulations are complex and their application will be different in each circumstance. The implications of failing to fully understand or comply with the TUPE regulations are very serious. It is very strongly recommended that you seek legal and/or HR advice if you are involved in the transfer of an undertaking.

This chapter is about a particularly technical area of employing people – TUPE transfers. This is when a project or service transfers into, or out of, your organisation. There are a number of legal obligations that arise in these circumstances. These obligations are set out in The Transfer of Undertakings (Protection of Employees) Regulations 1981 and 2006 ('TUPE').

Overview of TUPE Regulations

In the voluntary sector, funding for particular projects is often for a limited period of time. At the end of the funding period, the funding may be renewed, may cease, or the funding and responsibility for the project may pass to another organisation.

Voluntary sector organisations may also change in other ways. For example, one organisation may be taken over by another, or two organisations with similar charitable objectives may merge.

In the above situations where the transfer of a project, organisation or part of an organisation takes place, responsibility for the employees and all employment rights and liabilities is taken on by the new employer. This is called a Transfer of an Undertaking. The transferring employees will retain their original terms and conditions of employment, including their salary levels and benefits.

Do not assume that TUPE does not apply because you are a small charity. TUPE applies:

- regardless of whether an organisation operates to make a profit or has purely charitable objectives

- regardless of the size of the organisation (TUPE can involve just one employee).

The TUPE Regulations only cover employees and not volunteers. However, good practice in respect of volunteers who are affected by a transfer is covered later in this chapter.

The effects of TUPE

Below is a summary of the effects of TUPE:

- all employees employed in the undertaking to be transferred automatically become employees of the new employer (the transferee). An employer cannot pick and choose which employees to take on

- employees must transfer on the same terms and conditions (contracts of employment) as they had with their former employer (the transferor), except for certain occupational pension rights. Length of service is also maintained from the former employer

- the new employer takes over all liabilities (eg unfair dismissal or discrimination claims) arising from the contracts of employment, except for criminal liabilities

- any liabilities relating to employees who were dismissed before the transfer (for a reason connected with it) also transfer to the transferee. So if the transferor were to dismiss an employee immediately before the transfer, to avoid the employee having to transfer, the liability for unfair dismissal would fall to the transferee

Continued overleaf...

- any collective agreements made with recognised trade unions and any recognition agreements where the business retains a distinct identity following the transfer will also transfer
- there is special protection against dismissal. Employees who are transferred cannot, in most circumstances, be dismissed, if the dismissal is in connection with the transfer
- of course, the above provision does not mean that an employer cannot dismiss in any circumstances – a case of gross misconduct, for example, would warrant dismissal. A dismissal in this case would be for misconduct, not on account of the transfer
- employees may object to the transfer or resign and claim unfair dismissal if the transfer involves a detrimental change in their working conditions or terms of employment.

Determining whether TUPE applies

The 2006 TUPE Regulations have broadened the circumstances where the legislation will apply and there are only limited exceptions. Where the activities of the transferring organisation or service (undertaking) remain broadly similar after transfer, TUPE will apply to all:

- contracting-out exercises
- changes of service provider and
- contracting-in exercises.

TUPE may not apply if there is a single specific event or a task of short-term duration.

If you are in doubt as to whether TUPE may apply, you should take legal or human resources advice. It is wise not to simply accept the view of the other party to the transfer, or the view of the funding authority.

Managing the transfer process

Once you are in the process of managing a transfer, whether into or out of your organisation, there are certain obligations on you. The exact obligations will depend on whether you are the transferee or the transferor.

Obligations on the transferor to provide information to the transferee

If you are a transferor, you are obliged to give the transferee written information before the transfer about employees who are to transfer and all rights and obligations towards them. The information that must be provided is stated in the box opposite.

Information that must be provided by the transferor
*The identity and age of the employees who will transfer
*Information contained in the employees' written particulars of employment under section 1 of the Employment Rights Act 1996 (ie, the employee's 'contracts of employment')
*Information on any collective agreements affecting the employees that will apply after the transfer
*Information about any disciplinary proceedings taken against the employees or grievances brought by them in the last two years
* Information about any claims brought by the employees against the transferor in the last two years
* Information about any claims that the transferor reasonably believes might be brought.

The information should be given at least 14 days before the transfer or as soon as is reasonably practicable. The information must be no more than two weeks old. Clearly, it would be good practice, and helpful to the transferee, if the information is provided earlier than 14 days before the transfer is due to take effect. If you are the transferee, you may find it helpful to agree with the transferor an earlier date by which the information will be provided.

Once the relevant information has been provided, the transferor must provide written notification of any changes which occur up until the actual completion of the transfer.

One point to be aware of is to be absolutely clear which employees you believe to be involved in the transfer. Particular note should be taken of those employees who are temporarily assigned to the service or undertaking to transfer, or who work part of their time elsewhere. Advice should be taken if you are not sure which employees should and should not transfer.

If, as transferor, you do not provide the required statutory information, the transferee may apply to an employment tribunal for compensation. Compensation starts at a minimum of £500 for each employee in respect of whom the information was not provided or was defective.

Obligations to inform representatives of affected employees

The Regulations place a duty on both the transferor and transferee employers to inform and consult representatives of their own employees who may be affected by the transfer. Affected employees might include:

- those individuals who are to be transferred
- their colleagues in the transferor employer who will not transfer but whose jobs might be affected by the transfer
- their new colleagues in employment with the transferee whose jobs might be affected by the transfer (such as a manager who will be required to manage the transferee employees).

Continued overleaf...

'It would be good practice for the transferring employees, their representative(s) and their manager, to meet with the managers of the transferee organisation'

The information that must be given is outlined below.

> **Information that must be provided to employee representatives**
> Long enough before a relevant transfer to enable the employer to consult with the employees' representatives, the employer must inform the representatives:
>
> • that the transfer is going to take place, approximately when, and why
>
> • the legal, economic and social implications of the transfer for the affected employees
>
> • whether the employer envisages taking any action (reorganisation for example) in connection with the transfer which will affect the employees, and if so, what action is envisaged
>
> • the previous employer must also disclose to employee representatives whether the prospective new employer envisages carrying out any action (measures) which will affect the employees, and if so, what, eg change of uniform or office location. The new employer must give the previous employer the necessary information so that the previous employer is able to meet this requirement.

In reality, the employees to transfer may wish to know a lot more than the above information. For example, they may want to meet the managers of their new organisation and their new colleagues. The more the transferor and transferee organisations can co-operate, the smoother will be the transfer.

It would be good practice for the transferring employees, their representative(s) and their manager, to meet with the managers of the transferee organisation, to discuss the above. This direct communication with employees could be in addition to the statutory information that needs to be provided to workplace representatives. However, you should discuss and agree this approach with workplace representatives first, so that the possibility of miscommunication is minimised.

Obligations of both transferor and transferee to consult
Where actions (measures) are proposed in relation to affected employees, the present employer of these employees must consult with the appropriate representatives in good time before the transfer. An action might include a proposed change of rota arrangements or management structure, for example. No exact time is specified in the Regulations, although from an employee relations point of view, it is good practice to consult at the earliest opportunity. Actions, or measures mean any alteration to the status quo, such as proposals to change work location or to restructure.

If no actions are envisaged, then there is no obligation to consult, only to inform (see above).

The consultation on any actions to be taken must be with a view to seeking agreement. During the consultation, the employer must consider and respond to any representations made by the representatives. If the employer rejects these representations, the employer must also give reasons.

Appropriate representatives

The Regulations state that consultation should be with appropriate representatives of employees.

If your organisation recognises an independent trade union, the appropriate representatives will normally be trade union representatives. In the event that there is no recognition agreement, or any other elected consultation forum for consultation, you are required to make arrangements for employees to elect representatives for consultation purposes. This may seem inappropriate to you if the project to transfer only has, say, 3 employees. However, in practice, it is not as complicated as it seems and it is crucial that the affected employees are invited to elect a representative. Failure to do so may result in an employment tribunal claim for your failure to comply with the obligation to inform and consult.

If there is no recognised union and there are no employee representatives, you must invite employees to elect a representative or representatives for the purpose of conducting the TUPE information and consultation process. If the employees then fail to do so within a reasonable time, you must provide the relevant information to each affected employee individually. There is no obligation under TUPE to consult individually with each of the employees affected by the transfer. However there is nothing to stop you consulting with them individually and it is good practice to do so. So in the above case of 3 employees, the options are either that the employees elect one of themselves to be a representative, or if they fail to do so, you will provide the relevant information to each affected employee individually.

Further information about electing representative and about the rights of representatives is contained in a publication from the Department for Business, Enterprise and Regulatory Reform (DBERR): A Guide to the 2006 TUPE Regulations for Employees, Employers and Representatives, available from the DBERR website at www.berr.gov.uk/employment.

Failure to comply with the information and consultation regulations

The transferor and transferee are jointly and severally liable for any award of compensation made by an employment tribunal for failure to inform and consult.

Any possible award of compensation would be triggered by an employment tribunal claim raised by employee representatives or, in some cases, employees. The award is of up to 13 weeks' actual pay per employee. This is not subject to the statutory cap (as of 1 February 2008 £330 per week).

Due diligence

Due diligence is the process of checking out the transferring organisation or service. In particular, you will want to know about any liabilities that may transfer to you.

Earlier in this chapter, we have outlined that the transferor must provide certain statutory information to the transferee. However, this statutory information will not normally be enough to undertake full due diligence. Below are some other areas you may wish to review in your process of due diligence (please note this is not an exhaustive list):

- details of redundancy payments in excess of the statutory norms
- whether employer pensions contributions are up to date
- any current matters that may lead to a disciplinary case against an employee
- any outstanding employee loans
- details of those employees currently on maternity, adoption or paternity leave

- details of employees who are on sick leave
- details of individual promises, eg of promotion or ex-gratia payments, that may have been made
- information concerning staff who have signed opt-out agreements under the Working Time Regulations (see Chapter 11)
- confirmation that all staff (where relevant) have had CRB checks
- a copy of all personnel policies, including a statement of whether or not they are deemed to be contractual.

You are advised to seek legal advice on the due diligence areas you need to cover for your particular transfer.

Points of detail about TUPE

Below are a number of points of detail that may apply to the TUPE situation you are dealing with.

Pensions Act 2004

Occupational pension rights earned up to the time of the transfer are protected by social security legislation and pension trust arrangements.

Strictly speaking, ongoing pension provisions do not transfer under TUPE (although retirement-related terms and conditions such as the right to early retirement may transfer).

You do not therefore need to provide exactly the same pension as before, but the Pensions Act 2004 states certain minimum requirements. It states that where transferred employees were entitled to participate in an occupational pension scheme prior to the transfer, the transferee employer must establish a minimum level of pension provision for the transferred employees. This minimum safety net requires the transferee to match employee contributions, up to 6 per cent of salary, into a stakeholder pension, or offer an equivalent alternative. Further information on these aspects of the Pensions Act can be found on the Department for Work and Pensions (DWP) website: www.dwp.gov.uk.

Local authority and health authority transfers

If you are accepting employees who have local authority or health authority contracts, then the government requires transferee employers to provide a broadly comparable pension arrangement.

Many voluntary sector organisations do not have pension provisions that are broadly comparable with the generous public sector final salary pension schemes.

If your organisation does not have such a broadly comparable scheme, then you can apply for directions status (in respect of NHS transfers) or an admissions agreement (in respect of a local authority). This allows the transferring staff to remain in their NHS or local authority pension scheme after the transfer, although you as the employer would need to make the relevant contributions to the scheme.

A word of caution, though – make sure that the funding in the transfer agreement covers:

- your ongoing contributions into the pension scheme
- any additional administrative charge applied to the scheme
- indemnities to cover any past service deficit relating to service by employees in the scheme prior to the transfer

- indemnities to cover any additional costs relating to ill health retirement or early retirement on protected redundancy terms.

Trade union recognition

There are a number of scenarios that may occur with trade unions:

Neither employer recognise a trade union

There are no particular TUPE issues that arise in this scenario. The transferee employer continues to deal directly with employees.

Both employers recognise the same trade union

The same trade union will continue to be recognised post-transfer, for the service that is transferring. Note, however, that there will be two different recognition agreements (that of the transferor and the one that the transferee already has in place for its staff). It is appropriate to review the agreements and consider whether a single agreement can be reached.

The transferor employer does not recognise a trade union, but the transferee employer does

In this case, the transferee employer can invite employees in the transferring service to join the trade union and, if they wish, to be covered by collective bargaining.

The transferor employer recognises a trade union, but the transferee employer: either does not recognise a trade union; or recognises a different union.

Where the transferor employer voluntarily recognises an independent trade union in respect of some or all of the transferred employees, then at the point of transfer, the transferee employer will also be required to recognise that union to the same extent. It is, however, open to the transferee employer to then initiate a process of de-recognition, in the same way that any employer could de-recognise. See chapter 12 for derecognition process.

However, this requirement to recognise the union of the transferring employees only applies if the organised grouping of transferred employees maintains an identity distinct from the remainder of the transferee's business. If there is no distinct identity, the previous trade union recognition lapses, and it will then be up to the union and the employer to renegotiate a new recognition arrangement.

'A desire to harmonise the terms and conditions of existing and newly-transferred staff in your organisation is not a legitimate ground for changing terms and conditions.'

Dismissal of employees for a reason connected with the transfer

A dismissal of an employee by either the transferor or transferee because of the transfer will be automatically unfair unless there is an economic, technical or organisational (ETO) reason entailing changes in the workforce.

This means that a dismissal may only occur before or after a transfer where the sole or principal reason is either:

- entirely unconnected with the transfer or
- connected with the transfer, but for an ETO reason.

Examples of ETO reasons for dismissal include:

Economic reasons
where the demand for a service has fallen to such an extent that the service becomes unsustainable without dismissing staff

Technical reasons
where the transferee wishes to use new technology and the staff employed by the transferor in the entity do not have the requisite skills

Organisational reasons
where the transferee operates at a different location and it is not practical to transfer staff.

As with any dismissal, an employer must act reasonably and follow a fair procedure. Please note that employees with less than one year's service cannot present unfair dismissal claims under TUPE, as employment protection rights have not been accrued. Claims for discrimination, for example on the grounds of race, sex, disability etc, can however be made.

Changing terms and conditions for a reason connected with the transfer

The changing of an employee's terms and conditions for a reason connected with the transfer is prohibited under TUPE. A desire to harmonise the terms and conditions of existing and newly-transferred staff in your organisation is therefore not a legitimate ground for changing terms and conditions.

If there is a need to change the terms and conditions of employees for a reason related to the transfer, this is only possible if there is an economic, technical or organisational (ETO) reason that also entails changes to the workforce.

The change might be a change to the numbers of employees employed or their functions. For example, a functional change might be a new requirement on an employee who held a non-managerial position to move to a managerial position – or vice-versa. This may be considered to be a valid ETO reason justifying the change of terms and conditions.

In practice, the ETO circumstances where you could change terms and conditions are quite limited. Even if there is a valid ETO reason, the employee's agreement to changing the terms and conditions still needs to be gained. An employee may only agree to a change in terms and conditions if the new terms are equal to or better than, their existing terms. If you are contemplating changing terms and conditions for an ETO reason as outlined above, then you will need to consult with the employee and gain agreement to the change.

Insolvency

If you acquire all or part of an organisation that was insolvent, there are special rules that apply which are designed to make it easier to rescue aspects of insolvent organisations. Changes to terms and conditions may be agreed even where there are no economic, technical or organisational (ETO) reasons. There are certain conditions. The changes:

- must be designed to safeguard employment opportunities by ensuring the survival of the undertaking
- must be agreed with appropriate representatives of the employees and
- must not contravene UK law, for example the Working Time Regulations.

Employees with public sector contracts of employment

If the employees transferring to your organisation have public sector contracts, then specific rules apply. These are set out in the Code of Practice on Workforce Matters in Public Sector Service Contracts. The Code is intended to prevent a two tier workforce within a particular project, where transferred staff may be on better terms and conditions than staff recruited subsequently into that project.

The Code says that if you recruit new employees into a project, these employees must be offered terms and conditions of employment which are overall no less favourable than those of the transferred employees.

These requirements may lead to increased costs for your organisation in running the project, so it is really important that you are aware of the costs in advance and agree appropriate funding to be able to meet these costs.

Please note that the Code applies both to service transfers from the public sector and to second generation transfers between non-public sector employers. To see the full Code, use the following link: http://archive.cabinetoffice.gov.uk/ opsr/workforce_reform/code_of_ practice/index.asp.

Volunteers

The Transfer of Undertakings Regulations relate to employment and therefore do not cover volunteers. However, if there are volunteers in the service that is to be transferred, consider the following:

- if you are the transferor, consult with the volunteers about what they want. Do they wish to continue volunteering in the service, once it has transferred, or do they wish to stay with your organisation? Speak with the transferee organisation about the wishes of the volunteers and arrange a meeting between the transferee and the volunteers.
- if you are the transferee, consider how you might welcome volunteers who wish to continue volunteering in the service. Make sure they know of any changes and feel valued for their contribution.

Case study – TUPE transfer

The Westwich Association has been providing youth work services in Westwich for several years now.

In the neighbouring town, Westport, there is a similar but smaller charity, called Westport Y. Westport Y has two paid youth workers who are managed by a management committee.

Discussions have been going on for some time about how the two separate charities could work better together. It is felt that there are economies of scale in employing all the staff within one organisation. In addition, the trustees at Westport Y are finding the demands of employing the two youth workers to be higher than the time they have available to do it.

A decision is therefore taken in June 2007 that the Westwich Association will change its name to the Westwich and Westport Association and that Westport Y will cease to exist. The two youth workers from Westport Y will transfer to the Westwich and Westport Association as their new employer. It is intended that the transfer will take effect from 1 January 2008.

The two charities agree that the transfer falls under the TUPE regulations, as the service that will be provided by the two youth workers after transfer will be the same as the service provided prior to the transfer.

The process is managed as follows:

As the transferor, Westport Y gives the Westwich Association the statutory information about the two employees who are to transfer. This includes details of their terms and conditions of employment (see earlier in this chapter for the full list of statutory information).

The legal requirement is to give this statutory information at least 14 days in advance of the transfer. However, Westport Y provides the information much earlier than this – as soon as the decision is taken that a transfer will take place.

The Westwich Association and Westport Y are required to inform and consult the representatives of their own employees who may be affected by the transfer.

Both organisations give their employees the opportunity to elect representatives. The employees state that, given the small numbers of people involved, they do not wish to elect representatives, but for consultation to be with them directly. Since the employees have failed to elect representatives there is no obligation under TUPE to consult individually with each of the employees affected by the transfer, only an obligation to provide the relevant information to each affected employee individually. However both organisations agree to consult with the employees directly.

Consultation then proceeds. Westport Y consults with its two employees, the two youth workers.

The Westwich Association informs and consults with the following staff:

*The General Manager, who will manage the two transferring youth workers

*The two youth workers who are already employed by the WA

*The administrator and the part time accountant, who are likely to have an increased workload of, it is estimated, around 20%.

As a matter of good practice, the Westwich Association also keeps its other 5 staff informed about what is happening.

The informing and consulting process is in writing and in person and includes the following information:

That the transfer is to take place, when, and the reasons for the transfer.

The legal implications

The legal implications identified are: that the WA will change its name; that Westport Y will cease to exist; that the two youth workers from Westport Y will transfer to the Westwich and Westport Association; and that their existing contracts of employment will remain in force.

The economic implications

The economic implications identified are: that the finances of Westport Y will transfer to the Westwich and Westport Association; and that the Westport Y employees, who do not currently have access to a pension scheme, will be able to join the Westport and Westwich Association pension scheme after transfer.

The social implications

The main social implication is a proposal that the two Westport Y youth workers will in future be managed by the General Manager of the Westwich Association; and that existing financial support and administration at the Westport Y, to date undertaken on a voluntary basis by trustees, will in future be managed by the administrator and the part time accountant.

Measures that are envisaged in connection with the transfer that will affect the employees

The measures that are envisaged cover how the work may be structured. Specifically, there is a proposal that in future the youth workers would be required to cover for each other during absences, which may lead to increased travelling compared with currently.

The WA and Westport Y arrange for their youth workers to meet to discuss how they will work together. There is also a meeting of the youth workers of Westport Y and the whole staff team of the WA.

The youth workers make a couple of suggestions, which are about how work should be structured after the transfer. The WA and Westport Y consider these suggestions and respond to them.

In addition to the two youth workers, Westport Y has six volunteers. The transfer is explained to them and they are invited to continue volunteering, in the same capacity, but for the new organisation. They are happy to do this.

Hints and tips

Below are some suggestions which, although not legally required, may help to ensure that the transfer is successful.

Resources required to manage the transfer
Do not underestimate the resources required to manage a transfer of an undertaking. At the point of tendering for the transfer of a project to your organisation, make sure that the advantages of taking on the service outweigh the resource requirements (eg management time, cost of legal/ human resources advice etc).

During the transfer process
Meet with the other party or parties to the transfer as soon as you can. A working relationship with someone you have met should help to smooth the transfer process.

If you are the transferee, meet with the staff who will transfer to you as soon as possible. Plan the meeting carefully to make the staff welcome.

Think about the impact on service users
As the voluntary sector is about people, it is likely that there will be service users involved in the transfer. For example, the transfer of a care home, outreach project or supported living service will all involve service users.

Consider carefully how you will communicate with and reassure service users, as well as their families, close friends and advocates, about the transfer. Involve them early on and keep communicating with them throughout the process.

Transfer agreements and liabilities
Whether your organisation is a transferor or a transferee, you are strongly advised to enter into a legally-binding transfer agreement. This is particularly important if you are the transferee, since you will inherit all civil liabilities and obligations, including:

- liability for personal injury claims against the transferor
- liability for discrimination claims against the transferor
- liabilities for any breach of contract, such as arrears of overtime payments or salary
- all statutory rights and liabilities, such as unfair dismissal claims.

It is a relatively common practice for the transferee employer to require the transferor employer to provide an indemnity against any losses from any pre-transfer breaches of contracts or employment law. A legal adviser may be able to negotiate an appropriate indemnity on your behalf.

After the transfer
Having done all the work for a transfer of an undertaking, it might be tempting to sit back and consider the job done. However, there are further areas to consider:

- if you are the transferee employer remember that the transferring employees are moving to a new environment, with some new ways of doing things, new colleagues and perhaps different standards and expectations. Treat their induction as carefully as the induction of any new employee. Think also about existing staff, who may need to be reassured about the new staff transferring in
- if you are the transferor employer, consider the possible impact on morale of the loss of a service. Make sure you communicate with the remaining staff about the transfer, so that you are aware of, and can deal with, staff concerns.

Checklist

	Check whether TUPE applies to your particular transfer – note that the coverage of TUPE is wide and will apply to most service provision transfers
	If TUPE does apply, be aware that all employees in the undertaking will transfer to the transferee and that their existing terms and conditions of employment, plus length of service, will continue
	If you are the transferor, meet your legal obligations to provide written information to the transferee about the employees who are to transfer
	Both transferor and transferee must inform the representatives of their employees who are affected by the transfer
	If any measures/actions are envisaged in connection with the transfer, then there is also an obligation to consult with representatives
	Take advice if you are considering dismissing employees or changing their terms and conditions for a reason connected with the transfer – such actions are permitted in only limited circumstances
	If you are a transferee, undertake Due diligence
	Do not underestimate the resources required to manage a transfer. Remember that TUPE is a complicated area of the law. You are advised to take legal or HR advice on any TUPE situation you are contemplating or involved in
	Remember the human element of TUPE. Staff, service users, their families and advocates may be anxious about a transfer. Do your best to reassure them

Further information

The following organisations offer advice and resources about the subjects covered in this chapter to new and existing employers, often free of charge:

Acas
www.acas.org.uk

Business Link
Their website has a whole section on transfers of undertakings.
www.businesslink.gov.uk

Department for Business, Enterprise and Regulatory Reform (DBERR)
Their website has useful publication called A Guide to the 2006 TUPE Regulations for Employees, Employers and Representatives
www.berr.gov.uk

Department for Work and Pensions
Their website has information about pensions on a transfer of an undertaking, and the Pensions Act
www.dwp.gov.uk

A listing of all the useful organisations referred to in this Good Guide can be found at the back of this book with full contact details.

Fifteen

Collaborative Working

There are many employment implications to collaborative working. This chapter outlines some of these implications. The chapter covers the following areas:

- Why organisations might want to collaborate
- Types of collaborative project
- Staffing options for collaborative projects
- Points to consider when staffing a collaborative project

The information in this chapter is an abbreviated version of the free NCVO/Workforce Hub publication Staffing a Collaborative Project. The publication is available to download from the Collaborative Working section of the NCVO website, at www.ncvo-vol.org.uk /jointstaffing.

Collaborative working is an increasingly common way of working in the voluntary and community sector. NCVO's Collaborative Working Unit defines collaborative working as a spectrum of ways that two or more voluntary sector organisations can work together.

Why organisations might want to collaborate

Options range from informal networks and alliances, through joint delivery of projects to full merger. Collaborative working can last for a fixed length of time or can form a permanent arrangement.

Organisations can collaborate on any aspect of their work: sharing back office services or premises; running campaigns or fundraising initiatives together; or delivering joint projects or services.

Collaborative working may enable organisations to achieve more, by pooling resources or expertise. It may allow organisations to jointly pursue funding for specific projects which they wish to deliver together.

Collaborative working can also give increased opportunities to the employees from the organisations involved – for example in terms of training, taking on new roles or simply learning how another organisation does things.

Collaborative working may bring additional diversity, where voluntary organisations representing minority interests work with voluntary organisations that do not specialise in this way. An example might be a small voluntary organisation specialising in mental health issues for hearing impaired users, working with a larger organisation for all hearing impaired people, such as the Royal National Institute for Deaf People.

Types of collaborative project

Different forms of collaborative working will be appropriate in different circumstances and will involve various degrees of commitment.

At one end of the scale, collaborative working may simply involve two organisations co-operating with each other, with no heavy investment from either party. For example, each party may share training sessions, or may give each other access to facilities and services. In this case, there will typically be no shared staff.

At the other end of the scale, a full merger could take place, with a single new organisation resulting.

It is the middle ground of collaboration which most typically involves sharing staff. For example, two or more organisations may bid to undertake a particular project, where collaboration is required.

You should note that if the collaborative project involves staff moving from one employer to another (including in a merger), organisations may be affected by TUPE, the Transfer of Undertakings (Protection of Employment) Regulations 2006. See chapter 14 for further information.

'...it is important to be clear about who will manage the staff and to ensure that all partners are jointly accountable for project outcomes.'

Staffing options for collaborative projects

If you are looking to employ staff on collaborative projects, you will need to decide which of the project partners will be the employer of the project staff. Frequently, it is the larger partner organisation, with greater resources, which acts as the legal employer.

Alternatively, it may be that there are several project staff and some are employed by one partner, and some by the other.

In some circumstances, project staff may be employed by a separate organisation, eg a Council for Voluntary Service (CVS), to undertake common activities, such as training provision, on behalf of a group of partner organisations.

Whichever model you choose, it is important to be clear about who will manage the staff and to ensure that all partners are jointly accountable for project outcomes.

Here is one example of how a collaborative project may be staffed:

Case study – collaborative working staffing

This project involved a smaller local organisation (Action for Change) working with Addaction, a national organisation, to jointly provide services for drug and alcohol users in Brighton. The driver for jointly producing services was the opportunity to tender for a number of substance misuse services with a local Drug Advisory Team. The project is now at an end, having finished in March 2006.

An overall project manager co-ordinated the project and was employed by Addaction. Project staff reporting to the project manager were employed by either Addaction or Action for Change.

Project staff were put onto the Addaction pay scale, but other terms and conditions were those of their employing organisation. Some terms and conditions were different – for example annual leave was lower in Action for Change, but Action for Change staff had a more favourable pension scheme. These differences did not, in practice, cause any particular problems.

Points to consider when staffing a collaborative project

Regardless of which staffing model you choose, there are a number of factors you will need to consider if the staffing of the collaborative project is to be successful.

Resources
The establishment of a collaborative project is likely to take time. Those involved may have less time for their other work. It will be important to ensure that staffing resources are adequate to manage the change and to set up the project.

Change management
Change is not always easy. A substantial investment may have been made in what is rather than thinking what may be possible within a collaborative project. The key skills in change management are communication and consultation. It will help greatly to listen to people's concerns, learn from them, and make changes if needed. Genuine communication and consultation will help minimise some of the anxiety and conflict that can arise when a collaborative project is being developed and implemented.

Setting terms and conditions
Terms and conditions of employment (pay, hours of work, annual leave, notice periods and so on) for a joint employee or employees should be agreed between the partners.

The partners may agree that the terms and conditions of the partner who will employ the employee(s) are adopted. Alternatively, terms and conditions may be developed that are specific to the joint worker or workers. However, it is worth noting that this will require additional management time to agree each new term.

This latter approach may be most appropriate where salaries and other terms vary considerably between the partner organisations. If the salaries of the employing partner are particularly low or high relative to the other partners, for example, salaries might be set with reference to the mid point of salary rates for similar jobs in all the partner organisations.

There may also be specific provisions in the employment contracts of shared workers that are different from the terms of other workers of the employing partner. For example, the nature of the work may require the joint employee(s) to work from home and/or to have a mobile phone.

The partners will doubtless be constrained by the funding that they have available. As well as setting an appropriate salary, there will be other costs such as training, pension contributions, paid annual leave, sick pay and costs associated with maternity/paternity/adoption leave.

Physical location and equipment of a shared employee or employees
If the employee or employees are based at the offices of one of the partner organisations, then it will be especially important to communicate clearly that the employees are a shared resource, to fulfil the requirements of the partnership project.

There will also be a need to clarify who will be responsible for providing the employee's equipment, such as a desk, phone etc, especially when they work from more than one office. In many circumstances, it will make sense for the equipment to be provided by the partner organisation in whose office the employee is primarily based. With this approach, the health and safety responsibilities for both the equipment and premises are with one organisation. However, there will be a need to consider the cost of the equipment and how this should be shared between the partner organisations.

Continued overleaf...

Management style

Be aware that different organisations have different management styles, for example in respect of frequency of supervision, responsiveness to ideas from staff, employee consultation and involvement in decision making and approaches to personal/professional development.

It is especially important to clarify issues of management style, so that joint/shared workers receive consistent messages and expectations.

Cultural differences

The way in which one organisation may work will not necessarily be the way in which another organisation will work. There may be differences, for example, in the ways in which decisions are taken, the dress code, and the ways in which staff relate to users and volunteers. Differences may include issues of hierarchy, formality, value systems and communication style. A large organisation may sometimes need to make one size fits all decisions, whereas a smaller organisation, with a local hands-on approach, may be able to operate more quickly and flexibly. The differences in approach may bring about tensions.

It will be important to identify and address any differences in culture before they are a cause of conflict. Real or perceived differences can be a significant barrier if not addressed early on in an open and transparent manner. In particular, if one of the partner organisations in the collaborative project is larger than the other, there may be fears about takeover.

Organisational rules and procedures

You should clarify what rules any joint employee must adhere to. It is most common that the employee will follow the rules and procedures of the employing partner. However, there may be areas which are less clear. For example, if one member of a partnership allows internet access during lunchtime and the other does not, the employee needs to know the rules that apply to them, so that they do not inadvertently breach them.

Disciplinary and grievance procedures in particular should be explained to the employee. Should problems arise, the partners should consider carefully how they will deal with them. It may make sense that any disciplinary action is taken jointly by the parties. Alternatively, the employing partner may in some circumstances have the final say, because if dismissal results, then the employing organisation is the one which will be ultimately accountable for that dismissal in law.

It is the employing organisation that will need to deal with any employment tribunal claim, should a claim subsequently arise.

Balance of power in the staffing structure

If the partner organisations involved are significantly different in size, it may be hard to avoid the feeling that the larger organisation has the power. In structuring staffing and in considering management and supervision arrangements, it will be important to consider how to ensure that power is balanced between the parties.

Common understanding

All parties should have a clear understanding of how the employees allocated to the collaborative project will work. It can be very stressful to have more than one boss, with each giving a different interpretation of what should be done and how.

'In structuring staffing and in considering management and supervision arrangements, it will be important to consider how to ensure that power is balanced between the parties.'

Management responsibilities of a shared employee

A shared employee working across two or more partner organisations may also have some responsibility to co-ordinate employees across the partner organisations. For example, a project manager appointed as a shared employee of four organisations may need to co-ordinate the work of specific project workers in the four organisations. These project workers may also have a manager in their own organisation, as well as having other projects to run.

In such cases, the best approach is to clarify early on in the project how the arrangement will work, and to review it regularly. All parties – the project workers, their managers, and the shared project manager – need to appreciate the complexities of the situation and the variety of work that each may be involved in. Three-way supervision/review meetings with each project worker, their manager, and the shared project manager, will help to increase mutual understanding and reduce miscommunication, as well as setting consistent standards of work to the project worker.

Accountability

Consider carefully who is ultimately accountable for the delivery of the project. Where there are several partners, several project staff and more than one Trustee Board, accountability can become blurred – the project can either be everyone's responsibility or no-one's! In either of these scenarios, it is possible that the project will not deliver what is intended.

You should consider whether or not there should be an overall project manager and if so, to whom this post should report. Make sure that the project manager knows exactly for what they are accountable, and to whom.

Shared vision

Having a clear and commonly understood vision gives parties the opportunity to revisit it if things go off track. The shared vision may help in situations such as:

- where self-interest in your own organisation may adversely affect the shared aims of the partnership
- where the employee feels they are experiencing a conflict of loyalties
- where one organisation feels they are not getting a fair share of the employee's attention.

Clear leadership

Clear leadership is important in maintaining and explaining the shared vision; dealing with unanticipated problems; and finding solutions to staffing issues. Be clear about who is driving the partnership project in each of the partner organisations. For example, you might consider setting up a sub-group of your Board of Trustees to focus on the partnership and to report back to the main Board.

Managing reductions in staffing

Setting up a collaborative project may often be as a result of new sources of funding, or to seek new sources of funding. It may be a new activity, rather than a decrease in existing activity. Sometimes, however, there may be some rationalisation as a result of collaborative working. Two or more organisations may wish to share resources, in order to be more cost-effective.

Where this is the case, reductions in staffing may result, which may involve making redundancies. Make sure you consult about possible staffing reductions at the earliest possible opportunity. The legal and procedural position in respect of redundancies is relatively complex. See chapter 13 for further information.

Staff turnover

Think about how you will cope with turnover among the key individuals in the participating organisations – make sure collaborative arrangements are robust and do not just rely on individuals.

If individuals are employed on short-term contracts to undertake tasks for a group of organisations rather than for a single employer, this may carry a higher risk of difficulties in retention.

Formal written agreements

Using formal written agreements for collaborative projects can help ensure continuity and stability, even where there is staff or trustee turnover.

Formal written agreements can help because:

- they are a reference point if things go wrong
- the very act of writing the agreements helps to formulate thoughts and ideas
- putting faith in high levels of mutual trust can lead to misunderstandings
- key individuals may not continue to be involved – so it is important to have the agreement in writing.

Ongoing review

The largest amount of work in setting up a joint project will be at the early stages. However, don't forget to review progress and achievements on an ongoing basis, so that you can celebrate success and learn for the future.

Exit strategy

If the collaborative project is funded for a limited period, eg three years, then you will need to consider what will happen to the staff you have employed at the end of the period. If their employment is for two years or more, they will be entitled to statutory redundancy pay and you should make all efforts to redeploy them. It would be prudent to develop and consult on a redundancy policy prior to the event, so that everyone knows how the matter will be handled, and so that it is seen as fair.

Checklist

	Consider carefully the staffing resources required to set the project up and manage the change
	Agree with your partner organisation a clear and shared vision as to what the project is to achieve
	Establish who will be the legal employer of any staff and who will line manage the project manager. Make sure that the balance of responsibilities between the partners is clear and agreed
	Establish the employment terms and conditions that will apply
	Consider where you will locate your project workers, what equipment they may need and which of the partners will supply it
	Clarify how you will deal with any differences in organisational procedures, eg performance management, discipline and grievance
	Clarify any differences in management style or organisational culture between the partner organisations so that messages to and expectations of project workers are clear
	Address any staff anxieties about the new project with clear communication and consultation
	Clarify exactly who is accountable for which aspects of the project
	Use a formal written agreement to help ensure continuity and stability, even where there is turnover of staff or trustees
	Establish systems to review progress and achievements on an ongoing basis
	Consider your exit strategy at the end of the project, including any possible staff redundancies

Further information

The following organisation offers advice and resources about the subjects covered in this chapter to new and existing employers, often free of charge:

National Council for Voluntary Organisations (NCVO)
NCVO's Collaborative Working Unit (CWU) offers information and advice to help voluntary and community organisations make decisions about whether and how to work collaboratively.
The CWU has various publications on collaborative working, which you can download from the NCVO website, including the publication Staffing a Collaborative Project, which is a fuller version of this chapter, and guidance on developing joint working agreements.
www.ncvo-vol.org.uk

A listing of all the useful organisations referred to in this Good Guide can be found at the back of this book with full contact details.

Sixteen
Retirement

The Employment Equality (Age) Regulations, which came into force on 1 October 2006, not only outlawed discrimination in employment on the grounds of age (see chapter 2), but also established a national default retirement age of 65 and a set retirement procedure.

In essence, only a genuine retirement will be a fair dismissal, provided it is handled correctly.

Statutory retirement age

The national default retirement age is now 65. You can no longer force someone to retire before the age of 65.

If your written statements of terms and conditions (employment contracts) state a retirement age of earlier than age 65, this clause is no longer effective and you should amend the clause in the written statement.

For existing staff, you don't need to reissue the whole written statement, but you can simply write to inform them of their new retirement age, which must be 65 or above, and that your letter constitutes an amendment to their statement of main terms and conditions.

If you wish, you are free to state no retirement age at all in your written statements.

There are a few circumstances where you may be able to justify an earlier retirement age than 65, but there are very few such circumstances.

Recruiting and retaining older workers

The background to the retirement provisions of the Employment Equality (Age) Regulations 2006 is a recognition that:

- not all employees want to retire at a specific age, eg 60 or 65
- some people will want to stop work earlier than this and others will want to stop work later than this
- everyone is different – some people are more energetic at age 75 than others at age 45. It is therefore not appropriate to stereotype older workers as 'over the hill' and 'due for retirement'
- the demographics of the UK are changing – it is estimated that by 2025, half the adult population will be aged 50 and over. It simply no longer makes business sense not to employ older workers
- people are living longer, are healthier and will need to work for longer to save for pensions. As a result, a requirement that people retire at a set age, with no right to request to continue working, makes much less sense than in the past.

Many organisations, even before the Age Regulations, have adopted a policy of employing and retaining older workers. B&Q is a well-known example of this. Such organisations do not have a set retirement age.

You might wish to consider, within your own organisation, whether action could or should be taken to recruit and retain older workers. For example, you might place advertisements where they are more likely to be seen by older people. Think also about whether any policies or practices that you have may put barriers in the way of older workers.

It is good practice to recruit and retain workers of all ages who have the right skills and abilities for your jobs. However, please note that the law does say that where a person is older than, or within six months of, the employer's normal retirement age (which must be at least age 65), or 65 if the employer does not have a normal retirement age, then the employer may refuse to recruit that person.

Statutory retirement procedure

Retirement is now included as one of the potentially fair reasons for dismissal in law (the others being conduct, capability, redundancy, a legal reason or some other substantial reason).

If you intend to retire an employee, you can no longer just inform them that you are retiring them on their 65th birthday. Instead, there is now a statutory procedure that you must follow.

As long as you follow the statutory retirement procedure, the dismissal on grounds of retirement will be fair. If you do not follow the statutory retirement procedure and the employee makes an employment tribunal application, this could lead to a finding of unfair dismissal or a penalty of up to eight weeks' pay, depending on the nature of the breach.

The procedure is as follows:

Employer notification
Between 12 and 6 months before you intend to retire the employee, you should write to him or her to give notice of your intention. Your notice should inform the employee of their right to request not to retire and the right to work beyond retirement.

Employee request not to retire
The employee needs to exercise the right to request not to retire at least three months (but not more than six months) prior to the intended date of retirement. The employee must put their request in writing.
The employee's request may be to defer their retirement indefinitely, for a stated period or until a stated date.

Opposite is an example notification letter and form for the employee to state their intentions.

'If you intend to retire an employee, you can no longer just inform them that you are retiring them on their 65th birthday.'

Example notification of intention to retire an employee

Dear [employee]

I am writing to inform you that [employer] intends to retire you on [date], which is the date of your 65th birthday.

If you wish to continue to work, you can request not to retire. In order to be able to exercise this right, you should put your request in writing to [name], no later than three months before the intended retirement date set out above.

If you do request not to retire, we will meet to discuss your request. You can request that your employment continues:

• indefinitely
• for a stated period; or
• until a stated date.

Please return the slip below, indicating your intentions, no later than [date, three months prior to the intended retirement date].

Yours sincerely

[manager]

PLEASE DELETE THE SECTIONS OF THIS FORM THAT DO NOT APPLY

I intend to retire on [date], which is the date of my 65th birthday.
OR
I do not wish to retire and would like to keep working:

• indefinitely
• for further period of time of_____[please state]
• until_____ date [please state]

signed_____Employee

please also print your name_____

Meeting

Once you receive a request not to retire, you need to meet with the employee to discuss the request. The meeting should be held within a reasonable period of the request being received. The employee has the right to be accompanied by a work colleague at the meeting.

Decision

After the meeting, you need to take your decision. This could be:

• to refuse the employee's request and confirm the retirement on the date you originally stated
• to postpone the retirement date to a specified later date
• to postpone the retirement date indefinitely
• to agree to some other proposal from the employee, for example to reduce their working hours prior to retirement
• to offer an alternative to the employee. For example, you might decide that you do not wish to agree to the employee continuing in employment indefinitely, but you will agree to delay the retirement date for 6 months.

Continued overleaf...

Failure to notify the employee on time

The law does not require you to state your reasons for your decision, but it is good practice to do so.

Here are some of the reasons you may have:

Reasons why the request may be agreed:

* Savings to the organisation in respect of recruitment and training costs

* Retaining the valuable experience and knowledge of the employee

Reasons why the request may be refused:

* If there is or will be a restructure and there will no longer be a post for the employee

* If the employee is or has become less capable of meeting the requirements of the job and where there are no reasonable adjustments that can be made to enable the employee to remain in work (note that you would need to make reasonable adjustments under the Disability Discrimination Act)

* Where the employee requests a revised working pattern and it is not possible to accommodate this

* Where the employee's conduct or job performance is not satisfactory

Your written decision should include a statement that the employee has the right to appeal against your decision.

Appeal

If the employee appeals against your decision, a further meeting should be held, ideally with a more senior manager or a Trustee. The employee has the right to be accompanied by a work colleague or trade union representative at the meeting. That person should hear the appeal and take a decision. The decision should be confirmed in writing.

If you fail to follow the statutory procedure to notify the employee of their intended date of retirement between 12 and 6 months before the date you intend to retire them, you are still under a continuing duty to provide the written notification until the fourteenth day before the operative date of termination. The operative date of termination is either the date on which notice of termination given by the employer expires or, if no notice has been given, the date on which termination takes effect.

If you notify the employee late, then the employee can make their request not to retire at any time during the 6 months before the intended retirement date.

An employee may complain to an employment tribunal that their employer has failed to comply with the duty to notify. A claim must be lodged before the end of three months beginning with:

- the last day of the six-month window, if the employee knew their intended date of retirement by that date
- if the employee did not know of their intended date of retirement by the last day of the six-month window, with the first day on which they knew (or should have known) that date.

If successful, a tribunal must award the employee such amount as it considers just and equitable in all the circumstances, up to a maximum of eight weeks' pay.

Following retirement procedure more than once

You will need to follow the statutory retirement procedure more than once if the following circumstances apply:

- the employee has previously made a request to continue working after the normal age of retirement, which was accepted
- under that previous request, the employee was allowed to continue working for six months or more and
- you now want to retire the employee.

Circumstances where you do not need to follow the statutory retirement procedure

You may well have a conversation with an older worker who wishes to continue to work past your organisation's normal retirement age.

If you agree that the employee should continue to work, you do not need to follow the statutory procedure, although it would be good practice to write to the employee to confirm your discussion.

However, if in the future, you wish to retire the employee, you will at that stage need to follow the statutory procedure.

If the employee made a previous request and you agreed that the employee should continue working for less than six months, you do not need to follow the statutory procedure again. The retirement will simply take effect on the revised date.

'Avoid making stereotypical assumptions about what an older worker can and cannot do.'

Case study – dealing with a request not to retire

Freda Platt, General Manager of the Westwich Association, was due to reach her 65th birthday on 30 June 2007. The Vice Chair of the Trustees, who had a remit for employment matters at the WA, wrote to Freda in November 2006 to notify Freda of the WA's intention to retire her on 25 June 2007.

Freda wrote back in January 2007, with a request not to retire. In her request, she stated that she wished to continue to work for a further 18 months, until 31 December 2008, so that she could retire at the same time as her partner.

The Vice Chair of the Trustees met with Freda to discuss her request. The Vice Chair agreed the revised date with Freda. The meeting also provided the opportunity to discuss the appointment of a replacement for Freda's post. It was agreed that a replacement would be sought in September 2008, with a planned start date of the beginning of December 2008. This would allow for a reasonable handover period for this key position.

Freda also stated that she would like to reduce her hours to half time for the last month of her employment. The Vice Chair agreed to this, provided that a replacement had been found to start at the beginning of December 2008.

There was no need for an appeal, as Freda's request was accommodated.

The Vice Chair will need to go through the retirement procedure again, writing to Freda between 6 and 12 months prior to 31 December 2008.

Good practice in retirement situations

Here are some suggestions for good practice in dealing with retirement:

- handle the situation with tact and understanding
- avoid making stereotypical assumptions about what an older worker can and cannot do
- avoid making assumptions that an older worker would not want to work as hard as a younger worker
- try and be positive and open to requests not to retire, considering them with an open mind. Listen carefully to what the employee has to say. Consider each request on an individual basis
- follow the Acas guidelines that suggest that although the employee has no right to receive reasons for any refusal of the right to continue working, it is good practice to give a more detailed explanation of the reason and the policy. This is because it allows the employee to leave with some dignity and respect and it will help maintain good relationships with other employees

- if you decide to give reasons, think carefully about what you will say and how you will say it
- avoid discrimination on other grounds, such as race, gender, disability, sexual orientation or religion or belief. Such matters should not form a part of your decision, subconsciously or consciously
- treat retiring employees well (eg by arranging retirement events)
- encourage retiring employees to come back to work with you, for example on a short-term or consultancy basis
- consider having a flexible retirement process, where an employee might gradually reduce their hours of work in the few weeks before retirement.

Retirement and pensions

Employees who work beyond the normal retirement age may be able to continue to contribute to their pension scheme. For further information about pension schemes and retirement, please see chapter 6.

Checklist

	Update written statements of terms and conditions, if they currently include a retirement age of 65 or less
	Avoid making stereotypical assumptions about what an older worker can and cannot do
	Keep track of the ages and dates when your staff are due to retire, in order to give them statutory notification if you intend to retire them
	If you receive a request not to retire, or to delay retirement, consider it with an open mind. If you can agree to the request easily, inform the employee in writing that you agree. If not, follow the statutory procedure in full
	Make sure your retiring staff are able to retire with dignity – handle the process with tact and care

Further information

The following organisations offer advice and resources about the subjects covered in this chapter to new and existing employers, often free of charge:

Acas
The following publication can be downloaded from the Acas website:
• Age and the Workplace, which includes an explanation of the retirement procedure; a fair retirement flowchart; and examples of the letters needed for the retirement procedure. www.acas.org.uk

Age Partnership Group
Their website has a range of resources. www.agepositive.gov.uk

Chartered Institute of Personnel and Development (CIPD)
Their website has a fact sheet on age and employment, with good practice recommendations and an action plan. www.cipd.co.uk

Department for Business, Enterprise and Regulatory Reform (DBERR)
Their website has a number of resources on retirement and the Age Discrimination Regulations. www.berr.gov.uk

A listing of all the useful organisations referred to in this Good Guide can be found at the back of this book with full contact details.

Seventeen

Essential policies and employment documentation

The benefit of clear employment documentation is that all employees know what is expected of them and all managers know the procedure for dealing with particular situations. It is easier to achieve consistency of approach across an organisation if there are clear policies and procedures.

However, the number and type of policies you have is likely to be commensurate with the size of your organisation. If you have fewer than 10 employees, it is easier to adopt a consistent approach without formal policies. Once you have 30 or more employees, you are likely to need a number of written policies.

Essential minimum documentation

The following is essential documentation that you should give to each employee:

A written statement of terms and conditions

It is a legal requirement to issue a written statement of terms and conditions to each employee, within 2 months of the employee starting. For further information, see chapter 4.

A grievance procedure

You must implement and publish to your employees at least the statutory minimum procedure. For further information, see chapter 9.

A disciplinary procedure

You must implement and publish to your employees at least the statutory minimum procedure, but you are advised to have a fuller procedure, based for example on Acas guidelines. For further information, see chapter 9.

A health and safety policy

If you have more than 5 employees, you are legally required to have a health and safety policy. For further information, see chapter 11.

Health and safety poster

You must display a health and safety poster at all times, giving information about health, safety and welfare. For further information, see chapter 11.

Pensions information

From the time that you appoint your fifth employee, you must provide access to a Stakeholder Pension scheme, and give written information on this scheme. For further information, see chapter 6.

Equality and diversity policy

There is no legal requirement to have an equality and diversity policy, but you are advised to do so, to help you ensure that your workforce is representative of the community you serve. The policy may also be used as evidence that your organisation does not tolerate discrimination in the event that a discrimination claim is issued against the organisation. Funders may also require a statement of your policy on equality and diversity. For further information, see chapter 2.

Rules

You should publicise brief rules, covering matters such as making personal phone calls, confidentiality, non-harassment/bullying, data protection and use of computers. For further information, see chapter 9.

Sickness absence arrangements

You will need to specify in writing what procedures employees need to follow if they are sick. For further information, see chapter 10.

Annual leave arrangements

You will need to inform your employees in writing about booking and notification procedures for annual leave. For information about statutory requirements on annual leave, see chapter 6.

Additional documentation

As your organisation grows, you may find it useful to have some or all of the following documentation:

- **Application form, monitoring form other standard recruitment documentation** *(see chapter 3)*
- **Induction procedure** *(see chapter 5)*
- **Probation procedure** *(see chapter 5)*
- **Salary review policy** *(see chapter 6)*
- **Staff supervision and appraisal policy** *(see chapter 7)*
- **Standard staff supervision and appraisal forms** *(see chapter 7)*
- **Learning and development policy** *(see chapter 7)*
- **Learning and development plan** *(see chapter 7)*
- **Maternity, paternity, adoption and parental leave policies** *(see chapter 8)*
- **Policy on compassionate leave and emergency domestic leave** *(see chapter 8)*
- **Policy on requesting flexible working for parents of young children or for carers of adults** *(see chapter 8)*
- **Policies on communication and employee involvement** *(see chapter 12)*
- **Whistleblowing policy** *(see chapter 12)*
- **Absence policy** *(see chapter 10)*
- **Redundancy policy** *(see chapter 13)*

A format for your employment policies

Example format for your employment policies

Policy statement
Include here a brief statement of your organisation's stance concerning the policy area.

Scope
Explain here to whom the policy applies and in what circumstances.

Policy details
Here you can put the details of how your policy will work in practice.

Responsibilities under the policy
The responsibilities of managers and employees in implementing the policy should be stated here.

Date
State the date the policy was drafted.

Staff handbooks

Many employers produce a staff handbook for their employees. Staff handbooks take many forms, but a popular approach is to set out the main areas of employment in brief in the staff handbook, with cross-references to the full policies and where to find them.

**Example
Staff handbook**

**The Westwich Association
staff handbook – contents**

Introduction to the
Westwich Association
A letter of introduction from
the Chair of the Trustees

About the organisation
Brief history, mission, current
and future plans

Joining the Association
Induction and probation
Performance reviews and
supervision meetings
Staff benefits

Working at the Association
Equality and diversity
Harassment and bullying
Pay and payment method
Overtime
Flexitime
Parental rights
Sickness absence reporting
and sick pay
Annual leave entitlement
Arrangements for public holidays
Taking time off for religious festivals
Compassionate leave and emergency
domestic leave
Health and safety
Fire
Accidents

Rules and expectations
Drugs and alcohol
Smoking
Use of computers during
personal time
Use of the organisation's facilities
Computer security
Use of the internet
Confidentiality
Expenses
Acceptance of personal gifts

Dealing with problems
Grievance procedure
Disciplinary procedure
Whistleblowing
Complaints

Leaving employment
Redundancy
Giving notice
Return of Association property

Acas has a very useful guide on
producing a staff handbook.
It contains practical advice on
how to write a handbook, checklists
to help you to identify and review
your existing employment policies,
example sections which you can
customise for your own use, and
sources of further information.
You can see the guide at
www.acas.org.uk, and by
searching for 'staff handbook'.

Consulting and communicating about your employment documentation

Your new employment documentation is likely to be much more readily accepted if you consult and communicate with staff as you draft it. If you recognise trade unions, you should also consult with them.

Your staff will be able to tell you how things work in practice, and where things could be improved. You can build these comments into your policies and procedures.

You should also consider whether any proposed new policy may make a significant change to the existing terms and conditions of employment of your staff. If it does, then you will need the agreement of your staff before you can make the change. You cannot change terms without individual employees' agreement (see chapter 4).

Make sure that all your employees have access to your employment policies. You could display your policies on notice boards, include them in a staff handbook, or add them to your organisation's shared computer drive or intranet.

'Your staff will be able to tell you how things work in practice, and where things could be improved. You can build these comments into your policies and procedures.'

Checklist

	Make sure you have all the essential documentation outlined in this chapter
	Introduce new policies as your organisation grows and as needed
	Review existing policies from other organisations, to assist you with drafting your own policies
	Consult with your employees about any new documentation you want to introduce. Gain their agreement if there is a significant change to terms and conditions
	Communicate all your policies – make sure all staff have access to them

Further information

The following organisations offer advice and resources about the subjects covered in this chapter to new and existing employers, often free of charge:

Acas

The following publication can be downloaded from the Acas website:

- A guide to producing a staff handbook, including model policies and documents.

www.acas.org.uk

Chartered Institute of Personnel and Development (CIPD)

Their website has two guides that you may find of use:

- HR policies and procedures – which to consider?
- HR policies and procedures – why introduce them?

www.cipd.co.uk

Councils for Voluntary Service

Another source of information is your local Council for Voluntary Service. You can find their contact details in your local telephone directory or by looking on the National Association for Voluntary and Community Action website www.navca.org.uk

National Council for Voluntary Organisations

Their website has several example documents at the NCVO HR Bank.
www.ncvo-vol.org.uk

Other organisations

The chances are that if you are looking to draft a policy, another organisation may already have one! You could ask other organisations for a copy of their policies, to use as a basis for your own.

A listing of all the useful organisations referred to in this Good Guide can be found at the back of this book with full contact details.

Eighteen
Volunteers and employment

This chapter does not give comprehensive guidance about all aspects of managing volunteers, because the focus of this Good Guide is employment. However, reference is made to other sources of information and publications about volunteers.

Some of the information from this chapter is reproduced or adapted from much more extensive information provided by Volunteering England on their website www.volunteering.org.uk.

Considerations when thinking of taking on volunteers

If you are thinking of taking on one or more volunteers, here is a brief overview of some of questions you should consider:

- Are you ready for volunteers?
- Do you have a volunteer policy in place?
- How will you recruit?
- How will you induct volunteers?
- What ongoing training do you need to provide?
- Who will be responsible for supervising the volunteers?
- Have you taken health and safety into account?
- How will you deal with volunteer expenses?
- How will you deal with any problems?

There is lots of support available to help you think through these issues. As a first step, try looking at the Volunteering England website www.volunteering.org.uk, or contact them by phone on 0845 305 6979 or e-mail: information@ volunteeringengland.org.uk

The legal difference between a volunteer, an employee and a worker

Volunteers:
- support your organisation because they want to – there is no contract obliging them to do so
- do not have a contract of employment
- are not paid for what they do.

Employees:
- have a contract of employment, that is, the employee agrees to work in return for consideration, ie pay and other terms and conditions
- must come to work in accordance with the terms of their contract
- are paid to work.

Workers:
- have a lesser status than employees, but do have a contract to provide work for an organisation
- are generally engaged on a casual, as and when basis.

Employees enjoy many legal rights that have already been covered in this guide, such as protection against unfair dismissal, redundancy and discrimination on various grounds. Employees also have a right to parental leave, sick pay, the minimum wage and holidays. Workers do not have as many rights, but do have the right to paid annual leave and to the minimum wage. Further information on employees and workers is contained in chapter 4.

Volunteers do not have any of these rights. However, you still need to be just as careful in your recruitment and treatment of volunteers as you do with paid staff. Volunteers who feel that they are poorly treated will not stay around for very long.

You should be aware that the Protection of Children Act and the Care Standards Act apply to volunteers as well as paid employees. This means that if volunteers may have regular or substantial contact with children in a childcare organisation regulated by statute or vulnerable adults in a body regulated by the Commission for Social Care Inspection, you must seek Criminal Records Bureau checks (Disclosures) on them (see chapter 3 for further information).

Even where there is no legal requirement to seek Disclosures, it is likely to be a part of your duty of care, where your volunteers are working with children or vulnerable adults. See chapter 3.

Continued overleaf...

Procedures for taking on volunteers

From Autumn 2008 a new system for vetting and barring people considered unfit for working with children or vulnerable adults will be introduced. This will be run by the Independent Safeguarding Authority (ISA) and will mean that there will be a legal obligation to carry out checks for most employee and volunteering roles involving work with people from vulnerable groups. Please see chapter 3 for further information.

Although volunteers are not directly referred to by health and safety legislation, you do have a duty of care to them. You also have a duty to take account of their health and safety under section 3 of the Health and Safety at Work etc Act 1974, in the same way you have a duty to anyone who may be affected by your work. This means that you need to apply the same high standards of health and safety to your volunteers as to any paid employee (see chapter 11). Risk Assessments should be carried out on volunteer roles and activities. Volunteers should be included in health and safety policies. Training and support should be adequate to ensure that volunteers can carry out their roles safely.

Problems can arise if the status of your volunteer becomes unclear. A volunteer might become an employee or a worker if there is insufficient clarity.

Volunteers have in the past made employment tribunal claims for unfair dismissal and for employment rights such as the minimum wage.

Here are to the procedures for taking on volunteers, which make clear their status:

Application form
- don't use the same application form as you use for paid employees – it will probably make reference to employment, which is misleading when you are looking for volunteers not employees
- you may not need an application form at all. Consider whether you may be able to get the information you need when you meet the volunteer in person (this approach may also widen your pool of potential volunteers, as some volunteers may be put off by an application form or may have limited written English skills).

Volunteer agreement
It can be useful to have a volunteer agreement, because it sets out what volunteers can expect from the organisation and what the organisation expects from its volunteers. The following guidelines will help when you are developing a volunteer agreement:

- don't try to adapt the contract of employment that you may use for paid employees. Instead, use a volunteer agreement based on one of the model agreements provide by Volunteering England
- avoid any form of obligation or contractual language. Any hint of obligation – volunteers agreeing to volunteer for the next six months, for example – runs the risk of the document being seen as contractual
- talk of hopes and expectations, with the understanding that volunteers are free to come and go. For example, if you need volunteers to stay with you for a period, you could state 'we hope that you can stay with us for at least 3 months, for you, us and our clients to make the most of the volunteering opportunity. However, you are of course free to leave at any time.' This is better than saying 'you must volunteer with us for at least 3 months.'

'You may also find that if you pay a flat rate you are inadvertently creating a contract of employment, because the volunteers may be seen as working in return for a sum that exceeds their actual expenses'

- explain in the agreement that your organisation will reimburse volunteer expenses, provide adequate training and supervision, carry out adequate risk assessments, and treat volunteers in accordance with its equal opportunities policy
- explain in the agreement that volunteers are expected to follow the rules and procedures of the organisation, and meet time commitments, giving adequate notice if this is not possible
- consider putting some sort of disclaimer in the agreement, such as: 'this agreement reflects the hopes and intentions of the volunteer and the voluntary organisation, and is not contractually binding in any way on either party.'

A volunteer policy
A volunteer policy can help clarify exactly why volunteers are being used within an organisation, how they will work alongside paid staff and how they can expect to be treated by the organisation.

If yours is very small organisation, where everything is done on a face-to-face basis, you may not need a volunteer policy. However, once the organisation starts to get larger, consider producing a volunteer policy to help ensure consistency and good practice.

Volunteer expenses
It may seem easier to pay volunteers a flat rate, rather than reimbursing actual receipted expenses, but by doing this you are putting both your organisation and the volunteer at risk. Volunteers on benefits may lose part of their benefit if they receive anything over and above what they have actually spent. So, for instance, if your flat rate is £5 a day, but they have only spent £3.50, the entire sum may be seen to be income and could affect their benefits. HM Revenue and Customs also views money over and above actual out-of-pocket expenses as taxable income.

You may also find that if you pay a flat rate you are inadvertently creating a contract of employment, because the volunteers may be seen as working in return for a sum that exceeds their actual expenses – no matter by how little. Such a sum is called, in legal terms, a 'consideration.' By creating a contract you could make the volunteer a worker. If this is the case, they may be entitled to rights such as paid annual leave and the National Minimum Wage.

It is also possible that they could be considered to be an employee, in which case there are also additional rights such as the right not to be unfairly dismissed and other rights of employees listed in chapter 1. You must therefore take receipts and keep records so that you can prove that any money you have paid out is an actual reimbursement.

Volunteers paid cash for subsistence (the practice with almost all residential volunteering) do not qualify for the minimum wage if they have been recruited through another charity or similar body.

'...organisations should avoid giving training that is not relevant to the volunteer's role, as such a perk may be regarded as a form of payment'

Paying an honorarium

An honorarium is a lump sum amount of money that may be given as a 'thank you'. It is only acceptable to pay an honorarium if it is totally unexpected and there is no precedent surrounding it. However if it can be proved that there was an expectation that the payment would be made in return for a certain piece of work, length of service, or on leaving the organisation, then the payment would not be an honorarium, would be taxable and could indicate that the individual had employee status.

It is best to be extremely wary about paying honoraria. As well as the possibility of creating a contract it may cause other problems. Benefits offices generally see honoraria as a payment and may well reduce an individual's benefits accordingly.

Instead of paying out honoraria, you could make sure volunteers are able to claim expenses for meals, travel and care costs and that spare money is invested in making volunteer roles more rewarding. For example, offering more training (relevant to the job), social activities, extra resources, or equipment/adjustments to make the organisation more accessible.

Grievance and disciplinary procedures

It is generally better to have separate grievance and disciplinary procedures for volunteers. This helps clarify the non-employee status of volunteers.

You may wish to make the procedures for volunteers simpler, so that they are accessible and so that volunteers fully understand where they are in the process. You can look on the website of Volunteering England for advice on drafting these.

Having different procedures does not mean giving volunteers a lesser status, it simply recognises that they have different needs to those of paid staff.

Providing training

Following clarification in a recent employment tribunal decision, training is unlikely to be regarded as a consideration, but organisations should avoid giving training that is not relevant to the volunteer's role, as such a perk may be regarded as a form of payment. This might be the case if, for example, you pay for a volunteer gardener to go on computer training.

As training must be necessary for the volunteer role to not count as a consideration, it is important to make sure that any training is open to all volunteers and that being eligible for training is not reliant on them having volunteered for a set period of time.

Case study – unclear volunteer status

Amit has been a volunteer at Westwich Association (the WA) for about 9 years. He started by making teas and coffees and generally helping out. He now undertakes administration (mail-outs, newsletters and all responses to queries). He comes to the WA premises each Monday, Wednesday and Friday between 9.00am and 12.30pm.

The arrangement suits Amit, because, despite occasional part time jobs, he has not been able to secure regular paid employment. Going to the WA gives him a sense of purpose and a feeling of 'giving something back.' The WA has also been very supportive to him in his search for employment. For example on one occasion, they paid for a week-long advanced driving course, to assist him in his application to become a lorry driver.

The Trustees have, over the years, come to rely on Amit. In fact, the Trustee Board has changed in the 9 years of Amit's volunteering and no one is quite sure how he started or what arrangements are in place. There is nothing in writing between Amit and the WA.

Amit is not very accurate, but no one has liked to mention this to him, given all the support he gives the WA.

There is a long-standing unwritten agreement that Amit will be given a cash allowance of £10 per day as a thank you for his work. He takes holiday for about 6 weeks per year and he doesn't receive the allowance when on holiday.

The treasurer of the Board of Trustees is new. He thinks that the WA has now grown to such a size that a full-time paid administrator is needed.

The Board of Trustees discuss this with Amit. Amit decides to apply for the administrator job, but is not appointed. The Trustees tell him that they would be pleased if he would still undertake some other volunteering, but Amit feels his work has been taken away. He stops volunteering at the WA.

A week later, the WA receives an employment tribunal application from Amit. He is claiming: constructive unfair dismissal; breach of the Minimum Wage Act; failure to pay the statutory minimum 4.8 weeks holiday pay; and failure to issue a written statement of terms and conditions of employment.

Some points to consider:
Amit has received £30 per week from the WA for some time. This is not paid to reimburse receipted expenses; it is simply an allowance.

It is possible that the £30 per week could be considered to be a consideration in return for work undertaken, as could the payment for training which was not relevant to the volunteering.

It is quite possible that an employment tribunal could find that Amit was in reality an employee. If they were to find that he was an employee, it is possible that Amit's employment tribunal claims could succeed.

Alternatively, an employment tribunal may find that Amit is not an employee, but is a worker. In this case, Amit's claims for minimum wage and holiday pay may succeed.

Recruiting volunteers as employees

There is nothing to stop you from recruiting a volunteer as a paid employee. However, it may be poor equal opportunities practice to recruit only from your pool of volunteers, especially if your existing volunteers are not representative of your local community. Volunteers may come to expect they will be guaranteed paid work, as it becomes available.
This can affect volunteers' motives for volunteering and lead to people volunteering just to obtain paid work, like an unpaid apprentice. This again runs against equal opportunities, as not everyone is able to volunteer.

It is important to have a clear policy on this issue. If there is inconsistency, volunteers may have false hopes or expectations, or carry resentment that one volunteer was selected out of several.

Some organisations simply advertise all posts externally, encouraging volunteers to apply. Others have internal recruitment procedures, similarly encouraging volunteers to apply alongside paid staff. If no suitable candidate is found, the post is then advertised externally.

There are advantages and disadvantages to both approaches. External recruitment is purer in terms of equal opportunities, while internal recruitment allows staff and volunteers to develop within an organisation.

'...it may be poor equal opportunities practice to recruit only from your pool of volunteers, especially if your existing volunteers are not representative of your local community.'

Checklist

	Use volunteer application forms not employment application forms
	Use volunteer agreements not employment contracts
	Avoid contractual language – speak of hopes and expectations
	Draft a volunteer policy
	Reimburse expenses against receipts
	Only pay honoraria if they are totally unexpected, with no precedent surrounding them
	Provide training that is relevant to the voluntary work you need doing

Further information

The following organisations offer advice and resources about the subjects covered in this chapter to new and existing employers, often free of charge:

Criminal Records Bureau
www.crb.gov.uk

Equality and Human Rights Commission
Their website has guidance on recruiting and retaining disabled volunteers.
www.equalityhumanrights.com

Independent Safeguarding Authority
www.isa-gov.org

Volunteering England
Volunteering England has a very useful publication called Volunteers and the Law, which covers the information in this chapter in more detail. You can order it for £15, or download it from their website for free.

The Volunteering England website also has:

- A programme of professional level training for people who manage volunteers.
- A useful 'Frequently asked questions' section on their website.
- Information about important aspects of recruiting and managing volunteers, such as health and safety, impact on benefits and seeking criminal records checks.
- Sample volunteer agreements.
- Details of an extensive range of publications.
www.volunteering.org.uk

A listing of all the useful organisations referred to in this Good Guide can be found at the back of this book with full contact details.

Resources

Acas

Acas Publications
PO Box 235
Hayes
Middlesex
UB3 1DQ
www.acas.org.uk

E: acas@eclogistics.co.uk
T: 08702 42 90 90
F: 020 8867 3225
Helpline: 08457 47 47 47
Minicom: 08456 06 16 00

Services:
- Information for new
  and existing employers
- Free publications to download
  from website
- Equality Direct helpline
  – 0845 600 3444

Age Positive

Age Positive Team
Department for Work
and Pensions
Room W8d
Moorfoot
Sheffield
S1 4PQ
www.agepositive.gov.uk

Services:
- Information on pensions
  and retirement
- Promoting mixed-age workforces

Business Link

www.businesslink.gov.uk
T: 0845 600 9 006

Services:
- Information for new
  and existing employers
- Information on training

Care Standards Commission

Commission for
Social Care Inspection
33 Greycoat Street
London
SW1P 2QF
www.csci.org.uk/professional

T: 020 7979 2000
F: 020 7979 2111

Services:
- Recruitment information
  for employing social care workers

CELRE

Survey House
51 Portland Road
Kingston upon Thames
Surrey
KT1 2SH
www.celre.co.uk

E: info@celre.co.uk
T: 020 8549 8726
F: 020 8541 5705

Services:
- Voluntary sector
  salary survey

Charity Skills

www.charityskills.org

Services:
- Internet service
- Training

Chartered Institute of Personnel and Development (CIPD)

151 The Broadway
London
SW19 1JQ
www.cipd.co.uk

T: 020 8612 6200
F: 020 8612 6201

Services:
- Information on management;
  health in the workplace; maternity,
  paternity and adoption
- HR information
- Factsheets to download
  from website

Criminal Records Bureau (CRB)

PO Box 110
Liverpool
L69 3EF
www.crb.gov.uk

T: 0870 90 90 811
Minicom: 0870 90 90 344

Services:
- Information about Disclosure
  and checking potential employees

Croner Reward

www.croner-reward.co.uk
E: enquiries@croner-reward
  .co.uk
T: 01785 813566
F: 01785 817007

Services:
- Salary surveys for the
  not-for-profit sector

Department for Business, Enterprise and Regulatory Reform (DBERR)

Ministerial Correspondence Unit
1 Victoria Street
London
SW1H 0ET
www.berr.gov.uk

E: enquiries@berr.gsi.gov.uk
T: 020 7215 5000
F: 020 7215 0105
Minicom: 020 7215 6740

Services:
- Information for new and
  existing employers

Department for Work and Pensions

www.dwp.gov.uk

Services:
- Website service offering
  information on pensions
  and other employment
  information

Directory of Social Change

Directory of Social Change
24 Stephenson Way
London
NW1 2DP
www.dsc.org.uk

T: 08450 77 77 07
F: 020 7391 4808

Services:
- Training

Equality and Human Rights Commission (EHRC)
www.equalityhumanrights.com

England– disability
Freepost MID02164
Stratford upon Avon
CV37 9BR

E: englandhelpline2@
equalityhumanrights.com
T: 08457 622633
Textphone: 08457 622644
F: 08457 778878

England – race, age, gender,
sexual orientation and
religion and belief
Freepost RRLL-GHUX-CTRX
Arndale House
Arndale Centre
Manchester
M4 3EQ

E: englandhelpline@
equalityhumanrights.com
T: 0845 604 6610
Textphone: 0845 604 6620
F: 0845 604 6630

Wales
Freepost RRLR-UEYB-UYZL
1st Floor
3 Callaghan Square
Cardiff
CF10 5BT

E: waleshelpline@
equalityhumanrights.com
T: 0845 604 8810
Textphone: 0845 604 8820
F: 0845 604 8830

Scotland
Freepost RRLL-GYLB-UJTA
The Optima Building
58 Robertson Street
Glasgow
G2 8DU

E: scotlandhelpline@
equalityhumanrights.com
T: 0845 604 5510
Textphone: 0845 604 5520
F: 0845 604 5530

Services:
• *Equality rights and information*

Faculty of Occupational Medicine
6 St Andrews Place
Regents Park
London
NW1 4LB
www.facoccmed.ac.uk
T: 020 7317 5890

Services:
• *Information on
occupational medicine*

Fire Protection Association (FPA)
London Road
Moreton-in-Marsh
Gloucestershire
GL56 0RH
www.thefpa.co.uk
T: 01608 812500

Services:
• *Fire risk assessment*

Health and Safety Executive (HSE)
Information Centre
Broad Lane
Sheffield
S3 7HQ
www.hse.gov.uk
Helpline: 08701 545500

To order books:
HSE Books
PO Box 1999
Sudbury
Suffolk
CO10 6FS
T: 01787 881165

Services:
• *Health and safety information*
• *Book ordering service*
• *Free leaflets to download
from website*

HM Revenue and Customs
www.hmrc.gov.uk

Services:
• *Website information for new
and existing employers*

Border and Immigration Agency
Lunar House
40, Wellesley Road
Croydon
CR9 2BY
www.workingintheuk.gov.uk

E: indpublicenquiries@ind.
homeoffice.gsi.gov.uk
T: 0870 606 7766
Minicom: 0800 389 8289

Services:
• *Immigration, Asylum and
Nationality Act*
• *Information on your obligation
to check employee's right to work
in the UK*

Independent Safeguarding Authority
www.isa-gov.org

Services:
• *Information about the new vetting
service for employees working with
vulnerable adults and children*

Investors in People UK
7–10 Chandos Street
London
W1G 9DQ
www.investorsinpeople.co.uk

E: information@iipuk.co.uk
T: 020 7467 1900
F: 020 7636 2386

Services:
• *Run the Investors in People scheme*
• *People management assistance at
www.yourpeoplemanager.com*

Jobcentre Plus
www.jobcentreplus.gov.uk
Services:
- *Recruitment advice*
- *Disability employment advisers*

**Management
Standards Centre**
3rd Floor
17–18 Hayward's Place
London
EC1R 0EQ
www.managementstandards.
org
E: management.standards
@managers.org.uk
T: 020 7240 2826
Services:
- *Runs National Occupational
Standards (NOS) for
management and leadership*

**National Association for
Voluntary and Community
Action (NAVCA)**
www.navca.org.uk
Services:
- *Local Councils for
Voluntary Service*

National Centre for Diversity
C/o Leeds Trinity and All Saints
Brownberrie Lane
Horsforth
Leeds
LS18 5HD
www.nationalcentrefor
diversity.com
T: 0113 283 7100
F: 0113 283 7200
Services:
- *Runs the Investors in Diversity
(IiD) Standard*
- *Information about diversity
in the workplace*

**National Council for Voluntary
Organisations (NCVO)**
Regent's Wharf
8 All Saints Street
London
N1 9RL
www.ncvo-vol.org.uk
E: helpdesk@ncvo-vol.org.uk
T: 020 7713 6161
F: 020 7713 6300
Helpdesk: 0800 2 798 798
Textphone: 0800 01 888 111
Services:
- *Information and advice for
employers in the voluntary sector*
- *Free documents to download
from website*

NHS
www.NHSplus.nhs.uk
Services:
- *Information on
occupational health*

Public Concern at Work
Suite 306
16 Baldwins Gardens
London EC1N 7RJ
www.pcaw.co.uk
E: whistle@pcaw.co.uk
T: 020 7404 6609
F: 020 7404 6576
Services:
- *Information on whistle blowing*

**Royal Society for the
Prevention of Accidents
(Rospa)**
RoSPA House
Edgbaston Park
353 Bristol Road
Edgbaston
Birmingham
B5 7ST
www.rospa.com/
occupationalsafety
E: help@rospa.com
T: 0121 248 2000
F: 0121 248 2001
Services:
- *Information on safety
in the workplace*

Smoke free England
www.smokefreeengland.co.uk
Services:
- *Information on the
no smoking legislation*

The Daycare Trust
21 St George's Road
London
SE1 6ES
www.daycaretrust.org.uk
E: info@daycaretrust.org.uk
T: 020 7840 3350
F: 020 7840 3355
Services:
- *Information about childcare
voucher schemes*

The Pensions Regulator
Napier House
Trafalgar Place
Brighton
BN1 4DW
www.thepensionsregulator
.gov.uk
E: customersupport@
thepensionsregulator.gov.uk
T: 0870 606 3636
F: 0870 241 1144
Services:
- *Information about stakeholder
pension schemes*
- *Register of approved stakeholder
pension schemes*

**Third Sector
Leadership Centre**
Henley Management College
Greenlands
Henley-on-Thames
Oxfordshire
RG9 3AU
www.thirdsectorleadership.
org.uk
E: info@thirdsectorleadership.
   org.uk
T: 01491 571 454

Services:
- *Support for leaders
   in the third sector*

Trades Union Congress
Congress House
Great Russell Street
London
WC1B 3LS
www.tuc.org.uk

T: 020 7636 4030
F: 020 7636 0632

Services:
- *Represents trade
   unions in Britain*
- *Runs Worksmart website
   giving advice to union and
   non-union members –
   www.worksmart.org.uk*

UK Workforce Hub
Hosted by NCVO in England,
by NICVA in Northern Ireland,
by SCVO in Scotland and WCVA
in Wales.
www.ukworkforcehub.org.uk
E: help@ukworkforcehub.org.
   uk
T: 0800 652 5737

Services:
- *Information on learning & skills;
   human resources; leadership;
   volunteering*
- *E-briefings*

Unison
1 Mabledon Place
London
WC1H 9AJ
www.unison.org.uk

T: 0845 355 0845

Services:
- Public sector union
- Information on safety
   in the workplace

Volunteering England
Regents Wharf
8 All Saints Street
London
N1 9RL
www.volunteering.org.uk

E: volunteering@
   volunteeringengland.org
T: 0845 305 6979
F: 020 7520 8910
Helpline: 0800 028 3304

Services:
- *Advice and support for
   organisations working
   with volunteers*

Working Families
1–3 Berry Street
London
EC1V 0AA
www.workingfamilies.org.uk

T: 020 7253 7243
F: 020 7253 6253

Services:
- *Information on maternity,
   paternity, adoption, flexible
   working and childcare*

Workplace Health Connect
www.workplacehealthconnect.
co.uk

T: 0845 609 6006

Services:
- *Free website help
   for small businesses*